C000174706

About the Book

All the essential det
ready-reference for
showing an early in
by encouraging car

An up-to-date picture of each m̶o̶d̶e̶l
in the form of a concise summary, including origins. The format o̶
per page has been carefully designed to give the maximum information.

Completely up-dated for the 1991–92 model year, *Observers Cars* deals
with a broad cross-section of models on the market. Each new edition in
the series complements previous issues, since some models still in
production are dropped after a while to make way for more recent
introductions. For many car enthusiasts, this is an essential purchase
each year, to build up a mine of information about cars over the years.

Still more facts and figures are provided this year and, as usual, the
edition includes the very latest cars wherever possible, even in some
cases embracing a few models which were not introduced until the
Geneva Show in March 1991.

Among the particularly interesting cars in this 1991–92 edition are the
new Audi 100 V6 2.8, Honda NSX, Lancia Dedra Turbo, Mazda MX-5 and
BBR Turbo, Mitsubishi Sigma, Renault Chamade 16v, the 200 mph RJD
Tempest, and the car featured on the cover, Ford's Escort RS Cosworth,
due to start production next year.

About the Author

Stuart Bladon started 'driving' at the age of eight, when he used to
operate the clutch pedal, gear lever, steering and dipswitch of a Vauxhall
10 from the passenger seat while his tolerant aunt was allowed to control
the accelerator and brake. His first 'solo' was at the age of eleven, when
he brought his father's car out of the garage in a series of kangaroo leaps,
and this was followed by many drives on abandoned war-time airfields
and such places as Black Rock sands in North Wales.

His interest in cars developed, and after being in charge of a platoon of
staff cars and ambulances as a National Service officer, he joined the staff
of what was then *The Autocar* magazine, in 1955. In 26 years on the staff
of the journal, he drove and Road Tested an estimated total of more than
6,000 different cars, and his highest speed attained was 171 mph, in Italy,
in a Lamborghini Miura.

In 1981 he left *Autocar* to become a freelance motoring and travel
writer, and now contributes regularly to a number of specialist magazines
as well as writing the twice-weekly general interest motoring pages for
television teletext on Oracle, Channel 4. In preparing the material for this
book, he has the advantage that he has driven most of the cars it covers.

The *Observer's* series was launched in 1937 with the publication of *The Observer's Book of Birds*. Today, over fifty years later, paperback *Observers* continue to offer practical, useful information on a wide range of subjects, and with every book regularly revised by experts, the facts are right up-to-date. Students, amateur enthusiasts and professional organisations alike will find the latest *Observers* invaluable.

'Thick and glossy, briskly informative' – *The Guardian*

'If you are a serious spotter of any of the things the series deals with the books must be indispensable' – *The Times Educational Supplement*

CARS

Stuart Bladon

FREDERICK WARNE

FREDERICK WARNE

Published by the Penguin Group
27 Wrights Lane, London W8 5TZ, England
Penguin Books USA Inc., 375 Hudson Street, New York, New York 10014, USA
Penguin Books Australia Ltd, Ringwood, Victoria, Australia
Penguin Books Canada Ltd, 2801 John Street, Markham, Ontario, Canada L3R 1B4
Penguin Books (NZ) Ltd, 182–190 Wairau Road, Auckland 10, New Zealand

Penguin Books Ltd, Registered Offices: Harmondsworth, Middlesex, England

First published 1955
Thirty-fourth edition 1991

NOTE

The specifications contained in this book were collated on the basis
of material available to the compiler up to the start of 1991.
All information is subject to change and/or cancellation during the course
of the model year. Although every effort has been made to ensure
accuracy in compiling this book responsibility for errors and omissions
cannot be accepted by the compiler and publishers.

ISBN 0 7232 3795 6

Typeset, printed and bound in Great Britain by
William Clowes Limited, Beccles and London

CONTENTS

5

Mazda	121 GLX, 98; 323F 1.6 SE Executive, 99; 323 1.8 GT Hatchback, 100; 626 2.2i GLX Executive 4 × 4, 101; MX-5, 102; MX-5 BBR Turbo, 103; RX-7 2.6 Turbo Cabriolet, 104
Mercedes-Benz	190 2.5D automatic, 105; 190E 2.5 16V, 106; 300SL-24 5-Speed automatic, 107; 300TE 4-Matic, 108; 500E, 109; 300GD, 110; New S-Class, 111
Mercury	Sable LS, 112
Mitsubishi	Colt 1500-12V GLX, 113; Colt 1800 GTi 16V, 114; Galant Coupé Dynamic Four, 115; Lancer 1800 GLXi 4WD Liftback, 116; Shogun Turbo D, 117; Sigma, 118
Morgan	Plus 4 16V, 119
Nissan	Maxima 3.0, 120; Prairie 4 × 4, 121; Primera 1.6LS, 122; Sunny 100NX 1.6 Coupé, 123; 200 SX, 124; 300 ZX, 125
Oldsmobile	Bravada, 126
Peugeot	205 CTI Cabriolet, 127; 205 D Turbo, 128; 205 GTI 1.9, 129; 309 GTI, 130; 405 GLX4, 131; 405 GTDT, 132; 405 Mi16 × 4, 133; 605 SRi 2.0, 134; 605 SV24, 135
Pontiac	Trans Sport SE, 136
Porsche	911 Carrera RS, 137; 928 GT, 138; 944 S2 3.0, 139
Proton	1.5 SE Triple Valve, 140
Renault	19 Chamade TXE, 141; 19 Chamade 1.7 16v, 142; Clio 1.4 RT, 143; Espace Quadra TXE, 144; GTA V6 Turbo Le Mans, 145; 21 1.7 GTS Hatchback, 146; 21 2L Turbo Quadra, 147; 25 2.9 V6 Baccara, 148
RJD	Tempest, 149
Rolls-Royce	Silver Spirit II, 150
Rover	216GTi, 151; 414 SLi, 152; 820i, 153; 825D, 154; Metro 1.1C, 155; MG Maestro 2.0i, 156; Sterling, 157; Vitesse, 158
Saab	900S Turbo 16V, 159; 9000 2.3 Turbo, 160; 9000 2.3 Carlsson, 161
Seat	Ibiza SXi, 162
Skoda	Favorit 136LX, 163; Favorit Roadster, 164
Subaru	Justy GL II 4WD, 165; Legacy 2.2 GX 4WD, 166
Suzuki	Vitara JLX, 167
Toyota	Celica 2.0 GT-Four, 168; Corolla 1.6 GT-i 16V, 169; Corolla 1.6 4WD Estate, 170; Lexus LS400, 171; MR2 GT T-Bar, 172; Previa 2.4, 173; Supra 3.0i Turbo, 174
TVR	Griffith, 175; S3C, 176
Vauxhall	Astra GTE 2.0i Cabriolet, 177; Calibra 2.0i 16V, 178; Carlton 2.6i CDX, 179; Cavalier 2.0i 4 × 4, 180; Cavalier GSi 4 × 4 2.0i 16v, 181; Nova 1.5 Turbo Diesel, 182; Senator CD 3.0i 24v, 183
Volkswagen	Caravelle GL, 184; Corrado 1.8 16V, 185; Golf CL Umwelt Diesel, 186; Passat 2.0 GL Estate, 187; Polo GT 1.3, 188
Volvo	460GLi, 189; 480 Turbo, 190; 960, 191
Yugo	Sana, 192

COUNTRY OF MANUFACTURE

After each make, the country of origin is shown in brackets, and the key to the relevant countries, as established by International Convention, is shown below. In some cases, more than one country of origin is indicated; these are cars sourced from several countries, or using major components from another country, such as the Mazda MX-5 BBR Turbo, which is converted to turbocharging after arrival in Britain from Japan.

B	Belgium	J	Japan
CDN	Canada	K	Korea
CS	Czechoslovakia	MAL	Malaysia
D	Germany	NL	Holland (Netherlands)
E	Spain	S	Sweden
F	France	SU	Russia
GB	Great Britain	USA	United States of America
I	Italy	YU	Yugoslavia

AMERICA'S GALLON MYSTERY

It has become a tradition of this little booklet for each edition to explore possible reasons why America has a smaller gallon – identified by the single 'I' – than the British one. Fascinating theories on the subject continue to flood in from readers, at the rate of at least one a year. Some of these have seemed apocryphal, but the explanation offered by Mr G G Watkins of Pony Glen, Stirling, sounds more plausible than most.

There used to be two gallons in Britain, he writes, the ale gallon which was standardised at 282 cubic inches in 1611, and the wine gallon of 231 cubic inches, dating from 1707. The Americans, explains Mr Watkins, continued with the old Queen Anne gallon (and, perhaps, forgot how to spell 'gallon') in 1836, when the British established the new Imperial gallon at 277.274 cubic inches. This strange figure, incidentally, was derived from the volume of 10 lb of water weighed in air at 62 deg F, with the barometer at 30 in of mercury.

An earlier explanation, I recall, had something to do with wine, so perhaps we are getting nearer to the truth of this fascinating anomaly. The important thing to appreciate, however, is that throughout the book our gallon is the Imperial one, and American or Canadian readers should multiply by 1.2 to determine fuel tank capacity, or divide by this amount to find how far a car will travel on the US galon. To avoid confusion, the litre is taken as the standard measure established in 1791 (thank you, Mr Watkins); to convert mpg to litres per 100 km, simply divide the mpg figure into 282.5.

1991—THE THIRTY-FOURTH EDITION

What's new? That's the question we try to answer on this page, introducing yet another edition of *Observers Cars*. First, as far as the cars are concerned, we have a large number of new entries, with less than half of the cars covered being carried over from last year's edition. Those which are repeated from the 1990 edition have been checked, brought up to date where later information is available or where details have changed, and supplied with Road Test performance figures for those which have been tested in the meantime.

Again, I am grateful to the Editor of *Autocar & Motor* for permission to quote the journal's Road Test data, giving a reliable indication of the car's capabilities, provided a test has been published. When the term 'Works' appears in the 'Performance' section, it shows that Road Test information was not available at time of going to press, and the figures quoted are the manufacturer's claims.

Road Test fuel consumption figures are often far-removed from the official figures published by the Department of Transport, and they give a more reliable indication of 'real-life' consumption in consistently hard driving and test conditions. Of the DoT figures, the only one which seems to have any real meaning is the consumption at constant 75 mph, and this is given as well for each car, where available.

In last year's edition, I drew attention to the limitations of the long established 0 to 60 mph acceleration figure. The problem here is that cars have become so quick that the differences between cars on this sprint acceleration are often only fractions of a second. A much more useful figure is acceleration from 0 to 80 mph. So, to answer my initial question, the second important feature of this thirty-fourth edition change is that wherever available, acceleration time from rest to 80 mph is now included.

Why 80 mph? It has the merit of being high enough for aerodynamic shape to begin to take effect, and it gives a much more revealing indication of a car's performance. The oft-quoted 60 mph acceleration figure tends to be influenced by the ability of some cars to reach this speed without a change up into third gear.

Another important factor is that the metric conversion is very close: 80 mph and 130 km/h are almost identical, so it avoids the confusing difference – often ignored – between 60 mph and 100 km/h. Significant, too, is the fact that 80 mph is the motorway cruising speed in many countries. As a broad guide, acceleration to 80 mph in under 10 seconds is very quick indeed, 15 seconds is respectable, and over 20 is slow.

In the 'Identity' sections throughout the book, the word 'Show' is omitted to avoid repetition; 'introduced at Geneva 1991', for example, means introduced at the Geneva Show in 1991. Traditional Show dates are: Brussels in January, Amsterdam in February, Geneva in March, Frankfurt in September, and Birmingham or Paris in October. For 1990 only, the Birmingham Show was in September, but it moves back to October for 1992.

SETBACK YEAR

In the development of the car and motoring in general, there are the good years – many of them – punctuated by occasional periods of setback, when outside influences intervene to slow down progress. It's easy to identify 1990 as one of the disappointing years, with sales diminishing for the first time after a long run of growth. In Britain, the market was down by over 12 per cent, total sales of new cars were still over two million.

A sad result of the tougher market conditions was the disappearance of some of the more vulnerable products. The importer of the little Rumanian off-road vehicle, Dacia, ceased trading; very regrettable too was the collapse of Panther, whose once promising Solo mid-engined sports car had to be abandoned, following the regrettable decision to end the stylish and beautifully turned-out Kallista sports car.

Particularly lamentable, I thought, was the demise of the small Nuneaton-based manufacturer, Reliant, whose Scimitar 1800Ti was another contender to be crossed off the list in 1990 – like watching the drowning man whose valiant struggles to keep afloat fail just before the rescuers can reach him.

Not for all, though, was it a disastrous year, and companies offering attractive cars at the right prices still found ready demand, and managed to improve their competitiveness. Mitsubishi, for example, sold nearly 13,000 cars – an increase of 20 per cent over the 1989 figure. Other makes which beat the trend, to sell more cars in 1990 than in 1989, included Honda, Vauxhall (UK) – although Vauxhall imports were down – Isuzu, the Malaysian Proton, and Lotus – helped by the beginning of Elan sales.

Perhaps spurred on by the need to keep improving their products to make them competitive, manufacturers achieved a very active year for new car announcements. The most important launches of 1990 were the Ford Escort and Orion, Rover Metro and 400-Series, and the Renault Clio which went on the market in France in July.

The year started with Ford's addition of a saloon body style to the Granada and Scorpio range; thanks to Ford's co-operation, I was able to include this as a late entry in the 1990 edition. January also brought Volkswagen's *Umwelt* (environmental) diesel, fitted with catalyst, and in view of the interest in reduced pollution it was obviously right to include this car in the 1991 edition.

Highlights of February were the four-wheel drive versions of the Citroen BX, Fiat's saloon version of the Tipo, called Tempra, and the sleekly styled new Toyota Celica. In the following month, March, Peugeot staged a fascinating launch for additional versions of the new 605 model in Egypt, and a drive in the 605 SV24 across the desert provided some of the fastest motoring I have experienced for many years.

April brought the exciting little Ford Fiesta RS Turbo, and more additions to the impressive Citroën XM range: first the 12-valve turbo diesel, and then the automatic in May. This month also brought the much-improved new Rover Metro.

A significant new trend, threatened for some time, came in June, when the Japanese widened their continuous attack on the British market with a move into the luxury class and the Lexus LS400 was launched. It is, of course, a Toyota, though every effort is made to conceal its identity and make it appear a completely new marque. This is a technique which apparently works in America, but I suspect it might prove less successful in Europe, where the motoring public tend to be better informed and want to know what they are buying.

Also in June 1990 came two other significant new cars, the Honda CRX 1.6i-VT and the Vauxhall Calibra. The Honda is important for its introduction of a neat arrangement to give automatic adjustment of the engine's valve timing and amount of lift, leading to greater efficiency and a wider spread of power. The really outstanding car of June 1990, however, was the Vauxhall Calibra, introduced in the UK with its eye-catching styling and very secure handling.

Problems with the air traffic controllers' strike in France led Renault to cancel the international launch of the new Clio model, and an abbreviated one-day driving exercise was rushed through just before the Birmingham Show in September. It proved sound but not particularly inspiring.

August brought the most important launch of the year, with the new Ford Escort and Orion. Other important announcements were the 12-valve engines for the Mitsubishi Colt and Lancer, a 2-litre engine for the Volkswagen Passat, and Volvo's move to a new straight-six 3-litre engine, appearing in a less harshly styled addition to the range, the 960.

Audi, on the other hand, moved over to a V6 engine for the more powerful version of the new 100 model with 2.8-litre capacity. I was very taken with the new Audi 100, and at time of writing was looking forward to driving it in Britain, following the November launch in Germany, where an otherwise excellent new model launch was slightly marred by the rather dull choice of road route.

Mazda announced that they will be offering a luxury car in 1991, and at the Paris Show in October, Mitsubishi revealed the new big Sigma, which was announced on the UK market in April 1991.

November was memorable for me, as I was at last able to enjoy a long drive in the exciting BMW Z1 two-seater sports car. By the time I had my hands on the Z1, after an earlier disappointment, it had been announced that production would end this year, but it seemed appropriate to include the Z1 again this year in view of its exciting appeal and individuality.

The disappointment of the year came for me in December, when BMW launched the new 3-Series. A low-key international launch was arranged and, being excluded from the small British group invited to drive the car in France just before Christmas, I arranged to join a group from another country. Then, after making all arrangements and booking my own air flight, I was told that I had to be switched to another date which proved totally impossible.

Requests to be allowed to drive the new BMW while everyone was at lunch, or even during the night, were met with total inflexibility; I could go on the revised date, I was told, or not at all. So, with press day drawing near, I was obliged to cross the 3-Series entries off the contents list, which explains why there are only four pages for this make in the 1991 edition. I look back with sadness to the days when the BMW press department used to be the best in the industry; such lack of co-operation would not have happened then.

With this exception, all the significant new cars for the 1991 model year are included in this edition. Various other important but less radical changes are noted, too, such as the greatly improved Mercedes-Benz G-wagen, the Jaguar with new 3.2-litre engine, Saab's very fast new 2.3-litre turbo, and the 24-valve Ford Scorpio.

A slightly later publication date for this edition also made it possible to include a number of cars which did not appear until the Geneva Show in March 1991, in cases where their manufacturers cooperated by providing information in advance. Amongst these are the Audi Coupé S2, Bentley Continental R, Citroen ZX, Honda Legend, Mazda 121, and Mercedes-Benz 600SE (the new S-Class).

It has been a fruitful period for engineering progress, especially at the top end of the market. One of the most significant cars was the Mitsubishi Sigma, mentioned earlier, which uses the anti-lock brake sensors to detect a skid situation and – with computer control taking account of speed, steering angle and lateral grip – controls the car to prevent skidding.

It also restricts wheelspin by cutting engine power and applying the front brake at whichever side is proving most prone to spin. It isn't a substitute for four-wheel drive, but provides more grip than would have been thought possible with front drive alone, and contributes to safety on slippery roads.

Renault introduced electric closing of the tailgate on the 25 model, and a development of the year was the move by BMW and Mercedes-Benz to extend this to the side doors on the top models. Another innovation was double glazing for side windows, though it is difficult to believe this is worth the extra weight except in severe climates.

A significant engine development of the year was Honda's introduction of a simple system for varying both the timing and lift of valve gear; and more manufacturers are obtaining wider torque span from engines by varying the route for the induction air when the engine is turning at high revs.

In all respects – except for sales – it has been a fruitful year, producing over 100 new model introductions; and as many as possible of these are covered in the pages which follow.

ALFA ROMEO (I)   33 1.7 Boxer 16V

Identity: Latest version of the Alfa 33, launched Brussels 1990, has a more modern look, with traditional Alfa Romeo grille continued back into the bonnet swage lines and 16-valve engine available. The eight-valve engine continues, and a 1.5-litre injection engine was added September.

Engine: Front-mounted longitudinal four-cylinder with horizontally opposed pistons and twin ohc per bank working four valves per cylinder; Bosch Motronic ML 4.1 injection and ignition. Bore 87.0 mm, stroke 72.0 mm; capacity 1,712 cc. Power 139 PS (102 kW) at 6500 rpm; torque 119 lb ft (164 Nm) at 4600 rpm. Compression 9.5-to-1. Catalyst: not available.

Transmission: Front-wheel drive; five-speed manual gearbox. Automatic, not available. Top gear speed at 1000 rpm: 19.9 mph (32.0 km/h).

Suspension: Front, independent, MacPherson struts, anti-roll bar. Rear, dead beam axle on trailing arms with coil springs and Panhard rod.

Steering: Rack and pinion. Power assistance: standard. **Brakes:** Vented discs front, solid discs rear. ABS: not available. **Tyres:** 185/60 HR 14. **Fuel Tank:** 10.9 Imp. gall (50 litres). **Unladen weight:** 2138 lb (970 kg).

Dimensions: Length 160.4 in (4075 mm), width 63.5 in (1614 mm), height 53.1 in (1350 mm), wheelbase 97.4 in (2475 mm).

Performance *Autocar & Motor* test: Maximum speed 128 mph (206 km/h); 0 to 60 mph (97 km/h) 8.9 sec; 80 mph (130 km/h) 15.0 sec. Fuel consumption at constant 75 mph (120 km/h): 35.8 mpg; overall test, 29.7 mpg.

Features: Rear spoiler and aerodynamic sills identify the Boxer 16V, which also has alloy wheels as standard; but sunroof is an extra on both models. **Summary:** Although much improved, including a neater instrument layout, I still felt that the 33 was a dated design, with too much of its original Alfasud parentage. Still, it performs well and the standard power steering makes it much lighter to drive.

ALFA ROMEO (I)

75 3.0i V6

Identity: Last year we featured the 75 with the Twin Spark engine, which is now newly available in the 164, so a sensible switch seemed to be inclusion of the 75 in its most powerful form, with the big V6 engine. The 75 retains the classic Alfa layout of a rear transaxle (gearbox and final drive together at the rear).

Engine: Front-mounted longitudinal V6-cylinder with single ohc each bank and 12 valves. Bosch L Jetronic fuel injection. Bore 93.0 mm, stroke 72.6 mm; capacity 2959 cc. Power 182 PS (134 kW) at 5800 rpm; torque 182 lb ft (252 Nm) at 4500 rpm. Compression 9.5-to-1. Catalyst: standard.

Transmission: Rear-wheel drive; five-speed manual gearbox in unit with final drive. Automatic, not available. Top gear speed at 1000 rpm: 24.2 mph (38.9 km/h).

Suspension: Front, independent, wishbones and longitudinal torsion bars; anti-roll bar. Rear, De Dion axle with Watts linkage and coil springs; anti-roll bar.

Steering: Rack and pinion. Power assistance: standard. **Brakes:** Vented discs front, solid discs rear. ABS: not available. **Tyres:** 195/60 VR 14. **Fuel tank:** 15.0 Imp. gall (68 litres). **Unladen weight:** 2866 lb (1300 kg).

Dimensions: Length 174.0 in (4420 mm), width 65.3 in (1660 mm), height 55.1 in (1400 mm), wheelbase 98.8 in (2510 mm).

Performance *Autocar & Motor* test: Maximum speed 137 mph (221 km/h); 0 to 60 mph (97 km/h) 7.5 sec; 80 mph (130 km/h) 12.7 sec. Fuel at constant 75 mph (120 km/h): 30.7 mpg; overall test, 20.5 mpg.

Features: Since the test quoted above, the 75 V6 has become catalyst-equipped as standard; figures may not be quite so good now. **Summary:** Very impressive performance, with leisurely fast cruising, while the rear location of the gearbox also contributes to well-balanced handling. A curious mixture: very refined in some ways, but in others a rather dated saloon with its boxy styling.

ALFA ROMEO (I) 164 Cloverleaf

Identity: New top version of the Alfa Romeo 164 was introduced December 1990 and provided some superb motoring over the Yorkshire moors just before Christmas. Power is increased to the 'magic' 200 bhp, and the Cloverleaf has special equipment and additional aerodynamic skirts and spoilers.

Engine: Front-mounted transverse V6-cylinder with all-alloy construction and single ohc each bank; 12 valves. Bosch Motronic ML4.1 fuel injection/ignition. Bore 93.0 mm, stroke 72.6 mm; capacity 2959 cc. Power 203 PS (149 kW) at 5800 rpm; torque 198 lb ft (274 Nm) at 4400 rpm. Compression 10.0-to-1. Catalyst: standard.

Transmission: Front-wheel drive; five-speed manual gearbox. Automatic, not available. Top gear speed at 1000 rpm: 23.0 mph (37.0 km/h).

Suspension: Front, independent, MacPherson struts, anti-roll bar. Rear, independent, MacPherson struts with double transverse links and trailing arms.

Steering: Rack and pinion. Power assistance: standard. **Brakes:** Vented discs front, solid discs rear. ABS: standard. **Tyres:** 195/60 VR 15. **Fuel tank:** 15.5 Imp. gall (70 litres). **Unladen weight:** 180.0 lb (4560 kg).

Dimensions: Length 69.0 in (1760 mm), width 69.0 in (1760 mm), height 55.1 in (1400 mm), wheelbase 104.7 in (2660 mm).

Performance *Autocar & Motor* test: Maximum speed 143 mph (230 km/h); 0 to 60 mph (97 km/h) 7.8 sec; 80 mph (130 km/h) 12.7 sec. Fuel consumption at constant 75 mph (120 km/h): 30.4 mpg; overall test, 21.4 mpg.

Features: Automatic suspension control is standard, responding to speed and driving conditions; also fitted are air conditioning, electric sunroof and audio with compact disc unit. **Summary:** Standard 164 3.0 V6 continues, but this new Cloverleaf addition brings a more sporty concept. Hence no automatic version and slightly lower gearing. An extremely enjoyable high-performance car.

ALFA ROMEO (I)   164 Twin Spark

Identity: Additional version of the 164, first introduced with V6 engine Frankfurt 1987, came to the UK market in 1990 in less expensive form with an under 2-litre engine. Alfa's ingenious dual-ignition system allows the engine to run efficiently on weak mixtures.

Engine: Front-mounted transverse four-cylinder with twin overhead camshafts, eight valves, and Bosch Motronics with dual ignition. Bore 84.0 mm, stroke 85.5 mm; capacity 1962 cc. Power 150 PS (110 kW) at 5800 rpm; torque 137 lb ft (189 Nm) at 4000 rpm. Compression 10.0-to-1. Catalyst: not available.

Transmission: Front-wheel drive; five-speed manual gearbox. Automatic, not available. Top gear speed at 1000 rpm: 23.8 mph (38.3 km/h).

Suspension: Front, independent, MacPherson struts, anti-roll bar. Rear, independent, MacPherson struts, anti-roll bar.

Steering: Rack and pinion. Power assistance: standard. **Brakes:** Vented discs front and rear. ABS: optional. **Tyres:** 185/70 VR 14. **Fuel tank:** 15.4 Imp. gall (70 litres). **Unladen weight:** 2646 lb (1200 kg).

Dimensions: Length 179.5 in (4560 mm), width 69.0 in (1760 mm), height 55.0 in (1400 mm), wheelbase 105.0 in (2660 mm).

Performance *Autocar & Motor* test: Maximum speed 126 mph (202 km/h); 0 to 60 mph (97 km/h) 9.5 sec; 80 mph (130 km/h) 16.4 sec. Fuel consumption at constant 75 mph (120 km/h): 33.2 mpg; overall test, 23.4 mpg.

Features: Impressive interior styling and quite good standard equipment, especially on the Lusso version, which includes sunroof and ABS. **Summary:** In this form the 164 lacks the effortless performance of the V6, but it's still a very pleasant car to drive, with particularly crisp engine response, while handling benefits from the smaller engine.

ALFA ROMEO (I)   Spider Veloce

Identity: First launched at Geneva 1966 as the Duetto, the pretty little Alfa two-seater reappeared in updated, but still classic, form at the same show 24 years later. More practical bodywork and 2-litre engine. No rhd model is available from the factory, but in late 1990, a very well-engineered rhd conversion was developed by Seaking.

Engine: Front-mounted longitudinal four-cylinder with twin chain-driven ohc and Bosch Motronic ML 4.1 ignition/injection system. Bore 84.0 mm, stroke 88.5 mm; capacity 1962 cc. Power 128 PS (94 kW) at 5800 rpm; torque 123 lb ft (170 Nm) at 4200 rpm. Compression 10.0-to-1. Catalyst: optional.

Transmission: Rear-wheel drive; five-speed manual gearbox. Automatic, not available. Top gear speed at 1000 rpm: 21.8 mph (35.0 km/h).

Suspension: Front, independent, wishbones and coil springs; anti-roll bar. Rear, live axle on longitudinal links with central wishbone.

Steering: Recirculating ball. Power assistance: not available. **Brakes:** Solid discs front and rear. ABS: not available. **Tyres:** 195/60 R 15. **Fuel tank:** 10.1 Imp. gall (46 litres). **Unladen weight:** 2447 lb (1110 kg).

Dimensions: Length 167.6 in (4258 mm), width 64.2 in (1630 mm), height 50.8 in (1290 mm), wheelbase 88.6 in (2250 mm).

Performance Works: Maximum speed 118 mph (190 km/h); 0 to 62 mph (100 km/h) 9.4 sec. Fuel consumption at constant 75 mph (120 km/h): 32.5 mpg.

Features: Classic styling of the 60s is retained but cleverly brought up to date, and the Spider now features such items as electrically adjusted mirrors. **Summary:** Some of the 1960s features may be less desirable, such as the rather crude ventilator outlets, but the Spider is certainly a most eye-catching shape. The Seaking conversion to right-hand drive is well engineered, except for too-tight – and hence jerky – throttle cable action.

ASTON MARTIN (GB)　　Virage Volante

Identity: It took well over a year from the Birmingham 1988 launch of the Virage to get the car into production, but everything started happening in 1990, including launch of the convertible model, Volante, at the Paris Show. Magnificent for high-speed grand touring, but not so good in traffic and at lower speeds. 2 + 2 launched Geneva 1991.

Engine: Front-mounted longitudinal V8-cylinder with twin chain-driven ohc; four valves per cylinder. Weber Marelli fuel injection. Bore 100.0 mm, stroke 85.0 mm; capacity 5340 cc. Power 334 PS (246 kW) at 6000 rpm; torque 343 lb ft (475 Nm) at 3700 rpm. Comp. 9.5-to-1. Catalyst: standard.

Transmission: Rear-wheel drive; five-speed manual gearbox. Automatic, three-speed optional extra. Top-gear speed at 1000 rpm: 27.1 mph (43.7 km/h).

Suspension: Front, independent, wishbones and coil springs; anti-roll bar. Rear, de Dion axle with Watts linkage and triangulated radius arms; dual rate springs and damper units.

Steering: Rack and pinion. Power assistance: standard. **Brakes:** Vented discs front, solid discs rear. ABS: not available. **Tyres:** 225/60 ZR 16. **Fuel tank:** 26.0 Imp. gall (118 litres). **Unladen weight:** 3946 lb (1790 kg).

Dimensions: Length 186.8 in (4745 mm), width 72.8 in (1849 mm), height 52.0 in (1320 mm), wheelbase 102.8 in (2611 mm).

Performance *Autocar & Motor* test (saloon): Maximum speed 157 mph (252 km/h); 0 to 60 mph (97 km/h) 6.8 sec; 80 mph (130 km/h) 10.5 sec. Fuel consumption, overall test, 15.6 mpg.

Features: Superb finish and luxurious leather trimming, but a little short on modern refinements such as remote central locking. Neatly trimmed power hood. **Summary:** An all too brief one-day drive with the Virage was most exhilarating, especially at higher speed. Less good aspects are the big turning circle and difficulty of driving smoothly at low speeds, but it is certainly a most exciting and rewarding machine.

AUDI (D)   Coupé S2

Identity: Added to the Audi range in August 1990, the Coupé S2 is the natural successor to the Quattro, having four-wheel drive and 20-valve turbocharged engine. In one of these I enjoyed magnificent motoring to Geneva and back in 1991, and appreciated its superbly balanced and controllable handling over the mountains.

Engine: Front-mounted longitudinal five-cylinder with alloy head and twin ohc working four valves per cylinder. Bosch Motronics and turbocharger with intercooler. Bore 81.0 mm, stroke 86.4 mm; capacity 2226 cc. Power 220 PS (162 kW) at 5900 rpm; torque 223 lb ft (309 Nm) at 1950 rpm. Compression 9.3-to-1. Catalyst: standard.

Transmission: Four-wheel drive; five-speed manual gearbox. Automatic, not available. Top gear speed at 1000 rpm: 24.7 mph (39.7 km/h).

Suspension: Front, independent, MacPherson struts, anti-roll bar. Rear, independent, wishbones and coil springs; anti-roll bar.

Steering: Rack and pinion. Power assistance: standard. **Brakes:** Vented discs front, solid discs rear. ABS: standard. **Tyres:** 205/55 ZE 16. **Fuel tank:** 15.4 Imp. gall (70 litres). **Unladen weight:** 3130 lb (1420 kg).

Dimensions: Length 173.3 in (4401 mm), width 67.6 in (1716 mm), height 54.1 in (1375 mm), wheelbase 100.4 in (2549 mm).

Performance *Autocar & Motor* test: Maximum speed 148 mph (238 km/h); 0 to 60 mph (97 km/h) 5.9 sec, 80 mph (130 km/h) 10.5 sec. Fuel consumption at constant 75 mph (120 km/h): 30.4 mpg; overall test, 18.2 mpg.

Features: Comprehensive equipment includes 'one touch' electric sunroof. Permanent four-wheel drive with Torsen centre diff. and lockable rear diff. Procon-Ten safety system standard. **Summary:** An extremely fast and very safe car, able to cruise at 130 mph with excellent stability and brakes, plus very high standards of cornering.

AUDI (D)   Quattro 20V

Identity: At one time it looked as though the famous Audi Quattro (not to be confused with the small 'q' quattro versions of other Audis, which simply indicate four-wheel drive) was to be dropped; but it received a new lease of life in November 1989, with the 20-valve turbo engine. Production ends this year, but the Quattro remains a classic.

Engine: Front-mounted longitudinal five-cylinder with alloy head and twin ohc operating four valves per cylinder, through hydraulic tappets. Bosch Motronics and turbocharger with inter-cooler. Bore 81.0 mm, stroke 86.4 mm; capacity 2226 cc. Power 223 PS (164 kW) at 5900 rpm; torque 228 lb ft (315 Nm) at 1950 rpm. Comp. 9.3-to-1. Catalyst: standard.

Transmission: Four-wheel drive; five-speed manual gearbox. Automatic, not available. Torsen centre diff. and lockable rear diff. Top gear speed at 1000 rpm: 22.1 mph (35.6 km/h).

Suspension: Front, independent, MacPherson struts, anti-roll bar. Rear, independent, MacPherson struts, anti-roll bar.

Steering: Rack and pinion. Power assistance: standard. **Brakes:** Vented discs front, solid discs rear. ABS: standard. **Tyres:** 215/50 R 15 88V. **Fuel tank:** 19.8 Imp. gall (90 litres). **Unladen weight:** 2866 lb (1300 kg).

Dimensions: Length 173.4 in (4404 mm), width 67.8 in (1723 mm), height 52.9 in (1344 mm), wheelbase 99.3 in (2524 mm).

Performance *Autocar & Motor* test: Maximum speed 141 mph (227 km/h); 0 to 60 mph (97 km/h) 6.3 sec. Fuel consumption at constant 75 mph (120 km/h): 28.5 mpg; overall test, 19.1 mpg.

Features: 'Old' style coupé body with spoiler on rear, special alloy wheels, and fog lamps built into front apron. Full equipment, although sunroof is only winding type. **Summary:** Appearance now rather dated, but the Quattro is given even more staggering performance than before, now with 20-valve engine and turbocharging. With four-wheel drive it remains very manageable and safe even when driven extremely fast.

AUDI (D)   100 2.3E

Identity: Advanced replacement for the 100 model was launched in Germany November 1990, on UK market April 1991. Tremendous attention paid to sound-proofing, while suspension, handling and controls all show improvements. Appearance is confusingly similar to the V8, but identity point is the location of the indicators: adjacent to headlamps.

Engine: Front-mounted longitudinal five-cylinder with alloy head and single ohc; hydraulic tappets working ten valves. Bosch KE Jetronic injection. Bore 82.5 mm, stroke 86.4 mm; capacity 2309 cc. Power 133 PS (98 kW) at 5500 rpm; torque 135 lb ft (186 Nm) at 4000 rpm. Compression 9.2-to-1. Catalyst: standard.

Transmission: Front-wheel drive; five-speed manual gearbox. Automatic, optional extra. Quattro four-wheel drive version also available. Top gear speed at 1000 rpm: 22.0 mph (35.4 km/h).

Suspension: Front, independent, MacPherson struts; anti-roll bar. Self-correcting steering geometry. Rear, dead beam axle on trailing arms with Panhard rod; anti-roll bar.

Steering: Rack and pinion. Power assistance: standard. **Brakes:** Solid discs front, drums rear. ABS: optional. **Tyres:** 195/65 R 15 H. **Fuel tank:** 17.6 Imp. gall (80 litres). **Unladen weight:** 3020 lb (1370 kg).

Dimensions: Length 188.6 in (4790 mm), width 70.0 in (1777 mm), height 56.3 in (1431 mm), wheelbase 105.8 in (2687 mm).

Performance Works: Maximum speed 126 mph (202 km/h); 0 to 62 mph (100 km/h) 10.2 sec. Fuel consumption at constant 75 mph (120 km/h): 31.7 mpg.

Features: Clever body shape is even more aerodynamic than before, and offers generous boot space. Good equipment, except for lack of remote central locking. **Summary:** In this form, the 2.3 engine with catalyst lacked acceleration, but was exceptionally quiet and relaxed when cruising at 110 mph. Impeccable finish inside and out.

AUDI (D)   100 V6 quattro

Identity: In addition to the familiar four- and five-cylinder engines, Audi launched a delightfully smooth V6 to go with the new 100, giving high torque output, while enhancing the quietness of the car. It is available with front-drive or in quattro form (details follow). Quattro with automatic is expected to become available later.

Engine: Front-mounted longitudinal V6-cylinder with alloy heads and single ohc each bank. Ingenious multi-path intake manifold achieves high torque without spoiling peak power. MPI electronic fuel injection. Bore 82.5 mm, stroke 86.4 mm; capacity 2771 cc. Power 174 PS (128 kW) at 5500 rpm; torque 181 lb ft (250 Nm) at 3000 rpm. Compression 10.0-to-1. Catalyst: standard.

Transmission: Four-wheel drive; five-speed manual gearbox. Automatic, not available. Top gear speed at 1000 rpm: 22.1 mph (35.6 km/h).

Suspension: Front, independent, MacPherson struts; anti-roll bar. Self-correcting steering geometry. Rear, independent, four-joint trapezium arms with transverse links. Coil springs and anti-roll bar.

Steering: Rack and pinion. Power assistance: standard. **Brakes:** Vented discs front, solid discs rear. ABS: standard. **Tyres:** 195/65 R 15V. **Fuel tank:** 17.6 Imp. gall (80 litres). **Unladen weight:** 3307 lb (1500 kg).

Dimensions: Length 188.6 in (4790 mm), width 70.0 in (1777 mm), height 56.3 in (1431 mm), wheelbase 105.8 in (2687 mm).

Performance Works: Maximum speed 135 mph (218 km/h); 0 to 62 mph (100 km/h) 8.0 sec; 80 mph (130 km/h) 17.8 sec. Fuel consumption at constant 75 mph (120 km/h): 28.3 mpg.

Features: Six flap valves in the engine intake system open at 4,000 rpm to re-route the mixture path, giving better power. Comprehensive equipment and lockable centre differential. **Summary:** With this engine, the new Audi 100 is an outstanding car, providing effortless performance and high standards of quietness and refinement, especially for the smooth, snatch-free power train.

AUDI (D)   V8

Identity: Described as a 'new alternative in the luxury market', the V8 was launched Paris 1988, and introduced a magnificent specification, with four-wheel drive, high torque V8 32-valve engine, and automatic transmission. Reshaped bonnet and deeper front grille identify the V8 from the basically similar 100/200 range. On British market 1990.

Engine: Front-mounted longitudinal V8-cylinder with twin overhead camshafts each bank operating four valves per cyl.; all-alloy construction and Bosch Motronic injection/ignition system. Bore 81.0 mm, stroke 86.4 mm; capacity 3562 cc. Power 250 PS (184 kW) at 5800 rpm; torque 246 lb ft (340 Nm) at 4000 rpm. Compression 10.6-to-1. Catalyst: standard.

Transmission: Four-wheel drive. Automatic, four-speed standard. Manual transmission not available. Top gear speed at 1000 rpm: 26.1 mph (42.0 km/h).

Suspension: Front, independent, MacPherson struts, anti-roll bar. Rear, independent, trailing arms; coil springs, anti-roll bar.

Steering: Rack and pinion. Power assistance: standard. **Brakes:** Vented discs front, and rear. ABS: standard. **Tyres:** 215/60 VR 15. **Fuel tank:** 17.6 Imp. gall (80 litres). **Unladen weight:** 3770 lb (1710 kg).

Dimensions: Length 191.3 in (4861 mm), width 71.4 in (1814 mm), height 55.9 in (1420 mm), wheelbase 106.3 in (2702 mm).

Performance *Autocar & Motor* test: Maximum speed 144 mph (232 km/h); 0 to 60 mph (97 km/h) 9.0 sec; 80 mph (130 km/h) 14.0 sec. Fuel consumption at 75 mph (120 km/h): 25.9 mpg; overall test, 15.3 mpg.

Features: Three viscous couplings control the torque split to all four wheels. Top equipment including air conditioning and anti-lock brakes.
Summary: Wonderfully quiet car when cruising at 120 mph, and the new V8 is very definitely a rival in the top BMW, Mercedes, Jaguar class, while offering the superb traction an advanced four-wheel drive system makes possible. This was my superb transport to the Paris Show in 1990.

BENTLEY (GB) Continental

Identity: For many years the name of Bentley Continental spelled magic in the realms of luxury transport, and it is still one of the most exotic and eye-catching cars in production, adapted from the former Rolls-Royce model in mid-1984.

Engine: Front-mounted longitudinal V8-cylinder with alloy block and heads, and pushrod ohv; hydraulic tappets. Bosch K-Motronic fuel injection. Bore 104.1 mm, stroke 99.1 mm; capacity 6750 cc. Power and torque: no data released. Compression 8.0-to-1. Catalyst: no-cost option.

Transmission: Rear-wheel drive; three-speed GM automatic with R-R column-mounted electric control. Top gear speed at 1000 rpm: 30.0 mph (48.3 km/h).

Suspension: Front, independent, wishbones and coil springs with compliant controlled upper levers; anti-roll bar. Rear, independent, semi-trailing arms; coil springs and self-levelling struts; anti-roll bar.

Steering: Rack and pinion. Power assistance: standard. **Brakes:** Vented discs front, solid discs rear. ABS: standard. **Tyres:** 235/70 R 15. **Fuel tank:** 23.5 lmp. gall (107 litres). **Unladen weight:** 5360 lb (2430 kg).

Dimensions: Length 204.6 in (5196 mm), width 72.0 in (1829 mm), height 59.8 in (1518 mm), wheelbase 120.5 in (3061 mm).

Performance Works: Maximum speed 127 mph (205 km/h); 0 to 60 mph (97 km/h) 10.9 sec. Fuel consumption at constant 75 mph (120 km/h): 18.7 mpg.

Features: Power operated hood, though the folded hood still sticks up at the back a bit and has a rather tedious detachable tonneau cover.
Summary: The Continental always seems to lag slightly behind the other models in new developments and so does not yet get the electronic suspension control introduced for the rest of the range. But it does have the automatic parking brake release.

BENTLEY (GB)   Continental R

Identity: An unusually well-kept secret was Bentley's surprise announcement of a new model at Geneva 1991—the Continental R: familiar running gear, but entirely new body, owing much to the Project 90 special shown at Geneva 1985. It is the first uniquely styled Bentley since 1952.

Engine: Front-mounted longitudinal V8-cylinder with all-alloy construction and hydraulic tappets. Two valves per cylinder; Bosch K-Motronic fuel injection and Garrett TO4 turbocharger. Bore 104.1 mm, stroke 99.1 mm; capacity 6750 cc. Power and torque: no data released. Compression 8.0-to-1. Catalyst: standard.

Transmission: Rear-wheel drive. Automatic, four-speed, standard, with mode control. Top gear speed at 1000 rpm: 28.7 mph (46.2 km/h).

Suspension: Front, independent, coil springs and wishbones with electronically controlled dampers; anti-roll bar. Rear, independent, coil springs and semi-trailing arms; electronically controlled dampers and hydraulic self-levelling; anti-roll bar.

Steering: Rack and pinion. Power assistance: standard. **Brakes:** Vented discs front, solid discs rear. ABS: standard. **Tyres:** 255/60 ZR 16. **Fuel tank:** 23.5 Imp. gall (107 litres). **Unladen weight:** 5340 lb (2420 kg).

Dimensions: Length 210.3 in (5342 mm), width 80.5 in (2044 mm), height 57.6 in (1462 mm), wheelbase 120.5 in (3061 mm).

Performance Works: Maximum speed 145 mph (233 km/h); 0 to 60 mph (97 km/h) 6.6 sec. Fuel consumption at 75 mph (120 km/h): 19.3 mpg.

Features: Luxuriously trimmed and extravagantly equipped two-door coupé, most beautifully fitted out inside, with console flowing through from front into the rear compartment. **Summary:** The elegant new body of the Continental R is in steel with integral bumpers and front air dam. Flush glazing, but wipers are still visible, and the round headlamps look a bit dated. Nevertheless, the launch of the Continental R certainly caused a stir at Geneva.

Identity: Intermediate stage between the BMW 535i and the very high performance M5 model is this Sport version, launched early 1989, featuring the body styling embellishments and aerodynamic aids produced for the 5-Series by M-Technic, plus special alloy wheels and wide tyres.

Engine: Front-mounted longitudinal six-cylinder with alloy head and single ohc working 12 valves. Bosch Motronic system. Bore 92.0 mm, stroke 86.0 mm; capacity 3430 cc. Power 211 PS (157 kW) at 5700 rpm; torque 225 lb ft (305 Nm) at 4000 rpm. Compression 9.0-to-1. Catalyst: optional.

Transmission: Rear-wheel drive; five-speed manual gearbox. Automatic, optional extra. Top gear speed at 1000 rpm: 24.5 mph (39.4 km/h).

Suspension: Front, independent, double-jointed spring struts with anti-dive and self-compensating features; anti-roll bar. Rear, independent, semi-trailing arms with auxiliary trailing arms, featuring anti-dive and anti-squat geometry; coil springs and anti-roll bar.

Steering: ZF Recirculating ball. Power assistance: standard. **Brakes:** Vented discs front, and rear. ABS: standard. **Tyres:** 240/45 ZR 415. **Fuel tank:** 17.6 Imp. gall (80 litres). **Unladen weight:** 3362 lb (1525 kg).

Dimensions: Length 185.8 in (4720 mm), width 68.9 in (1751 mm), height 55.6 in (1412 mm), wheelbase 108.7 in (2761 mm).

Performance *Autocar & Motor* test: Maximum speed 141 mph (227 km/h); 0 to 60 mph (97 km/h) 7.4 sec; 80 mph (130 km/h) 12.6 sec. Fuel consumption at constant 75 mph (120 km/h): 29.4 mpg; overall test, 22.3 mpg.

Features: Front spoiler is integrated with bumper, and in body colour with fog lamps and air intakes. Wing on bootlid. Equipment as Special Equipment model. **Summary:** M-Technik additions to the bodywork enhance the appearance and avoid looking too much like 'add-ons'. The rear spoiler is claimed to make big reductions in aerodynamic lift at speed, contributing to better stability in cross winds.

BMW (D) 750i

Identity: At first, the new BMW V12 engine was available only in the long-wheelbase 7-Series; but in 1989 the 750i standard wheelbase model was added to the range, and I enjoyed a memorable journey to the Frankfurt Show in one in September that year.

Engine: Front-mounted longitudinal V12-cylinder with alloy block and heads; single chain-driven ohc per bank, and hydraulic tappets. Bosch Motronic injection-ignition system. Bore 84.0 mm, stroke 75.0 mm; capacity 4988 cc. Power 300 PS (223 kW) at 5200 rpm; torque 325 lb ft (450 Nm) at 4100 rpm. Compression 8.8-to-1. Catalyst: standard.

Transmission: Rear-wheel drive; four-speed automatic, standard. Top gear speed at 1000 rpm: 33.4 mph (53.8 km/h).

Suspension: Front, independent, double-jointed spring struts with anti-dive and self-compensating features; anti-roll bar. Rear, independent, semi-trailing arms with auxiliary arms and coil springs; anti-dive, anti-squat compensation.

Steering: Ball and nut. Power assistance: standard. **Brakes:** Vented discs front, solid discs rear. ABS: standard. **Tyres:** 255/60 VR 15. **Fuel tank:** 22.4 Imp. gall (102 litres). **Unladen weight:** 3968 lb (1800 kg).

Dimensions: Length 193.3 in (4910 mm), width 72.6 in (1845 mm), height 55.1 in (1400 mm), wheelbase 111.5 in (2833 mm).

Performance *Autocar & Motor* test: Maximum speed 152 mph (245 km/h); 0 to 60 mph (97 km/h) 7.3 sec; 80 mph (130 km/h) 11.2 sec. Fuel consumption at constant 75 mph (120 km/h): 25.9 mpg; overall test, 16.2 mpg.

Features: Leather upholstery and top equipment, including air conditioning and selectable suspension firmness. Electric seat adjustment. **Summary:** Impressive ability to cruise at very high speeds (120–130 mph seems to call for little effort from the engine), and supremely comfortable on a long journey; but the automatic transmission, with awkward selector, is disappointing in spite of having switchable mode control.

BMW (D)   850i

Identity: Exciting sports coupé launched Frankfurt 1989, to replace the respected 635CSi range. It appears first as the 850i, with V12 5-litre engine, but the 8-Series is expected to develop into a range, with six-cylinder engine versions later. Sleek four-seater two-door body.

Engine: Front-mounted longitudinal V12-cylinder with alloy block and heads; single chain-driven ohc per bank, and hydraulic tappets. Bosch Motronic injection-ignition system. Bore 84.0 mm, stroke 75.0 mm; capacity 4988 cc. Power 300 PS (223 kW) at 5200 rpm; torque 325 lb (450 Nm) at 4100 rpm. Compression 8.8-to-1. Catalyst: standard.

Transmission: Rear-wheel drive; six-speed manual gearbox. Automatic, optional, four-speed. Top gear speed at 1000 rpm: 34.4 mph (55.4 km/h).

Suspension: Front, independent, double-jointed spring struts with anti-dive and self compensating features; anti-roll bar. Rear, independent, five-link layout with coil springs and anti-dive, anti-squat compensation; anti-roll bar.

Steering: Ball and nut. Power assistance: standard. **Brakes:** Vented discs front, solid discs rear. ABS: standard. **Tyres:** 235/50 ZR 16. **Fuel tank:** 19.8 Imp. gall (90 litres). **Unladen weight:** 3946 lb (1790 kg).

Dimensions: Length 188.1 in (4780 mm), width 73.0 in (1855 mm), height 52.8 in (1340 mm), wheelbase 105.6 in (2684 mm).

Performance *Autocar & Motor* test: Maximum speed 157 mph (253 km/h); 0 to 60 mph (97 km/h) 7.2 sec; 80 mph (130 km/h) 11.0 sec. Fuel consumption at constant 75 mph (120 km/h): 27.2 mpg; overall test, 14.4 mpg.

Features: Many technical innovations, including six-speed gearbox, seat-belt system integrated with seats, and ellipsoid pop-up headlamps.
Summary: Worthy successor to the much-admired 635 CSi, though it's perhaps disappointing that it is again only produced as a closed car. Very high performance, and the 850i in manual form comes with automatic anti-wheelspin control. Automatic has stability control.

Identity: Great interest was aroused when a sneak picture of a charming little two-seater sports car was issued by BMW; then, at Frankfurt 1987, it was confirmed that it would go into production from June 1988. Sadly, it was built only in left-hand drive form and ceases production this year.

Engine: Front-mounted longitudinal six-cylinder with belt-driven ohc and inclined valves in hemi head. Bosch Motronic injection/ignition system. Bore 84.0 mm, stroke 75.0 mm; capacity 2494 cc. Power 170 PS (125 kW) at 5800 rpm; torque 163 lb ft (226 Nm) at 4000 rpm. Compression 9.7-to-1. Catalyst: standard.

Transmission: Rear-wheel drive; five-speed manual gearbox. Automatic, not available. Top gear speed at 1000 rpm: 24.5 mph (39.5 km/h).

Suspension: Front, independent, MacPherson struts, anti-roll bar. Rear, independent, trailing and semi-trailing arms; coil springs and telescopic dampers, anti-roll bar.

Steering: Rack and pinion. Power assistance: standard. **Brakes:** Vented discs front, solid discs rear. ABS: standard. **Tyres:** 205/55 VR 15. **Fuel tank:** 12.1 Imp. gall (55 litres). **Unladen weight:** 2425 lb (1100 kg).

Dimensions: Length 154.3 in (3921 mm), width 66.5 in (1690 mm), height 50.3 in (1277 mm), wheelbase 96.5 in (2450 mm).

Performance *Autocar & Motor* test: Maximum speed 136 mph (219 km/h); 0 to 60 mph (97 km/h) 7.9 sec; 80 mph (130 km/h) 13.5 sec. Fuel consumption at constant 75 mph (120 km/h): 34.5 mpg; overall test, 24.0 mpg.

Features: Bodywork in composite, and ingenious provision for the shallow doors to open downwards into the sills. Pop-up headlamps and neat folding hood. **Summary:** Intriguing new approaches to familiar problems such as door treatment for a small convertible two-seater, and use of a monocoque chassis. Engine is mounted well back in the frame, qualifying almost as 'mid-engined'.

BRISTOL (GB)   Britannia

Identity: Years pass and nothing much changes at Bristol, where the foursome – Brigand, Beaufort, Beaufighter turbo, and this model, the Britannia saloon – continue in production with traditional craftsmanship and American Chrysler engines. Welded steel chassis with aluminium panelling.

Engine: Front-mounted longitudinal V8-cylinder with chain-driven centre camshaft, pushrods and hydraulic tappets. Carter four-choke carb. Bore 101.6 mm, stroke 90.9 mm; capacity 5900 cc. No power or torque data revealed by Bristol. Compression 8.5-to-1. Catalyst: optional.

Transmission: Rear-wheel drive; three-speed manual gearbox. Automatic, standard. Top gear speed at 1000 rpm: 28.6 mph (46.0 km/h).

Suspension: Front, independent, wishbones and coil springs; anti-roll bar. Rear, live axle on longitudinal links with Watts linkage; torsion bar springs with self-levelling provision.

Steering: Recirculating ball. Power assistance: standard. **Brakes:** Solid discs front, and rear. ABS: not available. **Tyres:** 215/70 VR 15. **Fuel tank:** 18.0 Imp. gall (82 litres). **Unladen weight:** 3850 lb (1746kg).

Dimensions: Length 193.0 in (4902 mm), width 69.5 in (1765 mm), height 56.5 in (1435 mm), wheelbase 114.0 in (2895 mm).

Performance Works: Maximum speed 140 mph (225 km/h); 0 to 60 mph (97 km/h) 7.2 sec. Fuel consumption at constant 75 mph (120 km/h): 17.0 mpg.

Features: Interior finish is much as was applied to top quality cars some thirty years ago, with walnut veneered facia and leather upholstery.
Summary: The Bristol has moved with the times in such matters as bringing in electric seat adjustment, but the old traditional craftsmanship and construction methods continue. Britannia is the main seller of the range.

BUICK (USA)   Reatta Convertible

Identity: Addition to the Reatta range for 1990 was this elegant convertible model, which continues for 1991 with few changes. Restyled wheels are the chief identity point for the 1991 model.

Engine: Front-mounted transverse V6-cylinder with alloy heads and central chain-driven camshaft operating hydraulic tappets. Sequential fuel injection. Bore 96.5 mm, stroke 86.4 mm; capacity 3785 cc. Power 167 PS (123 kW) at 4800 rpm; torque 210 lb ft (290 Nm) at 2000 rpm. Compression 8.5-to-1. Catalyst: standard.

Transmission: Front-wheel drive; five-speed automatic, standard. Top gear speed at 1000 rpm: 35.0 mph (56.3 km/h).

Suspension: Front, independent, MacPherson struts, anti-roll bar. Rear, independent, modular assembly with single transverse leaf spring and deflected disc dampers; anti-roll bar.

Steering: Rack and pinion. Power assistance: standard. **Brakes:** Solid discs front, and rear. ABS: standard. **Tyres:** P215/65 R 15. **Fuel tank:** 15.2 Imp. gall (69 litres). **Unladen weight:** 3562 lb (1615 kg).

Dimensions: Length 183.7 in (4665 mm), width 73.0 in (1854 mm), height 51.2 in (1300 mm), wheelbase 98.5 in (2502 mm).

Performance (est): Maximum speed 120 mph (193 km/h). Fuel consumption (est), 25 mpg.

Features: Hood compartment has a rigid, hinged cover, with electric release; hood action is manual, but tensioning is also electric. **Summary:** Reatta is only a two-seater, and presents tidy appearance whether open or with hood raised. Although the instruments have changed to analogue, the speedometer reading is switchable, and can be digital, analogue, or both. Air bag, and many other special features.

CADILLAC (USA)   Allanté

Identity: Built by Pininfarina in Italy, and then the bodies are flown to America, a Jumbo-full at a time, to be fitted with running gear. For 1989, the Allanté was given a larger engine, 4½-litre instead of 4.1. Body in aluminium and galvanised steel. Two-seater, with hood and hardtop.

Engine: Front-mounted transverse V8-cylinder with alloy block and heads; cast iron cylinder liners. Pushrod valve gear and hydraulic tappets. Electronic sequential port fuel injection. Bore 92.0 mm, stroke 84.0 mm; capacity 4467 cc. Power 203 PS (149 kW) at 4300 rpm; torque 270 lb ft (366 Nm) at 3200 rpm. Compression 9.0-to-1. Catalyst; standard.

Transmission: Front-wheel drive; manual gearbox not available. Automatic, four-speed, standard. Top gear speed at 1000 rpm: 27.1 mph (43.5 km/h).

Suspension: Front, independent, MacPherson struts with lateral and trailing links; anti-roll bar. Rear, independent, struts, H-control arms and transverse composite leaf spring; telescopic dampers.

Steering: Rack and pinion. Power assistance: standard. **Brakes:** Vented discs front, solid discs rear. ABS: standard. **Tyres:** P225/55 VR 16 Goodyear Eagle. **Fuel tank:** 18.3 Imp. gall (83.3 litres). **Unladen weight:** 3492 lb (1584 kg).

Dimensions: Length 178.6 in (4537 mm), width 73.5 in (1866 mm), height 52.2 in (1327 mm), wheelbase 99.4 in (2525 mm).

Performance Works: Maximum speed 115 mph (185 km/h); 0 to 60 mph (97 km/h) 8.5 sec. Fuel consumption at constant 75 mph (120 km/h): 22 mpg.

Features: Power-operated hood was introduced mid-1990. Other new features include speed-dependent damping and air intake resonator to reduce engine noise. **Summary:** Wonderfully draught-free car when open, as a result of the swept back windscreen style. Body is also commendably taut for a convertible, with no scuttle-shake on bumps. Traction control system introduced for 1990.

CATERHAM CARS (GB) Super 7 HPC

Identity: Still higher goes the power/weight ratio of the little Caterham Seven, following the decision to adopt the Vauxhall 16-valve 2-litre engine in this special HPC model for 1991. The Super 7 continues, but moves to the Rover K-Series 16-valve engine.

Engine: Front-mounted longitudinal four-cylinder with alloy head and belt-driven twin ohc working 16 valves; twin Weber 45 DCOE carbs. Bore 86.0 mm, stroke 86.0 mm; capacity 1998 cc. Power 175 PS (129 kW) at 6000 rpm; torque 155 lb ft (214 Nm) at 4800 rpm. Compression 10.5-to-1. Catalyst: not available.

Transmission: Rear-wheel drive; five-speed manual gearbox. Automatic, not available. Top gear speed at 1000 rpm: 20.2 mph (32.5 km/h).

Suspension: Front, independent, wishbones and coil springs; anti-roll bar. Rear, de Dion axle with radius arms and lower diagonal links; coil springs and anti-roll bar.

Steering: Rack and pinion. Power assistance: not available. **Brakes:** Vented discs front and rear. ABS: not available. **Tyres:** 205/45 VR 16. **Fuel tank:** 10.0 Imp. gall (45.5 litres). **Unladen weight:** 1380 lb (626 kg).

Dimensions: Length 133.5 in (3390 mm), width 62.0 in (1580 mm), height 42.5 in (1080 mm), wheelbase 88.0 in (2230 mm).

Performance *Autocar & Motor* test: Maximum speed 126 mph (203 km/h); 0 to 60 mph (97 km/h) 5.2 sec; 80 mph (130 km/h) 8.4 sec. Fuel consumption, overall test, 17.3 mpg.

Features: Weather protection is rather basic, but much better than a motorcycle, which might be the nearest comparison! Alloy wheels are standard, and there is a roll-over cage. **Summary:** The heavy fuel consumption recorded in the test is a bit alarming, but perhaps reflects a lot of use of that staggering acceleration, with 80 mph coming up in only 8.4 sec from rest, and 120 mph in 25.7 sec.

CHEVROLET (USA)   Corvette ZR-1

Identity: After last year's edition, a reader wrote to suggest that I had grossly under-estimated the performance of the ZR-1, and this was confirmed when one of these cars raised the world 24-hour speed record from 161 mph to 176 mph. I blame the inadequacies of American press information, but this issue puts the record straight.

Engine: Front-mounted longitudinal V8-cylinder with alloy heads and block; twin ohc each bank, working four valves per cylinder. Multec fuel injection. Bore 99.0 mm, stroke 93.0 mm; capacity 5736 cc. Power 380 PS (279 kW) at 5800 rpm; torque 370 lb ft (511 Nm) at 4800 rpm. Compression 11.0-to-1. Catalyst: standard.

Transmission: Rear-wheel drive; six-speed manual gearbox. Automatic, not available. Top gear speed at 1000 rpm: 42.5 mph (68.3 km/h).

Suspension: Front, independent, wishbones and transverse glass-fibre reinforced plastic leaf spring; anti-roll bar. Rear, independent, five-link location with transverse glass-fibre plastic leaf spring; anti-roll bar.

Steering: Rack and pinion. Power assistance: standard. **Brakes:** Vented discs front and rear. ABS: standard. **Tyres:** Front: 275/40 ZR 17; rear: 315/35 ZR 17. **Fuel tank:** 16.7 Imp. gall (76 litres). **Unladen weight:** 3465 lb (1571 kg).

Dimensions: Length 178.5 in (4534 mm), width 73.2 in (1859 mm), height 46.7 in (1186 mm), wheelbase 96.2 in (2443 mm).

Performance *Autocar & Motor* test: Maximum speed 176 mph (283 km/h); 0 to 60 mph (97 km/h) 5.6 sec; 80 mph (130 km/h) 9.2 sec. Fuel consumption: overall (est), 20 mpg.

Features: Identity feature for 1991 model is the fitting of four horizontal louvres to the rear of the front wheel each side. Corvettes now have a cooler for the power steering fluid (!) and auxiliary power lead for cellular phone and other accessories. **Summary:** Very high performance for an American car, and the six-speed gearbox has automatic guidance from first direct to fourth on light throttle.

CHEVROLET (J+CDN)   Geo Storm

Identity: Produced in Japan for the American market and assembled in Canada, the Geo range took about 300,000 sales in America last year. The hatchback model is new for 1991, joining the GSi and 2+2 coupés. The tailgate is of glass; all models have an air-bag restraint system for the driver.

Engine: Front-mounted transverse four-cylinder with alloy head, and single ohc working three valves per cylinder. Multec fuel injection. Bore 80.0 mm, stroke 79.0 mm; capacity 1,589 cc. Power 96 PS (71 kW) at 5800 rpm; torque 97 lb ft (134 Nm) at 4800 rpm. Compression 9.1-to-1. Catalyst: standard.

Transmission: Front-wheel drive; five-speed manual gearbox. Automatic, optional extra. Top gear speed at 1000 rpm: 20.6 mph (33.1 km/h).

Suspension: Front, independent, MacPherson struts, anti-roll bar. Rear, independent, MacPherson struts.

Steering: Rack and pinion. Power assistance: standard. **Brakes:** Solid discs front, drums rear. ABS: not available. **Tyres:** 185/60 HR 14. **Fuel tank:** 10.3 Imp. gall (47 litres). **Unladen weight:** 2282 lb (1035 kg).

Dimensions: Length 163.4 in (4150 mm), width 66.7 in (1694 mm), height 51.1 in (1298 mm), wheelbase 96.5 in (2451 mm).

Performance (est): Maximum speed 105 mph (169 km/h). Fuel consumption: overall (est) 35 mpg.

Features: All models have electric windows and central locking, and a loadspace security cover is available for the hatchback. Rear side windows can be opened or removed. **Summary:** This is essentially a two-wheel drive version of the Geo Tracker sport and off-road vehicle. Trackers have a new anti-lock brake system, but this is not yet included on the Storm. Kits are built jointly by Suzuki, Isuzu and Toyota.

CHRYSLER (USA)   Voyager

Identity: At Paris 1990, one of the few new cars which had not been at Birmingham the week before was the new Chrysler Voyager multi-seater. Although there was much pomp at the launch, the design seemed very uninspiring compared with, for example, the Toyota Previa.

Engine: Front-mounted transverse V6-cylinder with alloy heads and single ohc on each bank. Multi-point fuel injection. Bore 91.1 mm, stroke 76.0 mm; capacity 2972 cc. Power 141 PS (104 kW) at 5200 rpm; torque 163 lb ft (225 Nm) at 2400 rpm. Compression 8.9-to-1. Catalyst: standard.

Transmission: Front-wheel drive; four-speed automatic; manual gearbox on 2.5-litre only. Top gear speed at 1000 rpm: 30.5 mph (49.1 km/h).

Suspension: Front, independent, MacPherson struts, anti-roll bar. Rear, dead beam axle on leaf springs; anti-roll bar.

Steering: Rack and pinion. Power assistance: standard. **Brakes:** Vented discs front, drums rear. ABS: not available. **Tyres:** P205/70 R 15. **Fuel tank:** 16.5 Imp. gall (75 litres). **Unladen weight:** 3527 lb (1600 kg)

Dimensions: Length 178.1 in (4525 mm), width 72.0 in (1830 mm), height 65.9 in (1673 mm), wheelbase 112.3 in (2853 mm).

Performance Works: Maximum speed 106 mph (170 km/h); 0 to 62 mph (100 km/h) 12.8 sec. Fuel consumption at constant 75 mph (120 km/h): 27.2 mpg.

Features: More front wheel castor has been incorporated in the design to give better stability than on the last model. Seating for five or seven, and air conditioning is optional. **Summary:** Sliding door is fitted on the right, and there is a top-hinged tail door as well as front doors. Also available is the LE model with 3.3-litre engine, four-wheel drive and anti-lock brakes.

CITROEN (F)   AX 14 TGD

Identity: Equipment of the little Citroën diesel models was improved for 1991, and five-door models are redesignated TGD and DTR. Otherwise it is mechanically the same as the 14RD in which I set the world fuel economy record for production cars at 112.01 mpg in 1989, after covering over 1000 miles on a tankful.

Engine: Front-mounted transverse four-cylinder with belt-driven ohc and alloy head. Ricardo precombustion chambers. Bore 75.0 mm, stroke 77.0 mm; capacity 1360 cc. Power 52 PS (38 kW) at 5000 rpm; torque 62 lb ft (86 Nm) at 2500 rpm. Compression 22.0-to-1. Catalyst: not available.

Transmission: Front-wheel drive; five-speed manual gearbox. Automatic, not available. Top gear speed at 1000 rpm: 20.4 mph (32.7 km/h).

Suspension: Front, independent, MacPherson struts, anti-roll bar. Rear, independent, trailing arms and transverse links with transverse torsion bars; telescopic dampers mounted horizontally for low floor height.

Steering: Rack and pinion. Power assistance: not available. **Brakes:** Solid discs front, drums rear. ABS: not available. **Tyres:** 145/70 R 13. **Fuel tank:** 9.5 Imp. gall (43 litres). **Unladen weight:** 1598 lb (725 kg).

Dimensions: Length 138.0 in (3505 mm), width 61.5 in (1562 mm), height 53.5 in (1359 mm), wheelbase 90.0 in (2285 mm).

Performance *Autocar & Motor* test: Maximum speed 91 mph (146 km/h); 0 to 60 mph (97 km/h) 16.2 sec; 80 mph (130 km/h) 36.2 sec. Fuel consumption at constant 75 mph (120 km/h): 56.5 mpg; overall test, 54.7 mpg.

Features: TGD is quite well equipped, and items such as a sunroof can be added; alternatively, there is the DTR, with higher level of equipment. **Summary:** Excellent engine, offering remarkable torque at low revs in fifth, which helped on those fuel-economy drives. Performance is impressively good for a 1.4-litre diesel, and once under way it no longer handles or sounds like a diesel. Impressive small car.

CITROEN (F)   AX GT

Identity: Performance version was added to the AX range at Motorfair 1987, identified by wheel arch and sill extensions, matching the composite material used for the bumpers. Power unit is the familiar 1,360 engine with carburettor, but in tuned form giving 85 bhp.

Engine: Front-mounted transverse four-cylinder with all-alloy construction and wet cylinder liners; single belt-driven ohc. Solex carb. Bore 75.0 mm, stroke 77.0 mm; capacity 1360 cc. Power 85 PS (62 kW) at 6400 rpm; torque 85 lb ft (118 Nm) at 4000 rpm. Compression 9.3-to-1. Catalyst: not available.

Transmission: Front-wheel drive; five-speed manual gearbox. Automatic, not available. Top gear speed at 1000 rpm: 18.3 mph (29.5 km/h).

Suspension: Front, independent, MacPherson struts, anti-roll bar. Rear, independent, trailing arms and transverse links, with transverse torsion bars; telescopic dampers mounted horizontally for low floor height. Anti-roll bar.

Steering: Rack and pinion. Power assistance: not available. **Brakes:** Solid discs front, drums rear. ABS: not available. **Tyres:** 165/65 R 13. **Fuel tank:** 9.5 Imp. gall (43 litres). **Unladen weight:** 1587 lb (720 kg).

Dimensions: Length 137.8 in (3500 mm), width 63.0 in (1600 mm), height 52.8 in (1340 mm), wheelbase 90.0 in (2285 mm).

Performance *Autocar & Motor* test: Maximum speed 107 mph (172 km/h); 0 to 60 mph (97 km/h) 9.0 sec; 80 mph (130 km/h) 17.6 sec. Fuel consumption at constant 75 mph (120 km/h): 42.8 mpg; overall test, 30.4 mpg.

Features: Wider tyres and firmer suspension settings. GT has different interior and gets bucket seats. **Summary:** GT also features improvements made to the AX since launch, which include lockable push button for tailgate. Available only as three-door. AX GT badge appears at the rear. Distinctive alloy wheels.

CITROEN (F)   BX GTi 4 × 4

Identity: Important additions to the BX range in 1990 were four-wheel drive versions of the GTi and 1.9-litre estate car. I used the GTi 4 × 4 for a caravan-towing job, on which the four-wheel traction proved a great advantage, but 4 × 4 brings a slight economy penalty.

Engine: Front-mounted transverse four-cylinder with eight-valve alloy head, alloy block, and wet cylinder liners. Bosch LE 3 fuel injection. Bore 83.0 mm, stroke 88.0 mm; capacity 1905 cc. Power 126 PS (93 kW) at 5500 rpm; torque 123 lb ft (170 Nm) at 2750 rpm. Compression 9.3-to-1. Catalyst: not available.

Transmission: Four-wheel drive; five-speed manual gearbox. Automatic, not available. Top gear speed at 1000 rpm: 20.7 mph (33.3 km/h).

Suspension: Front, independent, MacPherson struts, hydro-pneumatic springs with integral dampers; anti-roll bar. Rear, independent, trailing arms with hydropneumatic spring-damper units and automatic self-levelling, height adjustable; anti-roll bar.

Steering: Rack and pinion. Power assistance: standard. **Brakes:** Solid discs front and rear. ABS: standard. **Tyres:** 185/60 R 14. **Fuel tank:** 14.5 Imp. gall (66 litres). **Unladen weight:** 2502 lb (1135 kg).

Dimensions: Length 166.5 in (4230 mm), width 65.4 in (1660 mm), height 53.6 in (1361 mm), wheelbase 104.5 in (2655 mm).

Performance *Autocar & Motor* test: Maximum speed 115 mph (185 km/h); 0 to 60 mph (97 km/h) 10.6 sec; 80 mph (130 km/h) 18.9 sec. Fuel consumption at constant 75 mph (120 km/h): 31.7 mpg; overall test, 26.3 mpg.

Features: Drive is permanently engaged to all four wheels, with Torsen rear differential. Very comprehensive equipment, plus air conditioning as an option. **Summary:** Four-wheel drive gives an even more confident feel to the GTi on the road, and makes it a very competent all-weather car with excellent handling. It is also an ideal tow-car, for which the rather low gearing is perfect.

CITROEN (F)   BX TZD Turbo

Identity: As with the AX, Citroën revised the specifications and identity letters for some of the BX range, and the TZD is the top equipment model of the BX diesels for 1991. Mechanically it remains much as before, featuring the excellent 1.8-litre turbo diesel.

Engine: Front-mounted transverse four-cylinder with eight-valve alloy head and KKK or Garrett T2 turbocharger. Air-to-air heat exchanger immediately beneath the bonnet. Bore 80.0 mm, stroke 88.0 mm; capacity 1769 cc. Power 91 PS (67 kW) at 4300 rpm; torque 134 lb ft (185 Nm) at 2100 rpm. Compression 22.1-to-1. Catalyst: not available.

Transmission: Front-wheel drive; five-speed manual gearbox. Automatic, optional extra. Top gear speed at 1000 rpm: 25.9 mph (41.7 km/h).

Suspension: Front, independent, MacPherson struts, hydropneumatic springs with integral dampers; anti-roll bar. Rear, independent, trailing arms with hydropneumatic spring-damper units and automatic self-levelling, height adjustable; anti-roll bar.

Steering: Rack and pinion. Power assistance: standard. **Brakes:** Solid discs front and rear. ABS: optional. **Tyres:** 165/70 R 14. **Fuel tank:** 14.5 Imp. gall (66 litres). **Unladen weight:** 2260 lb (1025 kg).

Dimensions: Length 166.5 in (4230 mm), width 65.4 in (1660 mm), height 53.6 in (1361 mm), wheelbase 104.5 in (2655 mm).

Performance *Autocar & Motor* test: Maximum speed 104 mph (167 km/h); 0 to 60 mph (97 km/h) 11.9 sec; 80 mph (130 km/h) 23.2 sec. Fuel consumption at constant 75 mph (120 km/h): 44.8 mpg; overall test, 36.2 mpg.

Features: Already good, the existing specification was improved still further for the TZD, and air conditioning is available as an option. **Summary:** Remarkable combination of comfort, performance and economy. In 1988 I ran a controlled test to Scotland to check Citroën's claim of 900 miles a tankful, and covered nearly this mileage (847 to run-out) on a tankful at an average of 55 mph (58.4 mpg).

CITROEN (F)   XM 2.0 SEi

Identity: Replacing the CX range, the XM was launched Geneva 1989, and on the British market from Motorfair. It introduces advanced suspension control with automatic compression to counter roll forces on corners. This version has the injection engine and top equipment. Cheaper carb. model also available.

Engine: Front-mounted transverse four-cylinder with alloy head and single ohc, eight valves. Bosch fuel injection. Bore 86.0 mm, stroke 86.0 mm; capacity 1998 cc. Power 132 PS (97 kW) at 5600 rpm; torque 132 lb ft (182 Nm) at 4800 rpm. Compression 8.8-to-1. Catalyst: optional.

Transmission: Front-wheel drive; five-speed manual gearbox. Automatic, optional extra. Top gear speed at 1000 rpm: 20.9 mph (33.6 km/h).

Suspension: Front, independent, MacPherson struts with hydropneumatic units and Hydractive control of spring and damper rates; anti-roll bar. Rear, independent, trailing arms with hydropneumatic units, automatic self-levelling and Hydractive control; anti-roll bar.

Steering: Rack and pinion. Power assistance: standard. **Brakes:** Vented discs front, solid discs rear. ABS: standard. **Tyres:** 195/60 R 15. **Fuel tank:** 17.6 Imp. gall (80 litres). **Unladen weight:** 2888 lb (1310 kg).

Dimensions: Length 185.4 in (4708 mm), width 70.6 in (1794 mm), height 54.7 in (1390 mm), wheelbase 112.2 in (2850 mm).

Performance *Autocar & Motor* test: Maximum speed 120 mph (193 km/h); 0 to 60 mph (97 km/h) 11.2 sec; 80 mph (130 km/h) 20.2 sec. Fuel consumption at constant 75 mph (120 km/h): 34.9 mpg; overall test, 25.8 mpg.

Features: Lavish specification is included with the SEi trim, including remote central locking and air conditioning. Unusual feature is duplication of the rear window, giving saloon comfort with hatchback versatility.
Summary: Superbly comfortable car which is also very relaxing and easy to drive in spite of its size and roominess. It is also impressively quiet at speed. Very advanced design.

CITROEN   (F)   **XM 2.1 Turbo SED**

Identity: On the 1990 Land's End–John O'Groats trail I was involved in an interesting test drive, in which three Citröen diesels covered the 866 miles on a tankful. The new XM turbo diesel did it most easily of all, at 57.7 mph and 53.0 mpg. It's even more impressive when driven fast.

Engine: Front-mounted transverse four-cylinder with alloy head and single ohc working three valves per cylinder. Lucas Rotodiesel injection and Mitsubishi turbocharger with intercooler. Bore 85.0 mm, stroke 92.0 mm; capacity 2088 cc. Power 110 PS (80 kW) at 4300 rpm; torque 183 lb ft (253 Nm) at 2000 rpm. Comp. 21.5-to-1. Catalyst: not available.

Transmission: Front-wheel drive; five-speed manual gearbox. Automatic, not available. Top gear speed at 1000 rpm: 27.1 mph (43.6 km/h).

Suspension: Front, independent, MacPherson struts, hydropneumatic units with Hydractive control and integral dampers; anti-roll bar. Rear, independent, trailing arms with hydropneumatic spring-damper units and Hydractive control; anti-roll bar.

Steering: Rack and pinion. Power assistance: standard. **Brakes:** Vented discs front, solid discs rear. ABS: standard. **Tyres:** 195/65 R 15. **Fuel tank:** 17.6 Imp. gall (80 litres). **Unladen weight:** 3042 lb (1380 kg).

Dimensions: Length 185.4 in (4708 mm), width 70.6 in (1794 mm), height 54.7 in (1390 mm), wheelbase 112.2 in (2850 mm).

Performance *Autocar & Motor* test: Maximum speed 116 mph (187 km/h); 0 to 60 mph (97 km/h) 12.4 sec; 80 mph (130 km/h) 23.2 sec. Fuel consumption at constant 75 mph (120 km/h): 43.5 mpg; overall test, 32.0 mpg.

Features: SED version brings top-level equipment, matching the SEi petrol model, and includes air conditioning as standard besides the obvious features like remote central locking. **Summary:** This three-valve turbocharged and intercooled engine delivers enormous torque, and in conjunction with the high gearing and suspension comfort it makes the XM an outstanding car for covering long distances.

41

CITROEN (F)   XM 3.0 V6 24V

Identity: Last year we covered the 3-litre V6, which was then the top model of the XM range, and the comment was made that a 24-valve version was expected later. It came to the British market at Birmingham 1990, and offers noticeable extra punch for brisk acceleration.

Engine: Front-mounted transverse V6-cylinder with alloy heads and single ohc per bank working four valves per cylinder. Bendix Fenix 4 fuel injection. Bore 93.0 mm, stroke 73.0 mm; capacity 2975 cc. Power 200 PS (147 kW) at 6000 rpm; torque 192 lb ft (265 Nm) at 3600 rpm. Compression 9.4-to-1. Catalyst: standard.

Transmission: Front-wheel drive; five-speed manual gearbox. Automatic, not available. Top gear speed at 1000 rpm: 22.9 mph (36.8 km/h).

Suspension: Front, independent, MacPherson struts with hydropneumatic units and Hydractive control of spring and damper rates; anti-roll bar. Rear, independent, trailing arms with hydropneumatic units, giving automatic self-levelling, and Hydractive control; anti-roll bar.

Steering: Rack and pinion. Power assistance: standard. **Brakes:** Vented discs front, solid discs rear. ABS: standard. **Tyres:** 205/60 ZR 15. **Fuel tank:** 17.6 Imp. gall (80 litres). **Unladen weight:** 3245 lb (1745 kg).

Dimensions: Length 185.4 in (4708 mm), width 70.6 in (1794 mm), height 54.7 in (1390 mm), wheelbase 112.2 in (2850 mm).

Performance *Autocar & Motor* test: Maximum speed 143 mph (230 km/h); 0 to 60 mph (97 km/h) 7.5 sec; 80 mph (130 km/h) 12.4 sec. Fuel consumption at constant 75 mph (120 km/h): 27.7 mpg; overall test, 20.8 mpg.

Features: Equipment is much the same as for the SEi, but note the special sports alloy wheels, unique to the 24V. Citroën see this as the car for the performance driver, so it is available only with manual gearbox. **Summary:** Occasionally the ordinary V6 is a little lacking in low-down response, a failing which the 24V corrects wonderfully, giving vigorous answer to the throttle. But the gearing could be higher for more relaxed high-speed cruising.

CITROEN   (F)   ZX Avantage

Identity: New model line-up added to the Citroen range at Geneva 1991 was the ZX, perhaps the most important new model at the Show. Four versions are named Reflex, Aura, Volcane, and this one—likely to be the biggest seller—the Avantage with 1360 cc engine. Volcane has the 1.9-litre 130 bhp unit.

Engine: Front-mounted transverse four-cylinder with all-alloy construction and single ohc; two valves per cylinder. Single carb. Bore 75.0 mm, stroke 77.0 mm; capacity 1360 cc. Power 75 PS (55 kW) at 5800 rpm; torque 85 lb ft (118 Nm) at 3800 rpm. Compression 9.3-to-1. Catalyst: optional.

Transmission: Front-wheel drive; five-speed manual gearbox. Automatic, not available. Top gear speed at 1000 rpm: 20.6 mph (33.2 km/h).

Suspension: Front, independent, MacPherson struts; anti-roll bar. Rear, independent, trailing arms and torsion bar springs; anti-roll bar.

Steering: Rack and pinion. Power assistance: optional. **Brakes:** Solid discs front, drums rear. ABS: optional. **Tyres:** 165/70 R 13. **Fuel tank:** 12.3 Imp. gall (56 litres). **Unladen weight:** 2083 lb (945 kg).

Dimensions: Length 160.3 in (4072 mm), width 67.0 in (1702 mm), height 55.0 in (1397 mm), wheelbase 100.0 in (2540 mm).

Performance Works: Maximum speed 107 mph (172 km/h) ; 0 to 62 mph (100 km/h) 13.7 sec; 80 mph (130 km/h) 18.4 sec. Fuel consumption at constant 75 mph (120 km/h): 41.5 mpg.

Features: Same engine is available in the Reflex, but with less generous equipment. Wide range of options available. **Summary:** Neatly filling the Citroen range between AX and BX, the ZX is an attractive five-seater. Ingenious rear suspension design gives a small degree of rear wheel steering in the same direction as the front wheels when cornering hard, for better handling.

DAIHATSU (J)   Charade 1.3 CX

Identity: Asked by relatives to recommend a small car with automatic transmission, I suggested the Charade, on which automatic and power steering became available as options mid-1990. They bought one, and the advice has been applauded ever since.

Engine: Front-mounted transverse four-cylinder with alloy block and head, and single ohc working four valves per cylinder; twin-choke carb. Bore 76.0 mm, stroke 71.0 mm; capacity 1295 cc. Power 75 PS (55 kW) at 6500 rpm; torque 75 lb ft (104 Nm) at 3900 rpm. Compression 9.5-to-1. Catalyst: not available.

Transmission: Front-wheel drive; five-speed manual gearbox. Automatic, optional extra. Top gear speed at 1000 rpm: 18.4 mph (29.6 km/h).

Suspension: Front, independent, MacPherson struts; anti-roll bar. Rear, independent, MacPherson struts with parallel lower links; anti-roll bar.

Steering: Rack and pinion. Power assistance: optional. **Brakes:** Solid discs front, drums rear. ABS: not available. **Tyres:** 165/70 R 13. **Fuel tank:** 9.8 Imp. gall (44.6 litres). **Unladen weight:** 1850 lb (840 kg).

Dimensions: Length 142.1 in (3610 mm), width 63.0 in (1600 mm), height 54.5 in (1385 mm), wheelbase 92.1 in (2340 mm).

Performance *Autocar & Motor* test: Maximum speed 97 mph (156 km/h); 0 to 60 mph (97 km/h) 11.2 sec; 80 mph (130 km/h) 20.7 sec. Fuel consumption at constant 75 mph (120 km/h): 40.9 mpg; overall test 25.8 mpg.

Features: Quite good equipment for a small car, including steering-column rake adjustment and electric mirror adjustment; sunroof optional.
Summary: Lively performance as a result of the vigorous 16-valve engine. The Charade is particularly good as a town car in automatic form, and it's an advantage that power steering is available—something many older drivers appreciate.

DAIHATSU (J)   Charade GTti

Identity: With the new range launched May 1987, Daihatsu included a high performance model offering a promising specification, and a car which proved equally exciting on the road. Its near-100 bhp 1-litre engine gives phenomenal power/weight ratio, and it is one of the fastest of the 'pocket rockets'.

Engine: Front-mounted transverse three-cylinder with alloy head, and twin ohc operating four valves per cyl. Electronic fuel injection and IHI RHB51 turbocharger. Bore 76.0 mm, stroke 73.0 mm; capacity 993 cc. Power 99 PS (74 kW) at 6500 rpm; torque 96 lb ft (130 Nm) at 3500 rpm. Compression 7.8-to-1. Catalyst: not available.

Transmission: Front-wheel drive; five-speed manual gearbox. Automatic, not available. Top gear speed at 1000 rpm: 18.5 mph (29.8 km/h).

Suspension: Front, independent, MacPherson struts; anti-roll bar. Rear, independent, MacPherson struts; anti-roll bar.

Steering: Rack and pinion. Power assistance: not available. **Brakes:** Vented discs front, solid discs rear. ABS: not available. **Tyres:** 175/60 HR 14. **Fuel tank:** 8.8 Imp. gall (40 litres). **Unladen weight:** 1786 lb (810 kg).

Dimensions: Length 142.1 in (3610 mm), width 63.3 in (1615 mm), height 54.4 in (1385 mm), wheelbase 92.1 in (2340 mm).

Performance *Autocar & Motor* test: Maximum speed 114 mph (184 km/h); 0 to 60 mph (97 km/h) 7.9 sec; 80 mph (130 km/h) 14.3 sec. Fuel consumption at constant 75 mph (120 km/h) 37.3 mpg; overall test 28.8 mpg.

Features: Although the other Charade models have five doors, the sporting GTti is three-door only. Electric windows, central locking and sunroof optional. **Summary:** Outstandingly quick car, fun to drive with its combination of excellent handling, steering and brakes, plus outstanding performance for a small car. Test consumption a bit disappointing, but in swift driving that is not too fierce, over 35 mpg is obtainable.

DAIHATSU (J)   Sportrak EFi

Identity: An improved version of the Sportrak, introduced in the UK July 1990 to supplement the existing DX and EL models, the EFi has 16-valve engine and fuel injection, with catalyst as standard. '16 valve EFi' is lettered on the doors, and the injection engine copes much better with this tough little vehicle.

Engine: Front-mounted longitudinal four-cylinder with head and block of alloy, and single ohc working four valves per cylinder. Multipoint electronic fuel injection. Bore 76.0 mm, stroke 87.6 mm; capacity 1589 cc. Power 95 PS (70 kW) at 5,700 rpm; torque 95 lb ft (131 Nm) at 4800 rpm. Compression 9.5-to-1. Catalyst: standard.

Transmission: Four-wheel drive; five-speed manual gearbox. Automatic, not available. Four-wheel drive is selectable, with low-ratio transfer gearbox. Top gear speed at 1000 rpm: 16.9 mph (27.2 km/h).

Suspension: Front, independent, wishbones and torsion bars; anti-roll bar. Rear, beam axle on tapered leaf springs with gas-filled dampers.

Steering: Recirculating ball. Power assistance: standard. **Brakes:** Solid discs front, drums rear. ABS: not available. **Tyres:** 195 R 15 94S. **Fuel tank:** 13.2 Imp. gall (60 litres). **Unladen weight:** 2590 lb (1175 kg).

Dimensions: Length 149.9 in (3785 mm), width 64.4 in (1635 mm), height 67.7 in (1720 mm), wheelbase 85.6 in (2175 mm).

Performance Works: Maximum speed 93 mph (150 km/h). Fuel consumption at constant 75 mph (120 km/h): 23.7 mpg.

Features: Hardtop body includes a sunroof, but can also be removed altogether, leaving strong roll-over bar in place. Adjustable steering column; radio/cassette. **Summary:** With its lively performance and tidy handling, for an off-road vehicle, the Sportrak EFi is fun to drive. It has good off-road capability, although the ride is a bit lively on bad going.

DAIMLER (GB)   4.0

Identity: Top equipment of the luxury Jaguar range comes in the Daimler version, which is otherwise mechanically the same as the XJ6 and Sovereign 4.0, but not available with the smaller 3.2-litre engine. The Daimler comes with automatic transmission, or manual at no extra cost.

Engine: Front-mounted longitudinal six-cylinder with twin overhead camshafts and 24 valves. Lucas electronic fuel injection. Bore 91.0 mm, stroke 102.0 mm; capacity 3980 cc. Power 235 PS (175 kW) at 4750 rpm; torque 285 lb ft (387 Nm) at 3750 rpm. Compression 9.5-to-1. Catalyst: optional.

Transmission: Rear-wheel drive; four-speed automatic. Top gear speed at 1000 rpm: 29.2 mph (47.0 km/h).

Suspension: Front, independent, wishbones with anti-dive provision; coil springs and anti-roll bar. Rear, independent, wishbones with drive shafts acting as upper links; anti-squat and anti-lift provisions; coil springs concentric with dampers.

Steering: Rack and pinion. Power assistance: standard. **Brakes:** Vented discs front, solid discs rear. ABS: standard. **Tyres:** 220/65 VR 390 TD. **Fuel tank:** 19.5 Imp. gall (89 litres). **Unladen weight:** 3969 lb (1800 kg).

Dimensions: Length 196.4 in (4988 mm), width 71.3 in (1811 mm), height 53.5 in (1358 mm), wheelbase 113.0 in (2870 mm).

Performance *Autocar & Motor* test: (Jaguar Sovereign): Maximum speed 139 mph (224 km/h); 0 to 60 mph (97 km/h) 8.3 sec; 80 mph (130 km/h) 13.5 sec. Fuel consumption at constant 75 mph (120 km/h): 30.4 mpg; overall test, 18.5 mpg.

Features: Superbly equipped with every possible luxury fitting including air conditioning and electric sunroof; front foglamps and catalyst are the only listed options. **Summary:** One of the world's top saloons, offering highest standards of craftsmanship in its interior build quality, and providing supremely comfortable travel for five.

FERRARI (I)

Identity: Over the years, the V8 engine of the Ferrari coupé has increased in size, but the change to injection and emission control brought a disappointing power drop. This was made good at Frankfurt 1989, when the 348 was introduced, with power increased to 300 PS.

Engine: Mid-mounted longitudinal V8-cylinder with alloy block and cylinder heads; twin ohc each bank, operating four valves per cylinder. Bosch Motronic injection. Bore 85.0 mm, stroke 75.0 mm; capacity 3405 cc. Power 300 PS (221 kW) at 7200 rpm; torque 234 lb ft (323 Nm) at 4200 rpm. Compression 10.4-to-1. Catalyst: optional.

Transmission: Rear-wheel drive; five-speed manual gearbox. Automatic, not available. Top gear speed at 1000 rpm: 23.7 mph (38.2 km/h).

Suspension: Front, independent, wishbones and coil springs; anti-roll bar. Rear, independent, wishbones and coil springs; anti-roll bar.

Steering: Rack and pinion. Power assistance: not available. **Brakes:** Vented discs front, and rear. ABS: standard. **Tyres:** 215/50 (front), 255/45 (rear) ZR 17. **Fuel tank:** 20.8 Imp. gall (95 litres). **Unladen weight:** 3070 lb (1393 kg).

Dimensions: Length 166.5 in (4230 mm), width 74.6 in (1894 mm), height 46.0 in (1170 mm), wheelbase 96.5 in (2450 mm).

Performance *Autocar & Motor* test: Maximum speed 163 mph (262 km/h); 0 to 60 mph (97 km/h) 5.6 sec; 80 mph (130 km/h) 9.0 sec. Fuel consumption at constant 75 mph (120 km/h): 28.5 mpg; overall test, 18.4 mpg.

Features: Emphasis is very much on speed with safety, rather than luxury or extravagance of equipment. **Summary:** Extremely fast two-seater, available as the tb (Berlinetta) illustrated, or as 348ts, the Spyder with removable roof panel. Slats and scoops in the doors channel cooling air to the rear engine, but the radiator is at the front.

FERRARI (I)   **Mondial t Cabriolet**

Identity: Revised version of the Mondial, designated 't', was launched Geneva 1989 and shown at Motorfair. Seating four – it is claimed, though really more a 2 + 2 – the Mondial first appeared in 1980, and its V8 engine, increased to 3405 cc, now gives 300 bhp.

Engine: Mid-mounted longitudinal V8-cylinder with toothed belt drive to twin ohc each bank, working four valves per cylinder. Bosch Motronic injection. Bore 85.0 mm, stroke 75.0 mm; capacity 3405 cc. Power 300 PS (221 kW) at 7200 rpm; torque 234 lb ft (323 Nm) at 4200 rpm. Compression 10.4-to-1. Catalyst: not available.

Transmission: Rear-wheel drive; five-speed manual gearbox. Automatic, not available. Top gear speed at 1000 rpm: 19.9 mph (32.0 km/h).

Suspension: Front, independent, wishbones and coil springs; anti-roll bar. Three-position damper firmness control. Rear, independent, wishbones and coil springs; anti-roll bar. Three-position damper firmness.

Steering: Rack and pinion. Power assistance: standard. **Brakes:** Vented discs front, and rear. ABS: standard. **Tyres:** 205/55 (front), 225/55 (rear) ZR 16. **Fuel tank:** 21.1 Imp. gall (96 litres). **Unladen weight:** 3236 lb (1468 kg).

Dimensions: Length 178.5 in (4534 mm), width 71.2 in (1808 mm), height 48.6 in (1234 mm), wheelbase 104.3 in (2649 mm).

Performance *Autocar & Motor* test (coupé): Maximum speed 143 mph (230 km/h); 0 to 60 mph (97 km/h) 6.8 sec; 80 mph (130 km/h) 10.8 sec. Fuel consumption at constant 75 mph (120 km/h): 23.7 mpg; overall test, 16.8 mpg.

Features: Three-position selector switch gives choice of ride firmness; an electronic control box varies the setting according to speed and cornering forces. **Summary:** Unusual arrangement of the Mondial as re-launched 1989 was that the engine is mounted longitudinally while the transmission is transverse. In familiar Ferrari manner, the clutch and flywheel are on a shaft, the other side of the gearbox. Superb motoring.

Identity: One of the fastest cars of the 60s was recalled when Ferrari brought back the name Testarossa (redhead) for the new Pininfarina coupé, launched Paris 1984. Engine is a 'flat 12' developed from the 3-litre Ferrari V12 used in Formula 1 racing.

Engine: Mid-mounted longitudinal 12-cylinder with horizontal layout ('boxer') and toothed belt drive to twin ohc each bank, working four valves per cylinder. Bosch KE Jetronic injection. Bore 82.0 mm, stroke 78.0 mm; capacity 4942 cc. Power 390 PS (291 kW) at 6300 rpm; torque 362 lb ft (291 Nm) at 6300 rpm. Compression 9.3-to-1. Catalyst: not available.

Transmission: Rear-wheel drive; five-speed manual gearbox. Automatic, not available. Top gear speed at 1000 rpm: 26.5 mph (42.6 km/h).

Suspension: Front, independent, wishbones and coil springs; anti-roll bar. Rear, independent, wishbones and coil springs; anti-roll bar.

Steering: Rack and pinion. Power assistance: not available. **Brakes:** Vented discs front, and rear. ABS: not available. **Tyres:** 225/50 (front) 255/50 (rear) ZR 16. **Fuel tank:** 25.0 Imp. gall (115 litres). **Unladen weight:** 3675 lb (1668 kg).

Dimensions: Length 176.6 in (4485 mm), width 77.8 in (1976 mm), height 44.5 in (1130 mm), wheelbase 100.4 in (2550 mm).

Performance *Autocar & Motor* test: Maximum speed 171 mph (275 km/h); 0 to 60 mph (97 km/h) 5.2 sec; 80 mph (130 km/h) 7.9 sec. Fuel consumption at constant 75 mph (120 km/h): 24.8 mpg; overall test, 16.6 mpg.

Features: Strictly two-seater body, and the Testarossa runs to such features as height adjustable seats, electric windows and central locking.
Summary: One of the world's fastest and most exciting cars, yet it can also be very tractable and docile to drive, while the flat 12 engine brings shattering response when opened up. *Autocar & Motor* test saw the Testarossa reach 140 mph from rest in under 25 sec; that's acceleration!

FIAT (I)   Tempra 1.6 SX

Identity: Launched at Geneva, and on the British market from July, Tempra is the saloon version of Fiat's mid-range Tipo, and despatches the unloved Regatta to obscurity. Choice of 1.4, 1.6 or 1.8 injection engines, plus 1.9 diesel with or without turbo.

Engine: Front-mounted transverse four-cylinder with alloy head, single ohc, and Weber twin-choke carb. Bore 86.0 mm, stroke 67.0 mm; capacity 1581 cc. Power 86 PS (63 kW) at 6000 rpm; torque 96 lb ft (132 Nm) at 2900 rpm. Compression 9.2-to-1. Catalyst: not available.

Transmission: Front-wheel drive; five-speed manual gearbox. Automatic, optional extra. Top gear speed at 1000 rpm: 18.8 mph (30.0 km/h).

Suspension: Front, independent, MacPherson struts, anti-roll bar. Rear, independent, trailing arms and auxiliary cross member; coil springs and anti-roll bar.

Steering: Rack and pinion. Power assistance: standard. **Brakes:** Vented discs front, drums rear. ABS: not available. **Tyres:** 165/65 TR 14. **Fuel tank:** 14.3 Imp. gall (65 litres). **Unladen weight:** 2280 lb (1035 kg).

Dimensions: Length 171.4 in (4354 mm), width 66.7 in (1695 mm), height 56.9 in (1445 mm), wheelbase 100.0 in (2540 mm).

Performance *Autocar & Motor* test: Maximum speed 111 mph (179 km/h); 0 to 60 mph (97 km/h) 12.2 sec; 80 mph (130 km/h) 23.2 sec. Fuel consumption at constant 75 mph (120 km/h): 37.1 mpg; overall test, 28.1 mpg.

Features: Automatic transmission option is the Ford-Fiat continuously variable type. General equipment level is generous. **Summary:** Rather low overall gearing for a car with five-speed gearbox contributes to the heavy fuel consumption. Disappointing interior with fussy control layout and digital instruments, and the paint finish on cars I examined was not up to today's usual standard.

FIAT (I) Tempra 1.8ie SX Station Wagon

Identity: Following launch of the Tempra – a saloon version of the Tipo – on the British market in mid-1990, the Station Wagon was displayed at Birmingham in September, in anticipation of its arrival on the market in April 1991. It is available with seven-seater option.

Engine: Front-mounted transverse four-cylinder with alloy head and twin ohc working eight valves; IAW electronic injection/ignition. Bore 84.0 mm, stroke 79.2 mm; capacity 1756 cc. Power 110 PS (81 kW) at 6000 rpm; torque 103 lb ft (142 Nm) at 2500 rpm. Compression 9.5-to-1. Catalyst: not available.

Transmission: Front-wheel drive; five-speed manual gearbox. Automatic, not available. Top gear speed at 1000 rpm: 19.3 mph (31.1 km/h).

Suspension: Front, independent, MacPherson struts, anti-roll bar. Rear, independent, trailing arms and coil springs; anti-roll bar.

Steering: Rack and pinion. Power assistance: standard. **Brakes:** Solid discs front, drums rear. ABS: not available. **Tyres:** 175/65 R 14H. **Fuel tank:** 14.3 Imp. gall (65 litres). **Unladen weight:** 2513 lb (1104 kg).

Dimensions: Length 176.1 in (4472 mm), width 66.7 in (1695 mm), height 56.9 in (1445 mm), wheelbase 100.0 in (2540 mm).

Performance *Autocar and Motor* test (saloon): Maximum speed 122 mph (196 km/h); 0 to 60 mph (97 km/h) 10.6 sec. Fuel consumption at constant 75 mph (120 km/h): 34.0 mpg; overall test, 24.7 mpg.

Features: SX is top of the three trim levels available and gets good equipment, including alloy wheels and an electrically heated driving seat. **Summary:** Tailgate is horizontally divided on the Station Wagon, with the bumper integrated in the lower part, which folds down to facilitate loading. The Tempra Wagon is a spacious load carrier, but economy is poor for a 1.8.

FIAT   (I)   **Tipo 1.9T. ds**

Identity: Launched January 1988, Tipo is a five-door hatchback, available with 1.4 or 1.6 petrol engine, and a choice of 1.7 non-turbo diesel or the 1.9-litre turbocharged diesel engine in this top-of-the-range model. I still can't come to terms with the rear-end styling, but otherwise this diesel has appeal.

Engine: Front-mounted transverse four-cylinder with alloy head, single ohc, and indirect injection; KKK turbocharger with air–air intercooler. Bore 82.6 mm, stroke 90.0 mm; capacity 1929 cc. Power 93 PS (69 kW) at 4100 rpm; torque 136 lb ft (188 Nm) at 2400 rpm. Compression 19.2-to-1. Catalyst: not available.

Transmission: Front-wheel drive; five-speed manual gearbox. Automatic, not available. Top gear speed at 1000 rpm: 26.5 mph (42.6 km/h).

Suspension: Front, independent, MacPherson struts, anti-roll bar. Rear independent, trailing arms and auxiliary cross member; coil springs and anti-roll bar.

Steering: Rack and pinion. Power assistance: standard. **Brakes:** Solid discs front, drums rear. ABS: not available. **Tyres:** 175/65 R 14. **Fuel tank:** 12.1 Imp. gall (55 litres). **Unladen weight:** 2447 lb (1110 kg).

Dimensions: Length 155.8 in (3958 mm), width 66.9 in (1700 mm), height 56.7 in (1440 mm), wheelbase 100.0 in (2540 mm).

Performance *Autocar & Motor* test: Maximum speed 111 mph (179 km/h); 0 to 60 mph (97 km/h) 10.8 sec; 80 mph (130 km/h) 20.1 sec. Fuel consumption at constant 75 mph (120 km/h) 42.2 mpg; overall test, 35.4 mpg.

Features: Diesel cars are important in Italy, so the T.ds gets top equipment, and is also the only Tipo to have power steering as standard.
Summary: This is a very lively engine for a diesel, giving unusually good performance, but the penalty is a level of fuel consumption which most other diesels of this size can better. Apart from this, it is a pleasing model and responds well.

FIAT (I)   Uno Selecta

Identity: As first launched, the Uno with continuously variable, automatic transmission was powered by the 1116 cc engine, but is now also available with the 1372 cc engine. The larger capacity copes much better and meets the need for a small car with automatic transmission— there are still too few of these.

Engine: Front-mounted transverse four-cylinder with alloy head and single ohc; SPI-Bosch single-point electronic injection. Bore 80.5 mm, stroke 67.4 mm; capacity 1372 cc. Power 71 PS (52 kW) at 6000 rpm; torque 77 lb ft (106 Nm) at 3250 rpm. Compression 9.2-to-1. Catalyst: not available.

Transmission: Front-wheel drive; automatic, continuously variable, segmented steel belt drive. Top gear speed at 1000 rpm: 26.7 mph (42.9 km/h).

Suspension: Front, independent, MacPherson struts, anti-roll bar. Rear, semi-independent, torsion beam and trailing arms, coil springs.

Steering: Rack and pinion. Power assistance: not available. **Brakes:** Solid discs front, drums rear. ABS: not available. **Tyres:** 165/65 R 13. **Fuel tank:** 9.2 Imp. gall (42 litres). **Unladen weight:** 1874 lb (850 kg).

Dimensions: Length 145.2 in (3689 mm), width 61.5 in (1562 mm), height 56.1 in (1425 mm), wheelbase 93.0 in (2362 mm).

Performance _Autocar & Motor_ test: Maximum speed 98 mph (157 km/h); 0 to 62 mph (100 km/h) 14.0 sec. Fuel consumption at constant 75 mph (120 km/h): 40.4 mpg.

Features: Simple control lever to select Drive, with Low hold for hills. The S-level trim includes central locking and electric front windows. **Summary:** Quite a good choice where a five-door car that is easy to drive is wanted, but this type of automatic has the drawback of seeming a little fussy, with engine revving hard and transmission slipping, except on small throttle openings.

FIAT (I)   Uno Turbo i.e.

Identity: Although now competing against much stronger competition, the Fiat Uno Turbo is still one of the quickest of the 'pocket rockets' – high performance hatchbacks. In the new version introduced Frankfurt 1989, capacity goes up from 1299 to 1372 cc, and power is now 118 PS.

Engine: Front-mounted transverse four-cylinder with alloy head and belt-driven single ohc; eight valves. Bosch Jetronic fuel injection. Garrett T2 Turbocharger with intercooler. Bore 80.5 mm, stroke 67.4 mm; capacity 1372 cc. Power 118 PS (85 kW) at 6000 rpm; torque 116 lb ft (161 Nm) at 3500 rpm. Compression 7.7-to-1. Catalyst: not available.

Transmission: Front-wheel drive; five-speed manual gearbox. Automatic, not available. Top gear speed at 1000 rpm: 21.0 mph (33.8 km/h).

Suspension: Front, independent, MacPherson struts with gas-filled dampers; anti-roll bar. Rear, semi-independent, torsion beam and trailing arms, coil springs and gas-filled dampers.

Steering: Rack and pinion. Power assistance: not available. **Brakes:** Vented discs front, solid discs rear. ABS: optional. **Tyres:** 175/60 R 13. **Fuel tank:** 11.0 Imp. gall (50 litres). **Unladen weight:** 2040 lb (925 kg).

Dimensions: Length 145.2 in (3689 mm), width 61.5 in (1562 mm), height 55.3 in (1405 mm), wheelbase 93.0 in (2362 mm).

Performance _Autocar & Motor_ test: Maximum speed 126 mph (203 km/ h); 0 to 60 mph (97 km/h) 8.3 sec; 80 mph (130 km) 14.1 sec. Fuel consumption at constant 75 mph (120 km/h): 35.8 mpg; overall test, 25.9 mpg.

Features: Spoiler is incorporated in the front bumper of the Turbo model, and a red line below the doors leads into a 'Turbo i.e.' badge at the base of the rear side panels. **Summary:** Maker's figures for performance were largely confirmed by the road test, showing that the 1989 change to a larger engine made the new Turbo i.e. a fiery little hatchback. The Turbo is available only as a three-door.

FORD (GB, B)

Identity: New Escort and Orion models were launched Birmingham 1990, bringing greatly enhanced interior trim and design. More aerodynamic bodies are roomier inside, although external dimensions are almost the same as before. New suspension, and wider range of options.

Engine: Front-mounted transverse four-cylinder with alloy head and single ohc operating inclined valves in hemi head. Twin-choke carb. Bore 77.2 mm, stroke 74.3 mm; capacity 1392 cc. Power 73 PS (54 kW) at 5500 rpm; torque 78 lb ft (108 Nm) at 4000 rpm. Compression 8.5-to-1. Catalyst: optional.

Transmission: Front-wheel drive; five-speed manual gearbox. Automatic, optional extra. Top gear speed at 1000 rpm: 22.8 mph (36.7 km/h).

Suspension: Front, independent, MacPherson struts; anti-roll bar. Rear, semi-independent, trailing arms and torsion beam axle.

Steering: Rack and pinion. Power assistance: not available. **Brakes:** Solid discs front, drums rear. ABS: optional. **Tyres:** 175/70 R 13. **Fuel tank:** 12.1 Imp. gall (55 litres). **Unladen weight:** 2116 lb (960 kg).

Dimensions: Length 158.9 in (4036 mm), width 66.3 in (1684 mm), height 53.2 in (1352 mm), wheelbase 99.4 in (2525 mm).

Performance _Autocar & Motor_ test: Maximum speed 102 mph (164 km/h); 0 to 60 mph (97 km/h) 12.8 sec; 80 mph (130 km/h) 23.5 sec. Fuel consumption at constant 75 mph (120 km/h): 38.2 mpg; overall test, 29.0 mpg.

Features: Power steering became available for the first time on Escort, but is limited to 1.6-litre models; anti-lock brakes are offered across the range. **Summary:** Without power assistance, the steering is rather heavy as well as being low-geared, but in other respects I rated the new Escort a big improvement on its predecessor, especially because of better comfort and reduced noise levels.

FORD (GB, B, D)   Escort Cabriolet 1.6 EFi

Identity: Beautiful weather greeted my arrival in Switzerland to drive the new Escort and Orion models in August 1990, so I selected the Cabriolet for my first drive. This new and much-improved version provided thoroughly enjoyable open-top motoring.

Engine: Front-mounted transverse four-cylinder with alloy head and single ohc operating two valves per cylinder. Electronic fuel injection. Bore 80.0 mm, stroke 79.5 mm; capacity 1596 cc. Power 108 PS (80 kW) at 6000 rpm; torque 102 lb ft (141 Nm) at 4500 rpm. Compression 9.8-to-1. Catalyst: optional.

Transmission: Front-wheel drive; five-speed manual gearbox. Automatic, not available. Top gear speed at 1000 rpm: 24.3 mph (39.1 km/h).

Suspension: Front, independent, MacPherson struts with L-shaped strut-locating arms on double vertical bushes; anti-roll bar. Rear, semi-independent, trailing arms and torsion beam axle with coil springs.

Steering: Rack and pinion. Power assistance: standard. **Brakes:** Vented discs front, drums rear. ABS: optional. **Tyres:** 185/60 HR 14. **Fuel tank:** 12.1 Imp. gall (55 litres). **Unladen weight:** 2300 lb (1045 kg).

Dimensions: Length 158.9 in (4036 mm), width 66.3 in (1684 mm), height 53.2 in (1352 mm), wheelbase 99.4 in (2525 mm).

Performance Works: Maximum speed 115 mph (185 km/h) ; 0 to 60 mph (97 km/h) 10.4 sec. Fuel consumption at constant 75 mph (120 km/h): 38.7 mpg.

Features: This is the only one of the new Escort/Orion range to have power steering as standard. Leather seats, power-operated hood and alloy wheels all optional. **Summary:** Interior and map lights are built into the fixed roll bar, and the Cabriolet is structurally strong and very pleasant to drive. Neat tonneau cover can be fitted over the folded hood without a struggle, and complete hood raising or lowering takes only about a minute.

FORD (D, GB)   Escort RS Cosworth

Identity: Even as early as the original launch of the new Escort model, in September 1990, it was revealed that a high-performance version with Cosworth tuned engine and four-wheel drive would go on sale. This seemed an appropriate car for our cover, although it will not go on sale until the middle of 1992.

Engine: Front-mounted transverse four-cylinder with alloy head and twin ohc working four valves per cylinder. Turbocharger and electronic fuel injection. Bore 90.8 mm, stroke 77.0 mm; capacity 1993 cc. Power 240 PS (177 kW) at 6000 rpm; torque 217 lb ft (300 Nm) at 4000 rpm. Compression 8.0-to-1. Catalyst: standard.

Transmission: Four-wheel drive; five-speed manual gearbox. Automatic, not available. Top gear speed at 1000 rpm: 23.0 mph (37.0 km/h).

Suspension: Front, independent, MacPherson struts, anti-roll bar. Rear, independent, semi-trailing arms with coil springs.

Steering: Rack and pinion. Power assistance: standard. **Brakes:** Vented discs front, solid discs rear. ABS: standard. **Tyres:** 225/45–16. **Fuel tank:** 14.3 Imp. gall (65 litres). **Unladen weight:** 2712 lb (1230 kg).

Dimensions: Length 165.6 in (4205 mm), width 68.5 in (1740 mm), height 54.6 in (1387 mm), wheelbase 100.4 in (2550 mm).

Performance Works: Maximum speed 150 mph (241 km/h); 0 to 60 mph (97 km/h) 5.8 sec. Fuel consumption: no data.

Features: Aerodynamic aids, including high-level rear spoiler and distinctive paint finish, give a striking appearance to this special Escort. **Summary:** The main purpose of the Escort RS will be to head Ford's rally effort, hence the name Ford Motorsport on the side, but a number of the very fast RS Cosworths will be sold to private buyers.

FORD (D, E, GB)   Fiesta 1.4 Ghia

Identity: Completely new Fiesta range was launched Amsterdam 1989, and on UK market April. Choice of six engines, and for the first time a five-door as well as a three-door. The range was topped off by Ghia specification with the 1.4-litre engine at launch, until the XR2i became available later.

Engine: Front-mounted transverse four-cylinder with alloy head and single ohc operating inclined valves in hemi combustion chambers. Twin-choke carb. Bore 77.0 mm, stroke 74.0 mm; capacity 1392 cc. Power 75 PS (55 kW) at 5600 rpm; torque 80 lb ft (109 Nm) at 4000 rpm. Compression 9.5-to-1. Catalyst: not available.

Transmission: Front-wheel drive; five-speed manual gearbox. Automatic, optional extra. Top gear speed at 1000 rpm: 20.6 mph (33.1 km/h).

Suspension: Front, independent, MacPherson struts, anti-roll bar. Rear, independent, semi-trailing arms and coil springs.

Steering: Rack and pinion. Power assistance: not available. **Brakes:** Vented discs front, drums rear. ABS: optional. **Tyres:** 155/70 SR 13. **Fuel tank:** 9.2 Imp. gall (42 litres). **Unladen weight:** 1960 lb (890 kg).

Dimensions: Length 147.4 in (3743 mm), width 73.0 in (1854 mm), height 52.0 in (1320 mm), wheelbase 96.3 in (2446 mm).

Performance *Autocar & Motor* test: Maximum speed 98 mph (158 km/h); 0 to 60 mph (97 km/h) 13.4 sec; 80 mph (130 km/h) 27.2 sec. Fuel consumption at constant 75 mph (120 km/h): 42.2 mpg; overall test, 28.1 mpg.

Features: Ghia model gets good equipment for this size of car, but tailgate is self-locking with rather awkward electric release, and there is severe buffeting if the sunroof panel is taken out. **Summary:** Ford's new Fiesta jumped straight to the top of the sales league, and deserves its place as a very attractive small–medium size car.

FORD (E, GB)   Fiesta RS Turbo

Identity: At a brief but exciting launch in Northern Ireland, June 1990, Ford introduced what was proclaimed as the fastest Fiesta yet—a turbocharged version of the XR2i, with 133 PS output. Look for the louvres on the bonnet, and distinctive 'three-spoke' alloy wheels.

Engine: Front-mounted transverse four-cylinder with alloy head, belt-driven ohc, two valves per cylinder, and Garrett TO2 turbocharger. Bore 80.0 mm, stroke 79.5 mm; capacity 1596 cc. Power 133 PS (98 kW) at 5500 rpm; torque 132 lb ft (183 Nm) at 5500 rpm. Compression 8.2-to-1. Catalyst: not available.

Transmission: Front-wheel drive; five-speed manual gearbox. Automatic, not available. Top gear speed at 1000 rpm: 20.8 mph (33.5 km/h).

Suspension: Front, independent, MacPherson struts, anti-roll bar. Rear, semi-independent, trailing arms and torsion beam; coil springs, anti-roll bar.

Steering: Rack and pinion. Power assistance: not available. **Brakes:** Vented discs front, drums rear. ABS: optional. **Tyres:** 185/55 VR 14. **Fuel tank:** 9.2 Imp. gall (42 litres). **Unladen weight:** 2030 lb (920 kg).

Dimensions: Length 149.6 in (3801 mm), width 64.2 in (1630 mm), height 52.2 in (1326 mm), wheelbase 96.3 in (2446 mm).

Performance *Autocar & Motor* test: Maximum speed 129 mph (208 km/h); 0 to 60 mph (97 km/h) 7.9 sec; 80 mph (130 km/h) 12.7 sec. Fuel consumption at constant 75 mph (120 km/h): 34.0 mpg; overall test, 23.6 mpg.

Features: Special Recaro seats with dual-latch tracks are fitted for optimum location of front occupants. There are some other detail changes, such as the special small-diameter wheel and leather-trimmed gear knob. **Summary:** I felt Ford had gone to the extreme in making the suspension ultra-firm, but the instant punch of the turbocharged engine gave wonderfully zippy motoring. A great fun car.

FORD   (E, GB)   Fiesta XR2i

Identity: At the preview of the new Ford Fiesta towards the end of 1988, it was revealed that a fuel injection model would be launched, and it joined the range at Motorfair 1989. It has the 1.6 CVH (Compound Valve Hemi) engine, with advanced ignition system using no distributor.

Engine: Front-mounted transverse four-cylinder with ignition triggered directly from the flywheel, and electronic fuel injection. Alloy head, single ohc, and eight valves. Bore 80.0 mm, stroke 79.5 mm; capacity 1596 cc. Power 110 PS (81 kW) at 6000 rpm; torque 100 lb ft (138 Nm) at 2800 rpm. Compression 9.8-to-1. Catalyst: optional.

Transmission: Front-wheel drive; five-speed manual gearbox. Automatic, not available. Top gear speed at 1000 rpm: 20.3 mph (32.7 km/h).

Suspension: Front, independent, MacPherson struts with L-shaped locating arms mounted on double vertical bushes; anti-roll bar. Rear, semi-independent, trailing arms and torsion beam axle; coil springs.

Steering: Rack and pinion. Power assistance: not available. **Brakes:** Vented discs front, drums rear. ABS: optional (mechanical). **Tyres:** 185/60 HR 13. **Fuel tank:** 9.2 Imp. gall (42 litres). **Unladen weight:** 1962 lb (890 kg).

Dimensions: Length 149.6 in (3801 mm), width 64.2 in (1630 mm), height 52.2 in (1326 mm), wheelbase 96.3 in (2446 mm).

Performance *Autocar & Motor* test: Maximum speed 118 mph (190 km/h); 0 to 60 mph (97 km/h) 8.9 sec; 80 mph (130 km/h) 15.9 sec. Fuel consumption at constant 75 mph (120 km/h): 38.2 mpg; overall test, 28.4 mpg.

Features: Special bumpers incorporate an air dam at the front and house fog and driving lamps. A thin blue line runs along the top of the bumpers and continues along the body sides. **Summary:** Trying the XR2i on the bumpy roads of Northern Ireland, I again thought the suspension a little harsh, but it's a very sporty car with excellent handling and a superb range of performance.

FORD (D)   Granada 2.5 GL Turbo D Saloon

Identity: At Brussels 1990, Ford extended the Granada and Scorpio ranges with the launch of a new saloon version, considered by many to look more businesslike than the well-established hatchback. Prices are the same as for the hatchback, and the complete model palette is duplicated in the new saloon body.

Engine: Front-mounted longitudinal four-cylinder with alloy head and pushrod ohv. Garrett T.03 turbocharger. Bore 94.0 mm, stroke 90.0 mm; capacity 2498 cc. Power 92 PS (68 kW) at 4150 rpm; torque 150 lb ft (204 Nm) at 2250 rpm. Compression 21.1-to-1. Fuel: Derv.

Transmission: Rear-wheel drive; five-speed manual gearbox. Automatic, not available for diesel. Top gear speed at 1000 rpm: 24.3 mph (39.1 km/h).

Suspension: Front, independent, MacPherson struts, anti-roll bar. Rear, independent, semi-trailing arms and coil springs.

Steering: Rack and pinion. Power assistance: standard. **Brakes:** Vented discs front, solid discs rear. ABS: standard. **Tyres:** 185/70 R14 T. **Fuel tank:** 15.4 Imp. gall (70 litres). **Unladen weight:** 3065 lb (1390 kg).

Dimensions: Length 183.8 in (4669 mm), width 69.5 in (1766 mm), height 57.1 in (1450 mm), wheelbase 108.7 in (2761 mm).

Performance *Autocar & Motor* test: Maximum speed 106 mph (171 km/h); 0 to 60 mph (97 km/h) 13.4 sec; 80 mph (130 km/h) 25.2 sec. Fuel consumption at constant 75 mph (120 km/h): 47.1 mpg; overall test, 30.6 mpg.

Features: All equipment details and nearly every item of specification are the same for the saloon as for the hatchback. Comprehensive equipment and attractive furnishing. **Summary:** Diesel was selected for this representative of the new Granada saloon since the Peugeot-built turbo diesel engine is also a fairly new development for Granada. Previously it had no turbo, and power was borderline. Now, it is much more respectable.

FORD   (GB, B, D)   Orion 1.6 Ghia Injection

Identity: As before, the new Orion is essentially the saloon version of the Ford Escort, though the model is aimed higher up-market, and there are no Popular versions. Top trim is the Ghia model, available with the full range of 1.3, 1.4, 1.6 and 1.8 diesel engines, plus the injection Orion, available with or without catalyst.

Engine: Front-mounted transverse four-cylinder with alloy head and single ohc operating two valves per cylinder. Twin-choke carb. Bore 80.0 mm, stroke 79.5 mm; capacity 1596 cc. Power 90 PS (66 kW) at 5800 rpm; torque 94 lb ft (130 Nm) at 5800 rpm. Compression 9.5-to-1. Catalyst: optional.

Transmission: Front-wheel drive; five-speed manual gearbox. Automatic, optional extra. Top gear speed at 1000 rpm: 22.6 mph (36.4 km/h).

Suspension: Front, independent, MacPherson struts with L-shaped strut-locating arms on double vertical bushes; anti-roll bar. Rear, semi-independent, trailing arms and torsion beam axle with coil springs.

Steering: Rack and pinion. Power assistance: optional. **Brakes:** Vented discs front, drums rear. ABS: optional. **Tyres:** 175/70 R 13-T. **Fuel tank:** 12.1 Imp. gall (55 litres). **Unladen weight:** 2300 lb (1045 kg).

Dimensions: Length 166.5 in (4229 mm), width 66.3 in (1684 mm), height 53.0 in (1345 mm), wheelbase 99.4 in (2525 mm).

Performance Works: Maximum speed 110 mph (177 km/h); 0 to 60 mph (97 km/h) 10.3 sec. Fuel consumption at constant 75 mph (120 km/h): 39.8 mpg.

Features: Ghia specification is quite good, but even at this level, the Orion does not get power steering or anti-lock brakes as standard. **Summary:** Without assistance, the steering tends to be both low-geared and heavy to turn, so the power option has to be recommended, turning the Orion into a pleasant car. It offers more refinement, especially inside, than its predecessor.

FORD (GB, D)   Scorpio 2.9i Cosworth 24V

Identity: Last new model announcement of 1990 came just before Christmas: a more powerful version of the Scorpio with Cosworth engine, tuned to give 34 per cent more power but also to meet the world's toughest emission regulations. Look for the special wheels and tiny 24V badge on boot.

Engine: Front-mounted longitudinal V6-cylinder with cast-iron block, special Cosworth alloy heads, and twin ohc each bank. Ford injection and distributorless ignition. Bore 93.0 mm, stroke 72.0 mm; capacity 2933 cc. Power 195 PS (143 kW) at 5750 rpm; torque 199 lb ft (275 Nm) at 4500 rpm. Compression 9.7-to-1. Catalyst: standard.

Transmission: Rear-wheel drive; four-speed automatic, standard. Top gear speed at 1000 rpm: 25.5 mph (41.0 km/h).

Suspension: Front, independent, MacPherson struts, lower track control arms and rear-mounted anti-roll bar. Rear, independent, semi-trailing arms with coil springs and anti-roll bar.

Steering: Rack and pinion. Power assistance: standard. **Brakes:** Vented discs front and rear. ABS: standard. **Tyres:** 205/50 ZR 16. **Fuel tank:** 15.4 Imp. gall (70 litres). **Unladen weight:** 3053 lb (1385 kg).

Dimensions: Length 183.8 in (4669 mm), width 69.5 in (1766 mm), height 57.2 in (1453 mm), wheelbase 108.8 in (2765 mm).

Performance Works: Maximum speed 140 mph (225 km/h); 0 to 60 mph (97 km/h) 8.8 sec. Fuel consumption at constant 75 mph (120 km/h): 28.0 mpg.

Features: Special wheels are fitted, and top equipment includes CD player, electric seat adjustment front and rear, and fuel computer. **Summary:** Production started in February 1991, and the 24V went on sale in March. One objective of this special Scorpio was to show how higher power could be offered while also setting excellent emission control standards.

FORD (D)   Scorpio 4 × 4 2.9i

Identity: Slight increase in engine capacity for the new V6 engine launched October 1986 was achieved by lengthening the stroke; but engine also developed for more power, and catalyst-equipped version available for some markets including UK.

Engine: Front-mounted longitudinal 60 deg V6-cylinder with cast iron block and heads. Camshaft in block, and pushrod ohv. Bosch L-Jetronic fuel injection. Bore 93.0 mm, stroke 72.0 mm; capacity 2933 cc. Power 150 PS (110 kW) at 5700 rpm; torque 171 lb ft (233 Nm) at 3000 rpm. Compression 9.5-to-1. Catalyst: optional.

Transmission: Four-wheel drive; five-speed manual gearbox. No automatic option for 4 × 4. Top gear speed at 1000 rpm: 23.9 mph (38.4 km/h).

Suspension: Front, independent, MacPherson struts, lower track control arms and rear-mounted anti-roll bar. Coil springs and twin-tube telescopic dampers. Rear, independent, semi-trailing arms; coil springs and twin-tube telescopic dampers; anti-roll bar (larger dia. on 4 × 4).

Steering: Rack and pinion. Power assistance: standard, varying ratio. **Brakes:** Vented discs front, solid rear. ABS: standard. **Tyres:** 205/60 VR 15. **Fuel tank:** 15.4 Imp. gall (70 litres). **Unladen weight:** 3053 lb (1385 kg).

Dimensions: Length 183.8 in (4669 mm), width 69.5 in (1766 mm), height 57.2 in (1453 mm), wheelbase 108.8 in (2765 mm).

Performance *Autocar & Motor* test: Maximum speed 125 mph (201 km/h); 0 to 60 mph (97 km/h) 9.4 sec; 80 mph (130 km/h) 16.8 sec. Fuel consumption at constant 75 mph (120 km/h): 27.9 mpg; overall test, 19.2 mpg.

Features: Permanent four-wheel drive, with torque distributed 34 per cent front, 66 rear. **Summary:** Most impressive car, combining superb handling with admirable capability as a car for severe winter weather, plus restricted off-road use.

FORD (B, D)   Sierra Sapphire 2000E

Identity: Once the preserve of expensive high performance cars, a twin overhead camshaft engine was introduced for the Ford Sierra and Granada 2-litre models in mid-1989, bringing better performance and efficiency. At the same time, this lavishly equipped 2000E model was launched at the top of the Sapphire range.

Engine: Front-mounted longitudinal four-cylinder with alloy head and belt-driven twin ohc working two valves per cylinder; multi-point fuel injection. Bore 86.0 mm, stroke 86.0 mm; capacity 1998 cc. Power 125 PS (92 kW) at 5500 rpm; torque 128 lb ft (174 Nm) at 3000 rpm. Compression 10.3-to-1. Catalyst: optional.

Transmission: Rear-wheel drive; five-speed manual gearbox. Automatic, optional extra. Top gear speed at 1000 rpm: 21.7 mph (34.9 km/h).

Suspension: Front, independent, MacPherson struts, anti-roll bar. Rear, independent, semi-trailing arms and coil springs.

Steering: Rack and pinion. Power assistance: standard. **Brakes:** Vented discs front, drums rear. ABS: optional. **Tyres:** 195/65 HR 14. **Fuel tank:** 13.2 Imp. gall (60 litres). **Unladen weight:** 2690 lb (1220 kg).

Dimensions: Length 175.9 in (4467 mm), width 75.6 in (1920 mm), height 53.5 in (1358 mm), wheelbase 102.7 in (2608 mm).

Performance *Autocar & Motor* test: Maximum speed 119 mph (192 km/h); 0 to 60 mph (97 km/h) 10.0 sec; 80 mph (130 km/h) 18.0 sec. Fuel consumption at constant 75 mph (120 km/h): 38.7 mpg; overall test, 26.8 mpg.

Features: Top equipment and luxury furnishings in the 2000E include leather upholstery, leather-trimmed wheel, air conditioning and all-electric windows. **Summary:** Pleasant to drive, with the typical solid feel of the rear-drive mid-range Ford, and for the generous specification, the price is reasonable making this a popular choice for an executive 2-litre car. The DOHC engine is also available with carb., but not in 2000E spec.

FORD (B)   Sierra Sapphire RS Cosworth

Identity: The unlimited series production Cosworth appeared January 1988, using the Sierra Sapphire saloon body, with turbocharged 2-litre 16-valve engine by Cosworth Racing. Rear wing and special wheels identify this very fast version of the Sierra. Revised four-wheel drive version with more power, January 1990.

Engine: Front-mounted longitudinal four-cylinder with alloy head and twin belt-driven ohc operating four valves per cyl. Garrett TO3B turbocharger with air-air intercooler. Bore 90.8 mm, stroke 77.0 mm; capacity 1993 cc. Power 220 PS (162 kW) at 6250 rpm; torque 210 lb ft (290 Nm) at 3500 rpm. Compression 8.0-to-1. Catalyst: standard.

Transmission: Four-wheel drive; five-speed manual gearbox. Automatic, not available. Top gear speed at 1000 rpm: 22.8 mph (36.7 km/h).

Suspension: Front, independent, MacPherson struts, twin-tube gas-filled dampers; anti-roll bar. Rear, independent, semi-trailing arms and coil springs; gas-filled telescopic dampers, anti-roll bar.

Steering: Rack and pinion. Power assistance: standard, varying ratio.
Brakes: Vented discs front, solid discs rear. ABS: standard. **Tyres:** Dunlop D40 205/50 VR 15. **Fuel tank:** 13.2 Imp. gall (60 litres). **Unladen weight:** 2869 lb (1300 kg).

Dimensions: Length 176.9 in (4494 mm), width 66.9 in (1698 mm), height 54.2 in (1376 mm), wheelbase 102.7 in (2608 mm).

Performance *Autocar & Motor* test: Maximum speed 144 mph (232 km/h); 0 to 60 mph (97 km/h) 6.6 sec; 80 mph (130 km/h) 10.9 sec. Fuel consumption at constant 75 mph (120 km/h): 30.4 mpg; overall test, 21.6 mpg.

Features: Top equipment is included with such items as electric front windows, central locking, and glass sunroof. **Summary:** Fantastic performance on dry roads, and the handling was made much safer by the 1990 introduction of four-wheel drive. A very refined, swift, long journey car, but it can also be docile as well; a handy shopping car!

FORD (USA)   Thunderbird SC

Identity: Substantially revised for 1989, with new front, wheelbase 9 in longer, and all-independent suspension. All interior dimensions are larger than before; slats below bumper identify 1991 model. SC stands for Super Coupé, which brings turbocharger with inter-cooler.

Engine: Front-mounted longitudinal V6-cylinder with alloy heads and central chain-driven camshaft. Garrett turbocharger and intercooler. Bore 96.5 mm, stroke 86.4 mm; capacity 3791 cc. Power 210 bhp (SAE) (140 kW) at 4000 rpm; torque 315 lb ft (435 Nm) at 2600 rpm. Compression 9.0-to-1. Catalyst: standard.

Transmission: Rear-wheel drive; five-speed manual gearbox. Automatic, four-speed, optional. Top gear speed at 1000 rpm: 36.2 mph (58.2 km/h).

Suspension: Front, independent, wishbones and struts; coil springs and gas-filled telescopic dampers, anti-roll bar. Rear, independent, lower H-arm and upper arms; coil springs and gas-filled telescopic dampers; anti-roll bar.

Steering: Rack and pinion. Power assistance: standard. **Brakes:** Solid discs front, and rear. ABS: standard. **Tyres:** P225/60 VR 16. **Fuel tank:** 17.5 Imp. gall (80 litres). **Unladen weight:** 3542 lb (1607 kg).

Dimensions: Length 198.7 in (5047 mm), width 72.7 in (1847 mm), height 52.7 in (1339 mm), wheelbase 113.0 in (2870 mm).

Performance (est): Maximum speed 125 mph (201 km/h). Fuel consumption overall (est) 20.0 mpg.

Features: 'Handling' suspension has automatic ride control. Sports seats. Options include digital CD player and moon roof. **Summary:** A more exciting Thunderbird package, still with the sleek looks of the predecessor, but now bigger and with more power. The T-bird, as it is sometimes known, is also available in standard and LX form, automatic and without turbo.

GINETTA   (GB)   **G33 V8 Roadster**

Identity: High-performance lightweight convertible with body in glass-reinforced polyester resin on galvanised steel chassis. Power unit is a Rover V8 3.9-litre giving 200 bhp, and staggering performance figures include 0 to 80 mph (not 60 mph) in 7.2 sec.

Engine: Front-mounted longitudinal V8-cylinder with alloy block and heads, and electronic fuel injection. Bore 94.0 mm, stroke 71.1 mm; capacity 3947 cc. Power 203 PS (149 kW) at 5280 rpm; torque 220 lb ft (304 Nm) at 3500 rpm. Compression 10.5-to-1. Catalyst: optional.

Transmission: Rear-wheel drive; five-speed manual gearbox. Automatic, not available. Top gear speed at 1000 rpm: 27.0 mph (43.5 km/h).

Suspension: Front, independent, wishbones and coil springs; anti-roll bar. Rear, independent, lower wishbones, longitudinal links and fixed-length drive shafts; coil springs and anti-roll bar.

Steering: Rack and pinion. Power assistance: not available. **Brakes:** Vented discs front, solid discs rear. ABS: not available. **Tyres:** 195/50 ZR 15. **Fuel tank:** 12.0 Imp. gall (55 litres). **Unladen weight:** 1500 lb (680 kg).

Dimensions: Length 139.6 in (3547 mm), width 57.8 in (1469 mm), height 39.9 in (1013 mm), wheelbase 85.0 in (2160 mm).

Performance Works: Maximum speed 145 mph (233 km/h); 0 to 60 mph (97 km/h) 5.0 sec; 80 mph (130 km/h) 7.2 sec. Fuel consumption at constant 75 mph (120 km/h): 35.0 mpg.

Features: Interior trim is in leather, with pile carpet floors and traditional instrument layout. Pop-up headlamps in one-piece nose section. **Summary:** An exciting sports car from the well-established Ginetta company of Scunthorpe, suitable for use on road or track. Chassis is a multi-tubular backbone type, and the body has two doors and detachable hood.

HONDA (J)   Accord 2.2i

Identity: Launched Frankfurt 1989, the Accord appears in the fourth body style to carry the name, and has choice of 2.0-litre engine with carb. or injection, and 2.2-litre (details follow) with injection and catalyst. The new car is bigger, with longer wheelbase than its predecessor. All-wheel steering is standard.

Engine: Front-mounted transverse four-cylinder with alloy head and single ohc operating four valves per cylinder. PGM-F1 fuel injection. Bore 85.0 mm, stroke 95.0 mm; capacity 2156 cc. Power 150 PS (110 kW) at 5900 rpm; torque 143 lb ft (198 Nm) at 5000 rpm. Compression 9.8-to-1. Catalyst: standard.

Transmission: Front-wheel drive; five-speed manual gearbox. Automatic, optional extra.Top gear speed at 1000 rpm: 24.0 mph (38.7 km/h).

Suspension: Front, independent, wishbones and coil springs; anti-roll bar. Rear, independent, wishbones and coil springs; anti-roll bar.

Steering: Rack and pinion with shaft to rear steering box. Power assistance: standard. **Brakes:** Vented discs front, solid discs rear. ABS: standard. **Tyres:** 195/60 R 15. **Fuel tank:** 13.2 Imp. gall (60 litres). **Unladen weight:** 2920 lb (1325 kg).

Dimensions: Length 184.4 in (4685 mm), width 66.7 in (1695 mm), height 54.7 in (1390 mm), wheelbase 107.0 in (2720 mm).

Performance *Autocar & Motor* test: Maximum speed 123 mph (198 km/h); 0 to 60 mph (97 km/h) 9.9 sec; 80 mph (130 km/h) 17.1 sec. Fuel consumption at constant 75 mph (120 km/h): 33.2 mpg; overall test, 26.1 mpg.

Features: Even the 2.0i has anti-lock brakes, air conditioning, and cruise control; main added feature of the 2.2i is all-wheel steering. **Summary:** Angle change of the rear wheels occurs in the same direction, or opposite direction, according to amount of turning lock applied; the system is the same as for the Prelude EX, and contributes to excellent handling and manœuvrability. Rear spoiler identifies the 2.2i.

HONDA (J)   Civic Shuttle 1.6i-4WD

Identity: When I tried this first as an entry in the Caravan Club towcar contest I was very impressed, as it has a six-speed gearbox providing emergency low; but power was a little lacking and robbed it of a possible class win. Shuttle is the high roof version of Civic, available with two or four-wheel drive.

Engine: Front-mounted transverse four-cylinder with alloy block and head; twin belt-driven ohc operating four valves per cyl. Electronic fuel injection. Bore 75.0 mm, stroke 90.0 mm; capacity 1590 cc. Power 116 PS (85 kW) at 6300 rpm; torque 104 lb ft (141 Nm) at 5300 rpm. Compression 9.0-to-1. Catalyst: not available.

Transmission: Four-wheel drive; six-speed manual gearbox. Automatic, not available for 4WD version. Top gear speed at 1000 rpm: 19.2 mph (30.9 km/h).

Suspension: Front, independent, wishbones and coil springs, telescopic dampers, anti-roll bar. Rear, independent, trailing arms with compensator arms and upper links; coil springs and telescopic dampers.

Steering: Rack and pinion. Power assistance: standard. **Brakes:** Vented discs front, drums rear. ABS: not available. **Tyres:** 165 SR 13. **Fuel tank:** 9.9 Imp. gall (45 litres). **Unladen weight:** 2420 lb (1095 kg).

Dimensions: Length 161.6 in (4105 mm), width 66.5 in (1690 mm), height 59.6 in (1515 mm), wheelbase 98.4 in (2500 mm).

Performance *Autocar & Motor* test: Maximum speed 104 mph (167 km/h); 0 to 60 mph (97 km/h) 10.0 sec; 80 mph (130 km/h) 18.1 sec. Fuel consumption at constant 75 mph (120 km/h): 31.7 mpg; overall test, 22.9 mpg.

Features: Good equipment including all-electric windows, central locking, and divided folding rear seat. Steering wheel height adjustable.

Summary: Very practical family car giving a feeling of spaciousness inside. Remarkable traction with permanent four-wheel drive, and the standby very low gear for easy steep hill starts, especially when towing.

HONDA   (J)   CRX 1.6i-VT

Identity: A sporting coupé in the Civic range, the CRX was revised in 1990 with an ingenious control system for its valve gear. Valve timing and the amount of valve lift are altered for optimum efficiency, resulting in a remarkable 150 bhp from only 1.6-litre capacity.

Engine: Front-mounted transverse four-cylinder with alloy head and twin ohc working four valves per cylinder, with automatic control of valve timing and lift. Honda PGM electronic fuel injection. Bore 81.0 mm, stroke 77.0 mm; capacity 1595 cc. Power 150 PS (110 kW) at 7600 rpm; torque 106 lb ft (147 Nm) at 7100 rpm. Compression 10.2-to-1. Catalyst: standard.

Transmission: Front-wheel drive; five-speed manual gearbox. Automatic, not available. Top gear speed at 1000 rpm: 18.7 mph (30.1 km/h).

Suspension: Front, independent, wishbones and coil springs; anti-roll bar. Rear, independent, wishbones and coil springs; anti-roll bar.

Steering: Rack and pinion. Power assistance: not available. **Brakes:** Vented discs front, solid discs rear. ABS: standard. **Tyres:** 195/60 VR 14. **Fuel tank:** 9.9 Imp. gall (45 litres). **Unladen weight:** 2258 lb (1025 kg).

Dimensions: Length 148.6 in (3755 mm), width 65.9 in (1600 mm), height 50.0 in (1270 mm), wheelbase 90.5 in (2300 mm).

Performance *Autocar & Motor* test: Maximum speed 130 mph (209 km/h); 0 to 60 mph (97 km/h) 8.0 sec; 80 mph (130 km/h) 13.7 sec. Fuel consumption at constant 75 mph (120 km/h): 39.2 mpg; overall test, 28.1 mpg.

Features: Strictly 2+2 accommodation, but front seats are snug, and equipment is reasonable, with electric windows and small pop-up sunroof.
Summary: Extraordinarily free-revving engine, and the effect of the varying valve mechanism is shown by the fact that torque goes on building right up to 7,100 rpm. Good performance for a 1.6, but a bit heavy on fuel, due to all those revs!

HONDA   (J, GB)   Concerto 1.6i-16

Identity: Although the Concerto and Rover's equivalent 200-Series were not launched in Britain until Motorfair 1989, the Concerto first appeared Tokyo 1988, and the 1.4-litre was featured in the 1989 edition. This year Concerto is represented by the top 1.6i model.

Engine: Front-mounted transverse four-cylinder with alloy head and block; twin ohc operating four valves per cylinder. Honda PGM-F1 injection. Bore 75.0 mm, stroke 90 mm; capacity 1590 cc. Power 130 PS (96 kW) at 6800 rpm; torque 103 lb ft (143 Nm) at 5700 rpm. Compression 9.5-to-1. Catalyst: not available.

Transmission: Front-wheel drive; five-speed manual gearbox. Automatic, optional extra. Top gear speed at 1000 rpm: 20.2 mph (32.6 km/h).

Suspension: Front, independent, MacPherson struts, anti-roll bar. Rear, independent, wishbones and coil springs; anti-roll bar.

Steering: Rack and pinion. Power assistance: standard. **Brakes:** Vented discs front, solid discs rear. ABS: standard. **Tyres:** 175/60 R 14. **Fuel tank:** 12.1 Imp. gall (55 litres). **Unladen weight:** 2440 lb (1105 kg).

Dimensions: Length 167.9 in (4265 mm), width 66.5 in (1690 mm), height 54.9 in (1395 mm), wheelbase 100.3 in (2550 mm).

Performance *Autocar & Motor* test: Maximum speed 120 mph (193 km/h); 0 to 60 mph (97 km/h) 9.3 sec; 80 mph (130 km/h) 16.2 sec. Fuel consumption at constant 75 mph (120 km/h): 33.2 mpg; overall test, 25.7 mpg.

Features: All Concertos have an electric sunroof, but this top model also has a spoiler beneath the front bumper and twin exhaust pipes. **Summary:** This is certainly the performance model of the whole Honda-Rover range, offering brisk acceleration, and it feels a safe car at speed. All Concertos have power steering, but this is the only version to have an anti-roll bar at rear as well as front.

HONDA   (J)   Legend Coupé

Identity: All-new Legend was introduced at Geneva 1991, with more rounded body, and engine capacity increased to 3.2 litres and power now 205 PS. As before, the Legend is offered as saloon or in this attractive Coupé format. Both offer choice of manual or automatic.

Engine: Front-mounted longitudinal V6-cylinder with all-alloy construction and single ohc per bank, working four valves per cylinder. Distributorless ignition; varying intake system. Bore 90.0 mm, stroke 84.0 mm; capacity 3206 cc. Power 151 PS (205 kW) at 5500 rpm; torque 212 lb ft (293 Nm) at 4400 rpm. Compression 9.6-to-1. Catalyst: standard.

Transmission: Front-wheel drive; five-speed manual gearbox. Automatic, optional. Top gear speed at 1000 rpm: 34.6 mph (55.6 km/h).

Suspension: Front, independent, wishbones and coil springs with lateral arms; anti-roll bar. Rear, independent, wishbones and coil springs with lateral arms; anti-roll bar.

Steering: Rack and pinion. Power assistance: standard. **Brakes:** Vented discs front, solid discs rear. ABS: standard. **Tyres:** 205/65 ZR 15. **Fuel tank:** 15.0 Imp. gall (68 litres). **Unladen weight:** 3406 lb (1545 kg).

Dimensions: Length 192.3 in (4885 mm), width 71.3 in (1810 mm), height 53.9 in (1370 mm), wheelbase 114.6 in (2910 mm).

Performance Works: Maximum speed 140 mph (226 km/h) ; 0 to 62 mph (100 km/h) 8.1 sec. Fuel consumption: no data.

Features: Full equipment even includes an air bag on the driver's side, and there are heated front seats; doors have electric closing on Coupé.
Summary: Major change from the previous Legend is that the engine is now installed longitudinally (previously transverse). Promising new car introducing a number of special features.

HONDA (J)   NSX

Identity: At a Honda test day last year, everyone wanted to drive the NSX. I had given up waiting and was unlocking my car to leave when suddenly a chance presented itself, and I enjoyed a magnificent drive in this superbly competent, fast, very safe, high-performance GT. It is every bit as good as it looks – or better.

Engine: Mid-mounted transverse V6-cylinder with twin ohc each bank working four valves per cylinder, and varying valve timing. Programmed electronic ignition with varying volume induction system. Bore 90.0 mm, stroke 78.0 mm; capacity 2977 cc. Power 273 PS (201 kW) at 7300 rpm; torque 205 lb ft (284 Nm) at 5400 rpm. Compression 10.2-to-1. Catalyst: two standard.

Transmission: Rear-wheel drive; five-speed manual gearbox. Automatic, optional extra. Top gear speed at 1000 rpm: 24.1 mph (38.8 km/h).

Suspension: Front, independent, aluminium wishbones and coil springs; anti-roll bar. Rear, independent, aluminium wishbones and coil springs; anti-roll bar.

Steering: Rack and pinion. Power assistance: standard with automatic transmission. **Brakes:** Vented discs front and rear. ABS: standard. **Tyres:** 205/50 ZR 15 (front); 225/50 ZR 16 (rear). **Fuel tank:** 15.4 Imp. gall (70 litres). **Unladen weight:** 3020 lb (1370 kg).

Dimensions: Length 173. 4 in (4405 mm), width 71.3 in (1810 mm), height 46.1 in (1170 mm), wheelbase 99.6 in (2530 mm).

Performance *Autocar & Motor* test: Maximum speed 159 mph (256 km/h); 0 to 60 mph (97 km/h) 5.8 sec; 80 mph (130 km/h) 8.9 sec. Fuel consumption at constant 75 mph (120 km/h): 30.7 mpg; overall test, 19.6 mpg.

Features: Space is rather limited, but there's a small boot at each end and snug seats give good lateral location. Power steering on automatic models is electrically operated. **Summary:** Certainly an important addition to the ranks of the top supercars, offering fantastic grip on corners and very vigorous acceleration. A short but memorable drive.

Identity: One of the most significant new cars of 1987, introducing all-wheel steering. Ingenious rear steering box linked to front rack and pinion steers rear wheels either way, according to amount of turns of wheel. Even without this, it's also a very impressive four-seater coupé.

Engine: Front-mounted transverse four-cylinder with twin ohc working 16 valves; all-alloy construction and electronic PGM-FI fuel injection. Bore 81.0 mm, stroke 95.0 mm; capacity 1958 cc. Power 150 PS (110 kW) at 6000 rpm; torque 133 lb ft (180 Nm) at 5500 rpm. Compression 10.5-to-1. Catalyst: not available.

Transmission: Front-wheel drive; five-speed manual gearbox. Automatic, optional extra. Top gear speed at 1000 rpm: 20.7 mph (33.3 km/h).

Suspension: Front, independent, wishbones and coil springs, telescopic dampers, anti-roll bar. Rear, independent, wishbones and coil springs, telescopic dampers, anti-roll bar.

Steering: Rack and pinion with shaft to rear steering box. Power assistance: standard. **Brakes:** Vented discs front, solid discs rear. ABS: standard. **Tyres:** 195/60 VR 14. **Fuel tank:** 13.2 Imp. gall (60 litres). **Unladen weight:** 2524 lb (1145 kg).

Dimensions: Length 175.5 in (4460 mm), width 66.7 in (1695 mm), height 51.0 in (1295 mm), wheelbase 101.0 in (2565 mm).

Performance *Autocar & Motor* test: Maximum speed 128 mph (206 km/h); 0 to 60 mph (97 km/h) 8.5 sec; 80 mph (130 km/h) 14.4 sec. Fuel consumption at constant 75 mph (120 km/h): 33.6 mpg; overall test, 21.0 mpg.

Features: On small steering movements, rear wheels turn same way as front ones; beyond 140 deg turn of steering, they go in the opposite direction to improve manoeuvrability. **Summary:** Very pleasing car to drive, with much of the excellent handling owed to the clever AWS system. Rather low-geared in fifth, but lively performance to go with the excellent steering, handling and brakes.

HYUNDAI (K)   Pony X2 1.3 LS

Identity: When Korea's motor industry made its lightning debut, the first Pony was not a remarkable car, except for price. Then came a front-drive model which was much better, and Birmingham 1990 brought a rebodied, modern-looking successor. Choice of 1.3 or 1.5 engines, and three, four or five doors.

Engine: Front-mounted transverse four-cylinder with alloy head on cast-iron block. Single ohc, eight valves, twin-choke carb. Bore 71.0 mm, stroke 82.0 mm; capacity 1298 cc. Power 72 PS (53 kW) at 5500 rpm; torque 82 lb ft (114 Nm) at 3700 rpm. Compression 9.7-to-1. Catalyst: not available.

Transmission: Front-wheel drive; five-speed manual gearbox. Automatic, not available. Top gear speed at 1000 rpm: 20.8 mph (33.5 km/h).

Suspension: Front, independent, MacPherson struts, anti-roll bar. Rear, independent, trailing arms and coil springs; anti-roll bar.

Steering: Rack and pinion. Power assistance: not available. **Brakes:** Vented discs front, drums rear. ABS: not available. **Tyres:** 155 SR 13. **Fuel tank:** 9.9 Imp. gall (45 litres). **Unladen weight:** 2015 lb (914 kg).

Dimensions: Length 161.4 in (4100 mm), width 63.3 in (1607 mm), height 54.5 in (1385 mm), wheelbase 93.8 in (2382 mm).

Performance *Autocar & Motor* test: (1.5 GSi): Maximum speed 97 mph (155 km/h); 0 to 60 mph (97 km/h) 13.7 sec; 80 mph (130 km/h) 29.6 sec. Fuel consumption at constant 75 mph (125 km/h): 37.2 mpg; overall test, 28.0 mpg.

Features: S model also available, with three doors and four-speed gearbox, but LS has better equipment, including electric door mirrors, radio/cassette and rear wash/wipe. Data above is for 1.5 injection GSi.

Summary: This new Pony is a far better car than its predecessor, with a much more attractively styled body. The GSi brings good equipment and the 1.5 injection engine, as for the S Coupé. This LS model is the intermediate Pony, offering a good compromise on price.

HYUNDAI (K)   S Coupé GSi

Identity: After the surprise launch of the new S Coupé at Motorfair 1988, I tried to include details of it in the last edition, but no information was available. It finally came to the UK market at Birmingham 1990: an attractively styled, quite roomy family car.

Engine: Front-mounted transverse four-cylinder with alloy head on cast iron block. Single ohc and multi-point fuel injection. Bore 75.5 mm, stroke 82.0 mm; capacity 1468 cc. Power 84 PS (62 kW) at 5500 rpm; torque 89 lb ft (123 Nm) at 4000 rpm. Compression 9.4-to-1. Catalyst: standard.

Transmission: Front-wheel drive; five-speed manual gearbox. Automatic, optional extra. Top gear speed at 1000 rpm: 19.4 mph (31.2 km/h).

Suspension: Front, independent, MacPherson struts, anti-roll bar. Rear, independent, trailing arms and coil springs; anti-roll bar.

Steering: Rack and pinion. Power assistance: standard. **Brakes:** Vented discs front, drums rear. ABS: not available. **Tyres:** 185/60 HR 14. **Fuel tank:** 9.9 Imp. gall (45 litres). **Unladen weight:** 2094 lb (950 kg).

Dimensions: Length 165.8 in (4213 mm), width 64.0 in (1626 mm), height 52.3 in (1328 mm), wheelbase 93.8 in (2382 mm).

Performance *Autocar & Motor* test: Maximum speed 104 mph (167 km/h); 0 to 60 mph (97 km/h) 12.5 sec; 80 mph (130 km/h) 24.3 sec. Fuel consumption at constant 75 mph (120 km/h): 38.7 mpg; overall test, 30.8 mpg.

Features: Good equipment includes all the usual luxury items, such as electric windows and mirrors, but no sunroof. Cheaper LSi is also available. **Summary:** Sporty to look at, the S Coupé is also fun to handle. The test drive was spoilt only by a rather over-lively ride on undulations, but I was advised that better-damped suspension has been fitted to later models.

HYUNDAI (K)   Sonata 2.4i GLS

Identity: Entirely new model, launched Birmingham 1988, to replace the Stellar. Sonata is a front-drive car, and is offered with three engine sizes, two trim levels and manual or automatic transmission. Engines are 1.8, 2.0 and 2.4. Details follow for the 'big four'.

Engine: Front-mounted transverse four-cylinder with belt-driven single ohc and inclined valves; hydraulic tappets and alloy head. Electronic multi-point fuel injection. Bore 86.5 mm, stroke 100.0 mm; capacity 2351 cc. Power 110 PS (81 kW) at 4500 rpm; torque 140 lb ft (193 Nm) at 3500 rpm. Compression 8.6-to-1. Catalyst: not available.

Transmission: Front-wheel drive; five-speed manual gearbox. Automatic, four-speed optional, with electronic control. Top gear speed at 1000 rpm: 25.5 mph (41 km/h).

Suspension: Front, independent, MacPherson struts, anti-roll bar. Rear, torsion beam axle with trailing arms and Panhard rod; coil springs; anti-roll bar.

Steering: Rack and pinion. Power assistance: standard. **Brakes:** Solid discs front, drums rear. ABS: not available. **Tyres:** 185/70 SR 14. **Fuel tank:** 13.2 Imp. gall (60 litres). **Unladen weight:** 2684 lb (1217 kg).

Dimensions: Length 184.2 in (4680 mm), width 68.9 in (1750 mm), height 55.4 in (1408 mm), wheelbase 104.3 in (2650 mm.

Performance *Autocar & Motor* test: Maximum speed 112 mph (180 km/h); 0 to 60 mph (97 km/h) 12.3 sec; 80 mph (130 km/h) 22.4 sec. Fuel consumption at constant 75 mph (120 km/h): 29.4 mpg; overall test, 22.7 mpg.

Features: High specification including electric windows and mirrors; options to include cruise control, air conditioning and power sunroof.
Summary: Hyundai moved up the market some way with this new model, aiming at the executive buyer, hoping to tempt him or her with a well-furnished and equipped car at a highly competitive price. On UK market from May 1989.

ISUZU (J) Trooper Citation LWB Turbo Diesel

Identity: Following the collapse of the Isuzu importer in 1986, International Motors took over the concession in Britain, and the Trooper has become established as an important contender for the 4 × 4 market. Launched Paris 1986, it is offered with choice of petrol or diesel engine. Turbo diesel details follow. Citation is special top equipment model.

Engine: Front-mounted longitudinal four-cylinder with alloy head, belt driven ohc, and Garrett turbocharger. Bore 88.0 mm, stroke 92.0 mm; capacity 2238 cc. Power 74 PS (55 kW) at 4000 rpm; torque 114 lb ft (183 Nm) at 2500 rpm. Compression 21.0-to-1. Fuel: Derv.

Transmission: Four-wheel drive; five-speed manual gearbox. Automatic, not available. Top gear speed at 1000 rpm: 20.6 mph (33.2 km/h).

Suspension: Front, independent, wishbones and torsion bars. Rear, live axle on semi-elliptic leaf springs.

Steering: Recirculating ball. Power assistance: standard. **Brakes:** Vented discs front, drums rear. ABS: not available. **Tyres:** 215 SR 15. **Fuel tank:** 18.3 Imp. gall (83 litres). **Unladen weight:** 3640 lb (1655 kg).

Dimensions: Length 172.4 in (4380 mm), width 65.0 in (1650 mm), height 70.9 in (1800 mm), wheelbase 90.6 in (2300 mm).

Performance *Autocar & Motor* test: Maximum speed 78 mph (126 km/h); 0 to 60 mph (97 km/h) 26.1 sec; 80 mph (130 km/h) 47.1 sec. Fuel consumption at constant 75 mph (120 km/h): too slow to measure; overall test, 22.3 mpg.

Features: Good equipment for this kind of vehicle, with central locking and power steering on base model, and optional package providing limited slip diff, headlamp washers and splash guards. **Summary:** Good value for money, and a competent off-road vehicle. Rather noisy for a long journey, but the Citation model is acceptably comfortable.

JAGUAR (GB)   XJ6 3.2

Identity: Since introduction, the 2.9-litre had been the disappointing model of the new Jaguar XJ6 and Sovereign ranges, and for Birmingham 1990 it was replaced by a new and much better 24-valve engine with 3.2-litre capacity. Other changes included a sports suspension option.

Engine: Front-mounted longitudinal six-cylinder with head and block of alloy, and twin ohc working four valves per cylinder. Lucas fuel injection and ignition. Bore 91.0 mm, stroke 83.0 mm; capacity 3239 cc. Power 203 PS (149 kW) at 5250 rpm; torque 220 lb ft (304 Nm) at 4000 rpm. Compression 9.75-to-1. Catalyst: standard.

Transmission: Rear-wheel drive; five-speed manual gearbox. Automatic, optional extra. Top gear speed at 1000 rpm: 26.6 mph (42.8 km/h).

Suspension: Front, independent, unequal length wishbones giving anti-dive effect, coil springs; anti-roll bar. Rear, independent, wishbones with drive shafts as upper links, with anti-squat, anti-lift geometry; concentric coil springs and dampers.

Steering: Rack and pinion. Power assistance: standard. **Brakes:** Vented discs front, solid discs rear. ABS: standard. **Tyres:** 225/65 VR 15. **Fuel tank:** 19.0 Imp. gall (86.4 litres). **Unladen weight:** 3969 lb (1800 kg).

Dimensions: Length 196.4 in (4988 mm), width 71.3 in (1811 mm), height 54.3 in (1380 mm), wheelbase 113.0 in (2870 mm).

Performance *Autocar & Motor* test: Maximum speed 135 mph (217 km/h); 0 to 60 mph (97 km/h) 8.3 sec; 80 mph (130 km/h) 13.5 sec. Fuel consumption at constant 75 mph (120 km/h): 29.1 mpg; overall test, 19.9 mpg.

Features: Among the many changes introduced for the 1991 model were a better audio system with CD option, and new wheels and tyres. **Summary:** With its extra power and torque, this bigger engine is a much more acceptable alternative to the 4-litre, which continues. I tried a car with the sports handling pack but, although the extra tautness was appreciated, felt that it spoilt the superb ride of the standard model.

JAGUAR (GB)   Sovereign 4.0

Identity: One of the important new models of 1989 was the Jaguar in revised form with a host of minor improvements, headed by increase of capacity of the six-cylinder 24-valve engine to 4.0-litre, giving better response and quieter cruising. The 4-litre version is identified by the plinth badges at rear; 2.9 has free-standing letters.

Engine: Front-mounted longitudinal six-cylinder with twin overhead camshafts and 24 valves. Lucas electronic fuel injection. Bore 91.0 mm, stroke 102.0 mm; capacity 3980 cc. Power 235 PS (175 kW) at 4750 rpm; torque 285 lb ft (387 Nm) at 3750 rpm. Compression 9.5-to-1. Catalyst: standard.

Transmission: Rear-wheel drive; four-speed automatic, standard. Five-speed manual is no-cost option. Top gear speed at 1000 rpm: 29.2 mph (47.0 km/h).

Suspension: Front, independent, wishbones with anti-dive provision; coil springs and anti-roll bar. Rear, independent, wishbones with drive shafts acting as upper links; anti-squat and anti-lift provisions; coil springs concentric with dampers.

Steering: Rack and pinion. Power assistance: standard. **Brakes:** Vented discs front, solid discs rear. ABS: standard. **Tyres:** 220/65 VR 390 TD. **Fuel tank:** 19.5 Imp. gall (89 litres). **Weight:** 3969 lb (1800 kg).

Dimensions: Length 196.4 in (4988 mm), width 71.3 in (1811 mm), height 53.5 in (1358 mm), wheelbase 113.0 in (2870 mm).

Performance *Autocar & Motor* test: Maximum speed 140 mph (225 km/h); 0 to 60 mph (97 km/h) 8.3 sec; 80 mph (130 km/h) 13.5 sec. Fuel consumption at constant 75 mph (120 km/h): 30.4 mpg; overall, 18.5 mpg.

Features: Not quite as extravagantly equipped as the Daimler, but such items as electric sunroof and heated front seats can be specified.
Summary: One of the most improved cars of 1989 and considering how good the Sovereign was before, that's really saying something! Superb driver's car, yet also providing top quality and wonderful comfort.

JAGUAR (GB) XJ-S V12 Convertible

Identity: Previously, the open XJ-S was a cabriolet, with fixed side window frames and roll bar. Full convertible model with power hood was launched Geneva 1988, as one of the world's fastest open cars, looking magnificent open or closed. Reinforced chassis restores body strength.

Engine: Front-mounted longitudinal V12-cylinder with all-alloy construction and single ohc each bank. Lucas digital fuel injection. Bore 90.0 mm, stroke 70.0 mm; capacity 5345 cc. Power 291 PS (217 kW) at 5500 rpm; torque 317 lb ft (430 Nm) at 3000 rpm. Compression 12.5-to-1. Catalyst: standard.

Transmission: Rear-wheel drive; three-speed automatic, standard (no manual gearbox option). Top gear at 1000 rpm: 26.2 mph (42.2 km/h).

Suspension: Front, independent, wishbones with anti-dive geometry; coil springs, anti-roll bar. Rear, independent, lower transverse wishbones, driveshafts serve as upper links with radius arms; coil springs.

Steering: Rack and pinion. Power assistance: standard. **Brakes:** Vented discs front, solid discs rear. ABS: standard. **Tyres:** 235/60 VR 15. **Fuel tank:** 18 Imp. gall (82 litres). **Unladen weight:** 4055 lb (1835 kg).

Dimensions: Length 187.6 in (4765 mm), width 70.6 in (1793 mm), height 49.7 in (1262 mm), wheelbase 102 in (2590 mm).

Performance *Autocar & Motor* test: Maximum speed 144 mph (232 km/h); 0 to 60 mph (97 km/h) 8.0 sec; 80 mph (130 km/h) 12.9 sec. Fuel consumption at constant 75 mph (120 km/h): 22.5 mpg; overall test, 13.8 mpg.

Features: Hood operation takes only about 12 seconds. Electric action requires selector in Park and handbrake applied. Luxury equipment. **Summary:** Not quite as structurally taut as the previous model, but a superb car in every other way, providing wonderful open-top motoring. Special attention paid to such matters as security for the open car.

JAGUAR (GB)   XJ220

Identity: After its spectacular launch as a prototype at Birmingham 1988, the XJ220 was announced as a production car in late 1989, with the first ones to go to customers at the end of 1991. In production form it will be slightly less exciting, with V6 engine and rear-wheel drive instead of 4 × 4 and V12.

Engine: Mid-mounted.longitudinal V6-cylinder with all-alloy construction, twin ohc working four valves per cylinder, and twin water-cooled turbochargers. Electronic fuel injection. Bore 94.0 mm, stroke 84.0 mm; capacity 3498 cc. Power 500 PS (373 kW) at 6500 rpm; torque 472 lb ft (640 Nm) at 5000 rpm. Catalyst: standard.

Transmission: Rear-wheel drive; five-speed manual gearbox. Automatic, not available.

Suspension: Front, independent, wishbones and coil springs with concentric dampers; anti-roll bar. Rear, independent, wishbones; coil spring and concentric damper units mounted transversely; toe control links and anti-roll bar.

Steering: Rack and pinion. Power assistance: not available. **Brakes:** Vented discs front and rear. ABS: standard. **Tyres:** 245/40 ZR 17 (front), 345/35 ZR 18 (rear). **Fuel tank:** 20.0 Imp. gall (91 litres). **Unladen weight** (est.): 3448 lb (1560 kg).

Dimensions: Length 191.0 in (4860 mm), width 79.0 in (2000 mm), height 45.0 in (1150 mm), wheelbase 104.0 in (2640 mm).

Performance Works: Maximum speed 200 + mph (322 km/h); 0 to 60 mph (97 km/h) 4.0 sec. Fuel consumption, no data.

Features: All luxury equipment is included, with tinted flush glass all round, air conditioning, and leather upholstery. **Summary:** With the first car yet to be built, following the V12 prototype, performance data, weight, and so on are very much estimates; but the signs are that the XJ220 will be quite a nippy runabout! Initial run will be limited to 220 cars, priced at £290,000 each plus tax.

LADA (SU)   Samara 1500SLX

Identity: At Birmingham 1988 the Lada Samara three-door was supplemented by five-door versions and by a larger engine with 1500 c.c. capacity. The Lada gets better, but as it moves towards western standards so the prices move up, and it's no longer quite as good value as it used to be.

Engine: Front-mounted transverse four-cylinder with alloy head and belt-driven ohc. Downdraught twin-choke carb. Bore 82.0 mm, stroke 71.0 mm; capacity 1499 cc. Power 76 PS (56 kW) at 5600 rpm; torque 78 lb ft (108 Nm) at 3600 rpm. Compression 9.9-to-1. Catalyst: not available.

Transmission: Front-wheel drive; five-speed manual gearbox. Automatic, not available. Top gear speed at 1000 rpm: 21.0 mph (33.7 km/h).

Suspension: Front, independent, MacPherson struts. Rear, independent, trailing arms and coil springs, telescopic dampers.

Steering: Rack and pinion. Power assistance: not available. **Brakes:** Solid discs front, drums rear. ABS: not available. **Tyres:** 165/70 SR 13. **Fuel tank:** 9.5 Imp. gall (43 litres). **Unladen weight:** 1984 lb (900 kg).

Dimensions: Length 157.7 in (4006 mm), width 63.7 in (1620 mm), height 52.5 in (1335 mm), wheelbase 96.8 in (2460 mm).

Performance Works: Maximum speed 98 mph (158 km/h); 0 to 60 mph (97 km/h) 12.0 sec. Fuel consumption at constant 75 mph (120 km/h): 36.7 mpg.

Features: SL version gets better interior trim in tweed-style polyester, by Autotrim of Huddersfield. Stereo radio cassette standard. SLX, body styling kit. **Summary:** Compared with the 1300, which continues, the 1500 gives noticeably better performance, but it's still a rather basic car to drive. Side stripe and vented wheel trims identify the 1500.

LADA   (SU, B, GB)   San Remo Cabrio

Identity: Centrepiece of the Lada stand at Birmingham 1990 was the new Cabrio version of the Lada Samara, called San Remo. It's a cooperative effort, with conversion by a Belgian coachbuilder in conjunction with the Russian factory, and refinishing and trimming in Britain.

Engine: Front-mounted transverse four-cylinder with alloy head and belt-driven ohc. Downdraught twin-choke carb. Bore 82.0 mm, stroke 71.0 mm; capacity 1499 cc. Power 76 PS (56 kW) at 5600 rpm; torque 78 lb ft (108 Nm) at 3600 rpm. Compression 9.9-to-1. Catalyst: not available.

Transmission: Front-wheel drive; five-speed manual gearbox. Automatic, not available. Top gear speed at 1000 rpm: 21.0 mph (33.7 km/h).

Suspension: Front, independent, MacPherson struts. Rear, independent, trailing arms and coil springs.

Steering: Rack and pinion. Power assistance: not available. **Brakes:** Solid discs front, drums rear. ABS: not available. **Tyres:** 185/60 SR 13. **Fuel tank:** 9.5 Imp. gall (43 litres). **Unladen weight:** 2000 lb (907 kg).

Dimensions: Length 157.7 in (4006 mm), width 63.7 in (1620 mm), height 52.5 in (1335 mm), wheelbase 96.8 in (2460 mm).

Performance Works: Maximum speed 98 mph (158 km/h); 0 to 60 mph (97 km/h) 13.0 sec. Fuel consumption at constant 75 mph (120 km/h): 36.7 mpg.

Features: No fixed roll bar is fitted, and the hood folds neatly away beneath a tonneau cover. Four round headlamps and a single bar radiator grille give distinctive frontal appearance. **Summary:** The San Remo is based on the three-door body shell, and has a boot lid in glass fibre to replace the standard model's tailgate. A promising design for a low-cost convertible, it was exhibited at Birmingham to assess sales potential.

LANCIA (I)   Dedra 2000 Turbo

Identity: One of the last model announcements to be made in 1990 was the addition of a turbocharged version to the Dedra range, available as here with front-wheel drive, or as the Dedra integrale, having four-wheel drive. Engine features continuous modulation of turbo boost throughout the engine speed range.

Engine: Front-mounted transverse four-cylinder with alloy head and twin ohc; eight valves. Weber IAW fuel injection and Garrett 60/48 turbocharger with air–air heat exchanger. Bore 84.0 mm, stroke 90.0 mm; capacity 1995 cc. Power 165 PS (121 kW) at 5500 rpm; torque 199 lb ft (275 Nm) at 3000 rpm. Compression 7.5-to-1. Catalyst: not available.

Transmission: Front-wheel drive; five-speed manual gearbox. Automatic, not available. Top gear speed at 1000 rpm: 22.8 mph (36.7 km/h).

Suspension: Front, independent, MacPherson struts; anti-roll bar. Rear, independent, semi-trailing arms and coil springs with gas-filled dampers separate from coil springs; anti-roll bar.

Steering: Rack and pinion. Power assistance: standard. **Brakes:** Vented discs front, solid discs rear. ABS: optional. **Tyres:** 195/50 R 15V. **Fuel tank:** 13.9 Imp. gall (63 litres). **Unladen weight:** 2712 lb (1230 kg).

Dimensions: Length 171.0 in (4343 mm), width 66.9 in (1700 mm), height 56.3 in (1430 mm), wheelbase 100.0 in (2540 mm).

Performance Works: Maximum speed 134 mph (215 km/h); 0 to 62 mph (100 km/h) 8.3 sec. Fuel consumption at constant 75 mph (120 km/h): 30.7 mpg.

Features: The four-wheel drive integrale is distinguished by a boot-mounted spoiler. Higher level of equipment includes fog lamps and height-adjustable leather-trimmed steering wheel. **Summary:** In standard form, Dedra is a sporty car with crisp handling. This turbocharged version gives useful extra performance, with special control of turbo boost to spread the extra power and avoid 'peakiness'.

LANCIA (I)   Delta HF Integrale 16V

Identity: After its launch in June 1986, the HF 4WD version of the Lancia Delta went on to win three world championship rally titles, and was succeeded January 1988 by the HF Integrale. Changes include revised appearance, identified by the flared wheel arches to allow wider wheels and tyres, more power, plus better brakes and suspension.

Engine: Front-mounted transverse four-cylinder with alloy head on cast iron block and twin counter-rotating balance shafts. Twin ohc, and fuel injection with Garrett T3 turbocharger. Bore 87.0 mm, stroke 90.0 mm; capacity 1995 cc. Power 185 PS (136 kW) at 5300 rpm; torque 224 lb ft (310 Nm) at 2500 rpm. Compression 8.0-to-1. Catalyst: not available.

Transmission: Four-wheel drive; five-speed manual gearbox. Automatic, not available. Top gear speed at 1000 rpm: 23.9 mph (38.5 km/h).

Suspension: Front, independent, MacPherson struts. Rear, MacPherson struts with transverse links, longitudinal reaction rods, and anti-roll bar.

Steering: Rack and pinion. Power assistance: standard. **Brakes:** Vented discs front, solid discs rear. ABS: optional. **Tyres:** 195/55 VR 15. **Fuel tank:** 12.5 Imp. gall (57 litres). **Unladen weight:** 2645 lb (1200 kg).

Dimensions: Length 153.5 in (3900 mm), width 66.9 in (1700 mm), height 54.3 in (1380 mm), wheelbase 54.3 in (1380 mm).

Performance *Autocar & Motor* test: Maximum speed 128 mph (206 km/h); 0 to 60 mph (97 km/h) 6.4 sec; 80 mph (130 km/h) 11.2 sec. Fuel consumption at constant 75 mph (120 km/h): 27.7 mpg; overall test, 17.6 mpg!

Features: Turbocharger has water-cooled bearing and air–air intercooler. Over-boost control allows temporary increase of intake pressure to 14.5 psi (1 bar). **Summary:** Flared wheel arches and larger wheels give a more striking appearance to the HF Integrale, and the car features logical improvements to build on the success of the HF 4WD. Torque split of the standard four-wheel drive system is 56 per cent to front wheels, 44 rear.

LANCIA   (I)   Thema 2.0i.e. 16V

Identity: New zest came to the Thema range in mid-1989 with introduction of new lead-free burning 16-valve engines, available as turbo and as this injection version. As well as giving more power, the engines were developed for high torque at low revs; and ZF automatic became available.

Engine: Front-mounted transverse four-cylinder with alloy head and belt-driven twin ohc working 16 valves. Bosch LE 3.1 Jetronic injection. Bore 84.0 mm, stroke 90.0 mm; capacity 1995 cc. Power 150 PS (108 kW) at 6000 rpm; torque 136 lb ft (188 Nm) at 4000 rpm. Compression 9.9-to-1. Catalyst: not available.

Transmission: Front-wheel drive; five-speed manual gearbox. Automatic, optional extra. Top gear speed at 1000 rpm: 21.4 mph (34.4 km/h).

Suspension: Front, independent, MacPherson struts, anti-roll bar. Rear, independent, struts with twin transverse links; anti-roll bar.

Steering: Rack and pinion. Power assistance: standard. **Brakes:** Vented discs front, solid discs rear. ABS: not available. **Tyres:** 195/60 R 14H. **Fuel tank:** 15.4 Imp. gall (70 litres). **Unladen weight:** 2755 lb (1250 kg).

Dimensions: Length 180.7 in (4590 mm), width 69.0 in (1752 mm), height 56.4 in (1433 mm), wheelbase 104.7 in (2660 mm).

Performance *Autocar & Motor* test: Maximum speed 124 mph (199 km/h); 0 to 60 mph (97 km/h) 8.8 sec; 80 mph (130 km/h) 15.2 sec. Fuel consumption at constant 75 mph (120 km/h): 34.4 mpg; overall test, 24.4 mpg.

Features: Reduced noise levels, better brakes, and more use of zinc coated steel in the body were among features of the new Thema. Good equipment including central locking, but sunroof only on SE model. **Summary:** Substantially improved car with better performance and a lot more refinement. Although not on the standard options list, anti-lock brakes can be obtained to special order, also air conditioning and leather.

Identity: Announced at the end of 1989 was a new automatic Lancia Y10, selectronic (always with a small 's'), featuring the Ford-Fiat CVT transmission, which uses steel segment belts under compression, and pulleys of varying diameter, but with electronic control.

Engine: Front-mounted transverse four-cylinder with alloy head and belt-driven single ohc. Bosch Monojetronic fuel injection. Bore 70.0 mm, stroke 72.0 mm; capacity 1108 cc. Power 57 PS (41 kW) at 5500 rpm; torque 64 lb ft (88 Nm) at 3000 rpm. Compression 9.6-to-1. Catalyst: not available.

Transmission: Front-wheel drive. Automatic, standard, continuously variable, with segment steel belts, electromagnetic powder clutch; electronic control. Top gear speed at 1000 rpm: 24.5 mph (39.5 km/h), highest value on light load.

Suspension: Front, independent, MacPherson struts, anti-roll bar. Rear, semi-independent, centre-pivoted dead beam axle on semi-trailing arms with coil springs.

Steering: Rack and pinion. Power assistance: not available. **Brakes:** Solid discs front, drums rear. ABS: not available. **Tyres:** 135 SR 13. **Fuel tank:** 10.1 Imp. gall (46 litres). **Unladen weight:** 1786 lb (810 kg).

Dimensions: Length 133.5 in (3392 mm), width 59.3 in (1507 mm), height 49.0 in (1245 mm), wheelbase 85.0 in (2159 mm).

Performance Works: Maximum speed 93 mph (150 km/h); 0 to 62mph (100 km/h) 17.5 sec. Fuel consumption at constant 75 mph (120 km/h): 46.3 mpg.

Features: Simple selector control with P-R-N-D-L positions (L giving more effective engine braking for steep hill descents); and the electric clutch means that the engine is disengaged when idling. **Summary:** Lancia promise that the Y10 selectronic brings a new blend of liveliness with economy and smoothness. It came on to the UK market from April 1990.

LAND ROVER (GB)   Defender 110 Tdi

Identity: Following introduction of the new and much-praised direct injection diesel engine for the Discovery in 1989, the same engine was adopted for the Land Rover One Ten at Birmingham 1990. At the same time, the Defender name was introduced.

Engine: Front-mounted longitudinal four-cylinder with alloy head and single ohc; eight valves. Direct fuel injection and Garrett T25 turbocharger. Bore 90.5 mm, stroke 97.0 mm; capacity 2495 cc. Power 108 PS (80 kW) at 3800 rpm; torque 188 lb ft (260 Nm) at 1800 rpm. Compression 19.5-to-1. Catalyst: not available.

Transmission: Four-wheel drive; five-speed manual gearbox. Automatic, not available. Permanent four-wheel drive, with low-ratio transfer gearbox. Top gear speed at 1000 rpm: 21.7 mph (34.9 km/h).

Suspension: Front, live axle on radius arms with Panhard rod and long travel coil springs. Rear, live axle on radius arms with upper A-frame and long travel coil springs.

Steering: Worm and roller. Power assistance: optional. **Brakes:** Solid discs front, drums rear. ABS: not available. **Tyres:** 7.50-16. **Fuel tank:** 17.5 Imp. gall (79.5 litres). **Unladen weight:** 4257 lb (1931 kg).

Dimensions: Length 175.0 in (4445 mm), width 70.5 in (1790 mm), height 80.1 in (2035 mm), wheelbase 110.0 in (2795 mm).

Performance Works: Maximum speed 84 mph (135 km/h); 0 to 60 mph (97 km/h) 17.4 sec. Fuel consumption at constant 75 mph (120 km/h): 19.0 mpg.

Features: Elaborate paintwork of the Defender name three times across the door doesn't seem appropriate for an off-road vehicle. Interior still looks crude and unnecessarily basic in relation to the Discovery.
Summary: The direct injection diesel seemed notably harsher and more noisy in the new Defender than remembered from the Discovery, but it offers all-round improvements on the previous indirect injection engine.

LAND ROVER (GB)   Discovery V8i

Identity: A removals journey to south-east France was in prospect, and a Discovery with the five-door body, newly introduced at Birmingham 1990, filled the role admirably. Keeping the speed down to 80 mph helps to contain the fuel consumption, helped by the new fuel injection engine.

Engine: Front-mounted longitudinal V8-cylinder with alloy block and heads, and electronic fuel injection. Bore 89.0 mm, stroke 71.0 mm; capacity 3528 cc. Power 166 PS (122 kW) at 4750 rpm; torque 212 lb ft (293 Nm) at 2600 rpm. Compression 9.4-to-1. Catalyst: optional.

Transmission: Four-wheel drive; five-speed manual gearbox. Automatic, not available. Permanent four-wheel drive, with low-ratio transfer gearbox. Top gear speed at 1000 rpm: 25.1 mph (40.4 km/h).

Suspension: Front, live axle on radius arms with Panhard rod and long travel coil springs. Rear, live axle on radius arms with upper A-frame and long travel coil springs.

Steering: Recirculating ball. Power assistance: standard. **Brakes:** Vented discs front, solid discs rear. ABS: not available. **Tyres:** 205 R 16. **Fuel tank:** 19.5 Imp. gall (88 litres). **Unladen weight:** 4150 lb (1882 kg).

Dimensions: Length 178.0 in (4521 mm), width 70.6 in (1793 mm), height 75.6 in (1919 mm), wheelbase 110.0 in (2540 mm).

Performance *Autocar & Motor* test: Maximum speed 105 mph (169 km/h); 0 to 60 mph (97 km/h) 11.7 sec; 80 mph (130 km/h) 21.8 sec. Fuel consumption at constant 75 mph (120 km/h): 19.0 mpg; overall test, 16.5 mpg.

Features: Three-door body remains available. Attractive interior for this kind of vehicle: practical layout, good controls. Two sunroofs. **Summary:** Steering is the disappointing aspect of the Discovery; I found it very vague when trying to steer a tidy course between a lorry and the crash barrier. In other respects, however, it's comfortable as well as rugged, and performs well enough if the gears are used freely.

LAND ROVER (GB)   Range Rover Vogue SE

Identity: Land Rover keep on updating and improving the Range Rover; in a package of improvements announced December 1990, equipment was made even more comprehensive, especially on the top SE version. An important change was that anti-roll bars become standard.

Engine: Front-mounted longitudinal V8-cylinder with alloy block and heads. Pushrod valve gear with hydraulic tappets. Lucas L-Jetronic p fuel injection. Bore 94.0 mm, stroke 71.1 mm; capacity 3947 cc. Power 188 PS (138 kW) at 4750 rpm; torque 235 lb ft (319 Nm) at 2600 rpm. Compression 9.4-to-1. Catalyst: optional.

Transmission: Four-wheel drive; five-speed manual gearbox. Automatic, optional, no cost. Top gear speed at 1000 rpm: 26.8 mph (43.1 km/h).

Suspension: Front, live axle on radius arms with Panhard rod and coil springs; anti-roll bar. Rear, live axle on radius arms with upper A-bracket; coil springs and self-levelling Boge strut, anti-roll bar.

Steering: Worm and roller. Power assistance: standard. **Brakes:** Vented discs front, solid discs rear. ABS: standard. **Tyres:** 205 R 16 XM + S. **Fuel tank:** 18.0 Imp. gall (82 litres). **Unladen weight:** 4455 lb (2020 kg).

Dimensions: Length 175.0 in (4447 mm), width 72.0 in (1813 mm), height 71.0 in (1792 mm), wheelbase 100.0 in (2540 mm).

Performance _Autocar and Motor_ test (automatic): Maximum speed 108 mph (174 km/h); 0 to 60 mph (97 km/h) 11.3 sec; 80 mph (130 km/h) 21.3 sec. Fuel consumption at constant 75 mph (120 km/h): 21.0 mpg; overall test, 14.6 mpg.

Features: Extra equipment now included on the SE provides cruise control, a glass sunroof instead of a steel one, and automatically dipping rear mirror. **Summary:** All models gain the larger fuel tank of polyurethane and have heated front-door locks. The Range Rover goes on getting better—but I wish they would do something about the vague steering next!

LINCOLN (USA)   Continental

Identity: New body shape with more elegant styling instead of the former 'ruler design' was launched in 1988; and 1989 brought 3.8-litre V6 engine with multiple port fuel injection. Better automatic transmission with higher change points was among many improvements at the same time, and new electronic control was introduced 1991.

Engine: Front-mounted transverse V6-cylinder with pushrod ohv and roller tappets. Multi-port fuel injection and turbocharger with inter-cooler. Bore 96.7 mm, stroke 86.1 mm; capacity 3801 cc. Power 155 PS (114 kW) at 4000 rpm; torque 220 lb ft (304 Nm) at 2600 rpm. Compression 8.2-to-1. Catalyst: standard (dual).

Transmission: Front-wheel drive; four-speed automatic, standard. Top gear speed at 1000 rpm: 32.6 mph (52.4 km/h).

Suspension: Front, independent, MacPherson struts with nitrogen springs and computer controlled damping; anti-roll bar. Rear, independent, MacPherson struts with nitrogen springs and computer controlled damping, ride height and roll restriction.

Steering: Rack and pinion. Power assistance: standard. **Brakes:** Solid discs front and rear. ABS: standard. **Tyres:** P205/70 R 15. **Fuel tank:** 18.6 Imp. gall (85 litres). **Unladen weight:** 3663 lb (1661 kg).

Dimensions: Length 205.1 in (5210 mm), width 72.3 in (1847 mm), height 55.6 in (1412 mm), wheelbase 109.0 in (2769 mm).

Performance (est): Maximum speed 115 mph (185 km/h). Fuel consumption overall (est), 17.0 mpg.

Features: New instrument panel was introduced for 1989, with digital instrumentation. Electric seat adjustment with memory is optional.
Summary: Very spacious and comfortable executive car, and the air and nitrogen suspension system gives a luxuriously level ride.

LOTUS (D, GB)   Carlton

Identity: First revealed at Geneva 1989 as the Lotus Omega, this special version of the Carlton came to Britain at Birmingham 1990. Vauxhall, seeming almost embarrassed by its high speed potential, provided a half-hearted launch, and talked rather unenthusiastically about a product which not long ago might have seemed a great achievement.

Engine: Front-mounted longitudinal six-cylinder with alloy head and twin ohc; four valves per cylinder. Distributorless ignition; three coils. Two Garrett T25 turbochargers. Bore 95.0 mm, stroke 85.0 mm; capacity 3615 cc. Power 381 PS (281 kW) at 5200 rpm; torque 419 lb ft (579 Nm) at 4200 rpm. Compression 8.2-to-1. Catalyst: standard.

Transmission: Rear-wheel drive; six-speed manual gearbox. Automatic, not available. Top gear speed at 1000 rpm: 44.1 mph (71.0 km/h).

Suspension: Front, independent, MacPherson struts with gas-filled dampers; anti-roll bar. Rear, independent, multi-link layout with coil springs and gas-filled dampers; anti-roll bar.

Steering: Recirculating ball. Power assistance: standard. **Brakes:** Vented discs front, solid discs rear. ABS: standard. **Tyres:** 235/45 ZR 17 (front); 265/40 ZR 17 (rear). **Fuel tank:** 16.5 Imp. gall (75 litres). **Unladen weight:** 3640 lb (1650 kg).

Dimensions: Length 187.7 in (4768 mm), width 76.1 in (1933 mm), height 56.5 in (1435 mm), wheelbase 107.5 in (2730 mm).

Performance *Autocar & Motor* test: Maximum speed 164 mph (264 km/h); 0 to 60 mph (97 km/h) 5.1 sec; 80 mph (130 km/h) 7.8 sec. Fuel consumption at constant 75 mph (120 km/h): 27.5 mpg; overall, 14.3 mpg.

Features: Luxury interior trim and equipment, with upholstery all in Connolly leather, but some of the features one might expect for the money (such as electric seat adjustments) are not provided. **Summary:** Given more distance, this special Carlton might score a true 170 mph, and the fact that it achieved 164 mph on a 1.8-mile runway shows its magnificent performance, not to mention the superb brakes.

LOTUS (GB)   Elan SE

Identity: GM ownership of Lotus transformed the company's fortunes and made possible the long-postponed development of this exciting little two-seater sports car, launched Motorfair 1989; on UK market early 1990. Body is glass fibre, on a steel backbone chassis.

Engine: Front-mounted transverse four-cylinder with alloy head and twin ohc working four valves per cylinder. Electronic fuel injection and water-cooled turbocharger. Bore 80.0 mm, stroke 79.0 mm; capacity 1588 cc. Power 165 PS (123 kW) at 6600 rpm; torque 145 lb ft (200 Nm) at 4200 rpm. Compression 8.2-to-1. Catalyst: not available.

Transmission: Front-wheel drive; five-speed manual gearbox. Automatic, not available. Top gear speed at 1000 rpm: 20.9 mph (33.6 km/h).

Suspension: Front, independent, wishbones and coil springs; anti-roll bar. Rear, independent, upper links and wide-based lower wishbones; coil springs and anti-roll bar.

Steering: Rack and pinion. Power assistance: not available. **Brakes:** Vented discs front, solid discs rear. ABS: not available. **Tyres:** 205/50 ZR 15. **Fuel tank:** 10.2 Imp. gall (46.4 litres). **Unladen weight:** 2249 lb (1020 kg).

Dimensions: Length 149.7 in (3803 mm), width 68.3 in (1734 mm), height 48.4 in (1230 mm), wheelbase 88.6 in (2250 mm).

Performance *Autocar & Motor* test: Maximum speed 136 mph (219 km/h); 0 to 60 mph (97 km/h) 6.5 sec; 80 mph (130 km/h) 10.9 sec. Fuel consumption at constant 75 mph (120 km/h): 31.8 mpg; overall test, 20.1 mpg.

Features: Snug-looking interior with well-bolstered side seats and sporty flavour to the design and layout. Easy action folding hood.
Summary: Promising sports car, but I still look forward to an opportunity to drive the new Elan. The figures, especially very quick acceleration due to the low weight, look good, and if build quality matches the specification and appearance, the Elan should do well.

LOTUS   (GB)   Esprit Turbo SE

Identity: New version of mid-engined Esprit, launched Motorfair 1987 with choice of non-turbo or turbo 16-valve engine. Glass panel across rear behind back window identifies Turbo model. Many improvements, including more attractive interior with better seats and instruments.

Engine: Mid-mounted longitudinal four-cylinder with alloy head and block; twin ohc operating four valves per cyl.; two twin-choke Dellorto carbs and Garrett T3 turbocharger. Bore 95.3 mm, stroke 76.2 mm; capacity 2174 cc. Power 212 PS (160 kW) at 6000 rpm; torque 220 lb ft (298 Nm) at 4250 rpm. Compression 8.0-to-1. Catalyst: standard.

Transmission: Rear-wheel drive; five-speed manual gearbox. Automatic, not available. Top gear speed at 1000 rpm: 23.7 mph (38.1 km/h).

Suspension: Front, independent, wishbones and coil springs with coaxial dampers; anti-roll bar. Rear, independent, transverse links with box section trailing arms; coil springs and coaxial telescopic dampers.

Steering: Rack and pinion. Power assistance: not available. **Brakes:** Vented discs front, solid discs rear. ABS: standard. **Tyres:** 195/60 VR 15 (front), 235/60 VR 15 (rear). **Fuel tank:** 17.3 Imp. gall (78.6 litres). **Unladen weight:** 2795 lb (1268 kg).

Dimensions: Length 170.5 in (4331 mm), width 73.2 in (1859 mm), height 44.8 in (1138 mm), wheelbase 96.8 in (2459 mm).

Performance *Autocar & Motor* test: Maximum speed 150 mph (241 km/h); 0 to 60 mph (97 km/h) 5.4 sec; 80 mph (130 km/h) 8.2 sec. Fuel consumption at 75 mph (120 km/h): 26.6 mpg; overall test, 19.6 mpg.

Features: Knock resistant bumpers in body colour; tilt/remove glass roof panel. SE is special equipment model. **Summary:** Well-planned redesign of this exciting mid-engined two-seater GT, introduced sensible improvements while retaining the outstanding handling. Body in composite material with some Kevlar reinforcement, and bolted to backbone chassis.

MAZDA (J)   121 GLX

Identity: No one can say that the new Mazda 121, launched February 1991 in UK, does not look distinctively different; and the rounded body shape is also very practical, offering generous roominess and rear headroom in a small car. Available with automatic transmission only.

Engine: Front-mounted transverse four-cylinder with alloy head and single ohc working four valves per cylinder. Electronic single point fuel injection. Bore 71.0 mm, stroke 83.6 mm; capacity 1324 cc. Power 73 PS (54 kW) at 6000 rpm; torque 78 lb ft (108 Nm) at 370 rpm. Compression 9.4-to-1. Catalyst: standard.

Transmission: Front-wheel drive. Automatic, four-speed standard. Top gear speed at 1000 rpm: 24.5 mph (39.5 km/h).

Suspension: Front, independent, MacPherson struts. Rear, semi-independent, trailing arms and torsion beam; anti-roll bar.

Steering: Rack and pinion. Power assistance: not available. **Brakes:** Solid discs front, drums rear. ABS: not available. **Tyres:** 165/70 R 13. **Fuel tank:** 9.5 Imp. gall (43 litres). **Unladen weight:** 1841 lb (835 kg).

Dimensions: Length 149.6 in (3800 mm), width 65.1 in (655 mm), height 57.8 in (1470 mm), wheelbase 94.1 in (2390 mm).

Performance Works: Maximum speed 102 mph (164 km/h); 0 to 62 mph (100 km/h) 15.8 sec. Fuel consumption at constant 75 mph (120 km/h): 39.8 mpg.

Features: Rear seat centrally divided and folding. Standard equipment includes central locking and electric front windows, but no sunroof.
Summary: Automatic transmission has an unusual control system, with change-down and freewheel when selector is moved back, or change down with engine braking on pressing a button in the side of the selector. Pleasant small car, easy to drive.

MAZDA (J) 323F 1.6 SE Executive

Identity: To catch up with the new 323 before it came to Britain, I went to California and drove it there, and was very taken with this version – a 1.6-litre family car with hatchback tail and attractive styling, helped by having pop-up headlamps. 'F' denotes the Fastback style.

Engine: Front-mounted transverse four-cylinder with alloy head and single ohc working four valves per cylinder; hydraulic tappets. Twin-choke carb. Bore 78.0 mm, stroke 83.6 mm; capacity 1598 cc. Power 87 PS (64 kW) at 6000 rpm; torque 92 lb ft (127 Nm) at 3100 rpm. Compression 9.2-to-1. Catalyst: not available.

Transmission: Front-wheel drive; five-speed manual gearbox. Automatic, optional extra. Top gear speed at 1000 rpm: 20.5 mph (33.0 km/h).

Suspension: Front, independent, MacPherson struts, anti-roll bar. Rear, independent, coil spring struts with trailing arms and twin trapezoidal links; gas-filled dampers.

Steering: Rack and pinion. Power assistance: standard. **Brakes:** Vented discs front, drums rear. ABS: not available. **Tyres:** 175/70 SR 13. **Fuel tank:** 11.0 Imp. gall (50 litres). **Unladen weight:** 2377 lb (1078 kg).

Dimensions: Length 167.7 in (4260 mm), width 65.9 in (1675 mm), height 52.6 in (1335 mm), wheelbase 98.4 in (2500 mm).

Performance Works: Maximum speed 109 mph (175 km/h); 0 to 62 mph (100 km/h) 10.6 sec. Fuel consumption at constant 75 mph (120 km/h): 38.2 mpg.

Features: Good equipment includes electric sunroof, central locking, and electric windows front and rear. Neat instrumentation. **Summary:** Light to drive, with good roadholding and well-weighted power steering, the 323F in this Executive form is a very appealing car. A rear spoiler in body colour enhances the sporty appearance.

MAZDA (J)   323 1.8 GT Hatchback

Identity: In the new 323 range most models have the 1.6-litre engine, but there is also a 1.8-litre GT with injection engine and choice of hatchback or Fastback body. As Fastback, it has five doors and looks very similar to the 323F; but there are more differences than just the engine.

Engine: Front-mounted transverse four-cylinder with alloy head and twin ohc working four valves per cylinder; hydraulic tappets. Bosch L-Jetronic fuel injection. Bore 83.0 mm, stroke 85.0 mm; capacity 1840 cc. Power 140 PS (103 kW) at 6500 rpm; torque 120 lb ft (166 Nm) at 4700 rpm. Compression 9.8-to-1. Catalyst: not available.

Transmission: Front-wheel drive; five-speed manual gearbox. Automatic, not available. Top gear speed at 1000 rpm: 19.3 mph (31.1 km/h).

Suspension: Front, independent, MacPherson struts, anti-roll bar. Rear, independent, coil spring struts with trailing arms and twin trapezoidal links; gas-filled dampers and anti-roll bar.

Steering: Rack and pinion. Power assistance: standard. **Brakes:** Vented discs front, solid discs rear. ABS: not available. **Tyres:** 185/60 HR 14. **Fuel tank:** 12.1 Imp. gall (55 litres). **Unladen weight:** 2377 lb (1078 kg).

Dimensions: Length 167.7 in (4260 mm), width 65.9 in (1675 mm), height 52.6 in (1335 mm), wheelbase 98.4 in (2500 mm).

Performance *Autocar & Motor* test: Maximum speed 125 mph (201 km/h); 0 to 60 mph (97 km/h) 8.6 sec; 80 mph (130 km/h) 15.1 sec. Fuel consumption at constant 75 mph (120 km/h): 37.2 mpg; overall test, 28.6 mpg.

Features: Lack of anti-lock brakes is regrettable on this sort of car, but most other items are there, including alloy wheels. **Summary:** Impressive performance, with easy fast cruising and very good roadholding and steering; brakes cope well on good surfaces. In five-door form, the 1.8 GT gets the 323F badge at rear, but look for GT badge to rear of front wheel.

MAZDA (J)   626 2.2i GLX Executive 4 × 4

Identity: Additions to 626 range in January 1990 included air conditioning and anti-lock brakes; and this new version with four-wheel drive and 2.2-litre 12-valve engine topped off a model palette which now offers 14 versions. It is available only with hatchback body.

Engine: Front mounted transverse four-cylinder with alloy head and single ohc operating three valves per cylinder. Electronic fuel injection. Bore 86.0 mm, stroke 94.0 mm; capacity 2184 cc. Power 116 PS (86 kW) at 5000 rpm; torque 133 lb ft (184 Nm) at 4000 rpm. Compression 8.6-to-1. Catalyst: standard.

Transmission: Four-wheel drive; five-speed manual gearbox. Automatic, not available. Top gear speed at 1000 rpm: 23.9 mph (38.5 km/h).

Suspension: Front, independent, MacPherson struts; anti-roll bar. Rear, MacPherson struts with twin trapezoidal links and trailing links; anti-roll bar.

Steering: Rack and pinion. Power assistance: standard. **Brakes:** Vented discs front, solid discs rear. ABS: standard. **Tyres:** 195/60 HR 15. **Fuel tank:** 13.2 Imp. gall (60 litres). **Unladen weight:** 2877 lb (1305 kg).

Dimensions: Length 177.8 in (4515 mm), width 66.5 in (1690 mm), height 54.9 in (1395 mm), wheelbase 101.3 in (2575 mm).

Performance Works: Maximum speed 114 mph (183 km/h); 0 to 62 mph (100 km/h) 9.7 sec. Fuel consumption at constant 75 mph (120 km/h): 30.4 mpg.

Features: Very comprehensive equipment includes air conditioning, headlamp levelling, electric glass sunroof and central locking. **Summary:** This is not the most powerful version of the 626–that's the GT which develops 146 bhp; but it combines top equipment and four-wheel drive with an engine developed for high torque and a less sporty style of driving.

MAZDA   (J)   MX-5

Identity: Rationed to ten minutes' driving time during the Mazda 323 launch in America, I enjoyed my first brief experience of the little MX-5 sports car, and became enchanted with it on a proper appraisal opportunity later. It looks good, handles delightfully, and is a true return to the traditional image of an open sports car, for fun motoring.

Engine: Front-mounted longitudinal four-cylinder with alloy head and twin ohc working four valves per cylinder. Electronic fuel injection. Bore 78.0 mm, stroke 84.0 mm; capacity 1598 cc. Power 115 PS (85 kW) at 6500 rpm; torque 100 lb ft (138 Nm) at 5500 rpm. Compression 9.4-to-1. Catalyst: standard.

Transmission: Rear-wheel drive; five-speed manual gearbox. Automatic, not available. Top gear speed at 1000 rpm: 18.8 mph (30.3 km/h).

Suspension: Front, independent, wishbones and coil springs; anti-roll bar. Rear, independent, wishbones and coil springs; anti-roll bar.

Steering: Rack and pinion. Power assistance: standard. **Brakes:** Vented discs front, solid discs rear. ABS: not available. **Tyres:** 185/60 HR 14. **Fuel tank:** 10.0 Imp. gall (45.5 litres). **Unladen weight:** 2185 lb (990 kg).

Dimensions: Length 155.5 in (3950 mm), width 65.9 in (1675 mm), height 48.2 in (1230 mm), wheelbase 89.2 in (2265 mm).

Performance *Autocar & Motor* test: Maximum speed 114 mph (183 km/h); 0 to 60 mph (97 km/h) 9.1 sec; 80 mph (130 km/h) 17.0 sec. Fuel consumption at constant 75 mph (120 km/h): 36.2 mpg; overall test, 24.0 mpg.

Features: Hood fits snugly and folds very easily. Neat interior with full instrumentation. Bumpers are integral with the bodywork; pop-up headlamps. **Summary:** With its excellent controls and superbly balanced handling, helped by a return to 'old-fashioned' rear wheel drive for a car of this size, the MX-5 is very safe and extremely enjoyable to drive.

MAZDA   (J, GB)   MX-5 BBR Turbo

Identity: In conjunction with Brodie Brittain Racing (hence the BBR initials), this turbocharged version of the very successful little MX-5 sports car was developed for the UK market, and announced towards the end of 1990. Power is increased to 150 PS, giving sizzling acceleration.

Engine: Front-mounted longitudinal four-cylinder with alloy head and twin ohc working four valves per cylinder. Garrett T25 turbocharger with integral waste gate and water cooling. Bore 78.0 mm, stroke 84.0 mm; capacity 1598 cc. Power 150 PS (110 kW) at 6500 rpm; torque 154 lb ft (213 Nm) at 5500 rpm. Compression 9.4-to-1. Catalyst: standard.

Transmission: Rear-wheel drive; five-speed manual gearbox. Automatic, not available. Top gear speed at 1000 rpm: 18.8 mph (30.3 km/h).

Suspension: Front, independent, wishbones and coil springs; anti-roll bar. Rear, independent, wishbones and coil springs; anti-roll bar.

Steering: Rack and pinion. Power assistance: standard. **Brakes:** Vented discs front, solid discs rear. ABS: not available. **Tyres:** D40 M2 6.5 VR 15. **Fuel tank:** 10.0 Imp. gall (46 litres). **Unladen weight:** 2170 lb (985 kg).

Dimensions: Length 156.5 in (3975 mm), width 65.9 in (1675 mm), height 48.4 in (1230 mm), wheelbase 89.2 in (2265 mm).

Performance *Autocar & Motor* test: Maximum speed 122 mph (196 km/h); 0 to 60 mph (97 km/h) 7.8 sec; 80 mph (130 km/h) 13.5 sec. Fuel consumption overall test, 24.1 mpg.

Features: Extensive modifications include a modified sump with oil return from the turbocharger and reprogramming of electronic settings for injection and ignition. **Summary:** In standard form, the MX-5 is quite a nippy little sports car. Turbocharging moves it into a different class altogether, increasing the appeal, while retaining the charm of this little two-seater.

MAZDA (J)   RX-7 2.6 Turbo Cabriolet

Identity: As the first to run a Wankel-engined car in Britain, back in 1965, I have always been fascinated by the rotary concept, which continues only in the Mazda RX-7 (as far as cars are concerned). In the latest turbo form, power has been increased to an impressive 200 PS. Coupé and cabriolet available.

Engine: Front-mounted longitudinal twin-rotor rotary engine with die-cast housing, fuel injection, and Hitachi twin-scroll turbocharger with inter-cooler. Chamber capacity 654 cc; direct equivalent, 2616 cc; rated equivalent, 2254 cc. No valves; circumferential porting. Power 200 PS (147 kW) at 6500 rpm; torque 195 lb ft (270 Nm) at 3500 rpm. Compression 9.0-to-1. Catalyst: standard.

Transmission: Rear-wheel drive; five-speed manual gearbox. Automatic, not available. Top gear speed at 1000 rpm: 24.3 mph (39.1 km/h).

Suspension: Front, independent, MacPherson struts; anti-roll bar. Rear, independent, semi-trailing arms and multi-link layout with coil springs; anti-roll bar.

Steering: Rack and pinion. Power assistance: standard. **Brakes:** Vented discs front and rear, ABS: standard. **Tyres:** 205/55 ZR 16. **Fuel tank:** 15.8 Imp. gall (72 litres). **Unladen weight:** 2933 lb (1330 kg).

Dimensions: Length 169.9 in (4315 mm), width 66.5 in (1690 mm), height 49.8 in (1265 mm), wheelbase 95.7 in (2430 mm).

Performance *Autocar & Motor* test: Maximum speed 148 mph (238 km/h); 0 to 60 mph (97 km/h) 6.7 sec; 80 mph (130 km/h) 11.0 sec. Fuel consumption at 75 mph (120 km/h): 26.2 mpg; overall test, 14.3 mpg.

Features: Equipment improved for latest version, including a small electric sunroof for the coupé; the cabriolet has a fully folding hood with no fixed roll bar. **Summary:** The smoothness of a Wankel rotary engine has to be experienced to be appreciated and, with turbocharging, the RX-7 has the performance to match the top super cars. Heavy fuel consumption, however, has always been a problem of the Wankel engine.

MERCEDES-BENZ (D)

190 2.5D

Identity: In the summer of 1989 I used this model for a drive to the West Country in heavy rain and strong wind, and was a bit disappointed at the way in which it blew about on the road. In other respects, it is a comfortable car, and one of the quietest diesels I have ever driven.

Engine: Front-mounted longitudinal five-cylinder with alloy head and single ohc operating two valves per cylinder. Engine totally encapsulated to reduce noise. Bore 87.0 mm, stroke 84.0 mm; capacity 2497 cc. Power 90 PS (66 kW) at 4600 rpm; torque 113 lb ft (154 Nm) at 2800 rpm. Compression 22.0-to-1. Catalyst: not available.

Transmission: Rear-wheel drive; five-speed manual gearbox. Automatic, optional extra. Top gear speed at 1000 rpm: 24.9 mph (40.0 km/h).

Suspension: Front, independent, MacPherson struts, anti-roll bar. Rear, independent, five-link location; coil springs and anti-roll bar.

Steering: Recirculating ball. Power assistance: standard. **Brakes:** Solid discs front, drums rear. ABS: optional. **Tyres:** 185/65 R 15. **Fuel tank:** 12.1 Imp. gall (55 litres). **Unladen weight:** 2712 lb (1230 kg).

Dimensions: Length 175.1 in (4448 mm), width 64.2 in (1033 mm), height 54.7 in (1390 mm), wheelbase 104.9 in (2665 mm).

Performance Works: Maximum speed 108 mph (174 km/h); 0 to 62 mph (100 km/h) 16.1 sec. Fuel consumption at constant 75 mph (120 km/h): 36.7 mpg (automatic).

Features: Tidy interior finish, excellent controls and general driving layout; equipment still a little basic in relation to price. **Summary:** Reshaping of the seats at Paris 1988 resulted in a little more room in the back, but the 190 is still rather more a four-seater than a five. In diesel automatic form, performance is a little leisurely but the car cruises fast once speed has built up.

MERCEDES-BENZ (D)

190E 2.5-16V

Identity: At the same time as the 190 range was revised in 1988, Mercedes increased the power of the 16-valve performance model by extending the stroke and raising capacity to 2½-litre. Already a very fast car, it gains a lot more torque for better low-speed response.

Engine: Front-mounted longitudinal four-cylinder with alloy head and twin chain-driven ohc operating four valves per cyl. Bosch K-Jetronic fuel injection. Bore 95.5 mm, stroke 87.3 mm; capacity 2498 cc. Power 200 PS (147 kW) at 6200 rpm; torque 176 lb ft (242 Nm) at 4500 rpm. Compression 9.7-to-1. Catalyst: not available.

Transmission: Rear-wheel drive; five-speed manual gearbox. Automatic, four-speed, optional. Top gear speed at 1000 rpm: 23.5 mph (37.8 km/h).

Suspension: Front, independent, MacPherson struts, anti-roll bar. Rear, independent, five-link system with anti-dive, anti-squat control; coil springs, anti-roll bar.

Steering: Recirculating ball. Power assistance: standard. **Brakes:** Vented discs front, solid discs rear. ABS: standard. **Tyres:** 205/55 ZR 15 TL. **Fuel tank:** 15.4 Imp. gall (70 litres). **Unladen weight:** 2866 lb (1300 kg).

Dimensions: Length 174.4 in (4430 mm), width 67.2 in (1706 mm), height 53.5 in (1361 mm), wheelbase 104.9 in (2665 mm).

Performance *Autocar & Motor* test: Maximum speed 142 mph (229 km/h); 0 to 62 mph (100 km/h) 7.2 sec; 80 mph (130 km/h) 11.8 sec. Fuel consumption at constant 75 mph (120 km/h): 32.8 mpg; overall test, 22.0 mpg.

Features: Many refinements to make this quick version of the 190 very enjoyable. Snug sports seats give good location. **Summary:** Close ratio gearchange with offset first, and upper four gears in H layout, takes a little familiarisation; but it is certainly a most exciting car and one that gobbles up long journeys in fine style.

MERCEDES-BENZ (D)

300SL-24 5-Speed automatic

Identity: In the last edition we covered the fabulously fast 500SL with 32-valve engine. Now here is the later arrival: the six-cylinder version of this lovely sports car with the unusual feature of a five-speed automatic transmission.

Engine: Front-mounted longitudinal six-cylinder with alloy head and block and twin ohc working four valves per cylinder. Bosch KE5 CIS fuel injection. Bore 89.0 mm, stroke 80.0 mm; capacity 2960 cc. Power 231 PS (170 kW) at 6300 rpm; torque 200 lb ft (277 Nm) at 4600 rpm. Compression 10.0-to-1. Catalyst: not available.

Transmission: Rear-wheel drive; five-speed automatic, standard. Top gear speed at 1000 rpm: 28.9 mph (46.5 km/h).

Suspension: Front, independent, MacPherson struts, anti-roll bar. Rear, independent, five-link location with coil springs and anti-roll bar. Anti-squat and anti-dive control.

Steering: Recirculating ball. Power assistance: standard. **Brakes:** Vented discs front, solid discs rear. ABS: standard. **Tyres:** 225/55 ZR 16. **Fuel tank:** 17.6 Imp. gall (80 litres). **Unladen weight:** 3725 lb (1690 kg).

Dimensions: Length 175.9 in (4470 mm), width 71.3 in (1812 mm), height 51.2 in (1303 mm), wheelbase 99.0 in (2515 mm).

Performance *Autocar & Motor* test: Maximum speed 134 mph (216 km/h); 0 to 60 mph (97 km/h) 8.6 sec; 80 mph (130 km/h) 14.1 sec. Fuel consumption at constant 75 mph (120 km/h): 26.6 mpg; overall test, 19.2 mpg.

Features: Five-speed transmission selector has only four positions, no first gear hold, and is moved sideways for fifth, which is marked OD (overdrive). **Summary:** Most of the superb furnishings and safety features are the same as for the 500SL, though leather upholstery is an option on the six-cylinder. Automatic transmission has the usual Mercedes mode control switch offering E (Economy) or S (Sport).

MERCEDES-BENZ (D)   300TE 4-MATIC

Identity: This is four-wheel drive 'on demand', brought in progressively when required. The 4-Matic system became available in 1988 on all the 200-300 Series. The 300TE illustrated here shows the versatile estate in the 200-300 range, designated 'T'. 24-valve engine, Frankfurt 1989.

Engine: Front-mounted longitudinal six-cylinder with alloy head and belt-driven twin ohc working four valves per cylinder. Bosch KE 5 fuel injection. Bore 88.5 mm, stroke 80.3 mm; capacity 2962 cc. Power 220 PS (162 kW) at 6400 rpm; torque 197 lb ft (265 Nm) at 4500 rpm. Compression 10.0-to-1. Catalyst: not available.

Transmission: Four-wheel drive. Automatic, four-speed standard. Electrically operated differentials under computer control add progressive drive to front wheels when needed. Top gear speed at 1000 rpm: 22.3 mph (35.9 km/h).

Suspension: Front, independent, MacPherson struts, anti-roll bar. Rear, independent, five-link system with anti-dive, anti-squat control; coil springs and telescopic dampers, anti-roll bar.

Steering: Recirculating ball. Power assistance: standard. **Brakes:** Vented discs front, solid discs rear. ABS: standard. **Tyres:** 195/65 VR 15. **Fuel tank:** 15.4 Imp. gall (70 litres). **Unladen weight:** 3443 lb (1558 kg).

Dimensions: Length 187.6 in (4765 mm), width 74.2 in (1884 mm), height 58.7 in (1490 mm), wheelbase 110.2 in (2800 mm).

Performance *Autocar & Motor* test: (Saloon): Maximum speed 134 mph (216 km/h); 0 to 60 mph (97 km/h) 8.3 sec; 80 mph (130 km/h) 14.4 sec. Fuel consumption at constant 75 mph (120 km/h): 30.1 mpg; overall test, 18.6 mpg.

Features: 4-Matic is an expensive option, but gives remarkable traction without affecting normal handling. **Summary:** A light comes on when 4-Matic is doing its work, otherwise you'd hardly know; but permanent four-wheel drive would perhaps be better and benefit handling even when grip is good. An outstandingly competent car.

MERCEDES-BENZ (D) 500E

Identity: It came as something of a surprise to hear at the Paris Show 1990 that the Porsche factory at Zuffenhausen was to build a Mercedes – but that is what is happening with the very special 5-litre V8 500 model. It is produced by craftsmen for enthusiasts, at the rate of only 12 a day.

Engine: Front-mounted longitudinal V8-cylinder with alloy block and heads, and twin ohc each bank, working four valves per cylinder. Bosch LH Jetronic fuel injection. Bore 96.5 mm, stroke 85.0 mm; capacity 4973 cc. Power 326 PS (240 kW) at 5700 rpm; torque 347 lb ft (480 Nm) at 3900 rpm. Compression 10.0-to-1. Catalyst: standard.

Transmission: Rear-wheel drive; five-speed automatic, standard. Top gear speed at 1000 rpm: 25.9 mph (41.7 km/h).

Suspension: Front, independent, MacPherson struts with anti-dive control; anti-roll bar. Rear, independent, five-link system with anti-dive, anti-squat control; self-levelling, coil springs and anti-roll bar.

Steering: Recirculating ball. Power assistance: standard. **Brakes:** Vented discs front and rear. ABS: standard. **Tyres:** 225/55 ZR 16. **Fuel tank:** 19.8 Imp. gall (90 litres). **Unladen weight:** 3748 lb (1700 kg).

Dimensions: Length 187.0 in (4750 mm), width 70.7 in (1796 mm), height 55.4 in (1408 mm), wheelbase 110.2 in (2800 mm).

Performance Works: Maximum speed 156 mph (251 km/h); 0 to 62 mph (100 km/h) 5.9 sec. Fuel consumption: no data.

Features: Elaborate standard equipment provides such items as air conditioning and electric seat adjustment, and a new 'world first' is that all the electronic systems constantly communicate with each other.
Summary: A car for the very discerning buyer. A lot of attention has been paid to road handling, including moving the battery to the boot for optimum weight balance; the Mercedes wheelspin control system is standard.

MERCEDES-BENZ (D)   300 GD

Identity: Always very competent, if rather basic in its performance on the road, the Geländewagen – commonly known as the G-wagon – was vastly improved in 1990. In September the importers arranged a spectacular mountain drive of the new version in Scotland. Sidelamps recessed in the bumper identify the new model, which now has permanent four-wheel drive.

Engine: Front-mounted longitudinal six-cylinder with cast iron head and block, and single ohc; indirect fuel injection, no turbo. Bore 87.0 mm, stroke 84.0 mm; capacity 2,996 cc. Power 113 PS (83 kW) at 4600 rpm; torque 141 lb ft (195 Nm) at 2700 rpm. Compression 22.0-to-1. Catalyst: not available.

Transmission: Four-wheel drive; five-speed manual gearbox. Automatic, optional extra. Four-wheel drive is permanently engaged, with low ratio transfer gearbox. Top gear speed at 1000 rpm: 18.8 mph (30.3 km/h).

Suspension: Front, live axle on trailing arms with Panhard rod; coil springs. Rear, live axle on trailing arms with Panhard rod; coil springs, anti-roll bar.

Steering: Recirculating ball. Power assistance: standard. **Brakes:** Solid discs front, drums rear. ABS: standard. **Tyres:** 205 R 16. **Fuel tank:** 20.1 Imp. gall (95 litres). **Unladen weight:** 4905 lb (2225 kg).

Dimensions: Length (lwb) 173.0 in (4395 mm), (swb): 155.3 in (3945 mm), width 66.9 in (1700 mm), height 77.8 in (1975 mm), wheelbase 112.2 in (2850 mm).

Performance *Autocar & Motor* test: Maximum speed 84 mph (135 km/h); 0 to 60 mph (97 km/h) 25.4 sec. Fuel consumption at constant 75 mph (120 km/h): 17.7 mpg; overall test, 17.1 mpg.

Features: Differential locks (front, centre and rear) have electric switch control on facia. Much better interior trim and layout, derived from the W123 car range. **Summary:** Still the same rather angular body, but very impressive cross-country ability, helped by the huge ground clearance.

MERCEDES-BENZ (D)   New S-Class

Identity: Introduced Geneva 1991, the replacement for the larger model of the Mercedes range presents a more aerodynamic body, with many special features. Range of engines from a new six-cylinder of 3.2-litre capacity to the V12 6-litre detailed here.

Engine: Front-mounted longitudinal V12-cylinder with alloy block and heads, twin ohc per bank, and four valves per cylinder; varying intake valve timing. Advanced ignition/injection control system. Bore 89.0 mm, stroke 80.2 mm; capacity 5987 cc. Power 408 PS (300 kW) at 5200 rpm; torque 420 lb ft (580 Nm) at 3800 rpm. Compression 10.0-to-1. Catalyst: standard.

Transmission: Rear-wheel drive. Automatic, four-speed standard. Top gear speed at 1000 rpm: 29.5 mph (47.5 km/h).

Suspension: Front, independent, wishbones and coil springs with anti-dive control and gas-filled dampers; anti-roll bar. Rear, independent, multi-link layout with coil springs and gas-filled dampers. Anti-squat and anti-lift control plus self-levelling; anti-roll bar.

Steering: Recirculating ball. Power assistance: standard. **Brakes:** Vented discs front and rear. ABS: standard. **Tyres:** 235/60 ZR 16. **Fuel tank:** 22.0 Imp. gall (100 litres). **Unladen weight:** 4806 lb (2180 kg).

Dimensions: Length 201.3 in (5113 mm), width 74.3 in (1886 mm), height 58.7 in (1490 mm), wheelbase 119.7 in (3040 mm).

Performance Works: Maximum speed 155 mph (250 km/h); 0 to 62 mph (100 km/h) 6.0 sec. Fuel consumption at constant 75 mph (120 km/h): 20.6 mpg.

Features: Every item of luxury equipment is standard at the top level of the range represented by the 600SE and long-wheelbase 600SEL.
Summary: Superbly engineered car achieving very high standards of safety, performance, luxury and quietness. Advanced systems in the new S-Class include electric throttle control, automatic seat belt adjustment, wipers clearing 90 per cent of the screen, and filtered ventilation.

MERCURY (USA) Sable LS

Identity: It should be easy to tell that a Sable is approaching at night, on account of its all-across lighting scheme. Sable is available as four-door saloon or estate car, and seats five (or up to eight in the estate with optional third seat). Sable first appeared in 1985. GS and LS trim available.

Engine: Front-mounted transverse V6-cylinder with pushrod ohv and hydraulic tappets. Electronic sequential multi-point fuel injection. Bore 88.9 mm, stroke 78.7 mm; capacity 2982 cc. Power 140 PS (103 kW) at 4800 rpm; torque 160 lb ft (221 Nm) at 3000 rpm. Compression 9.3-to-1. Catalyst: standard.

Transmission: Front-wheel drive; four-speed automatic standard. Top gear speed at 1000 rpm: 31.3 mph (50.3 km/h).

Suspension: Front, independent, MacPherson struts; anti-roll bar. Rear, independent, MacPherson struts with parallel arms; anti-roll bar.

Steering: Rack and pinion. Power assistance: standard. **Brakes:** Solid discs front, drums rear. ABS: not available. **Tyres:** P205/70 R 14. **Fuel tank:** 13.3 Imp. gall (60 litres). **Unladen weight:** 3112 lb (1411 kg).

Dimensions: Length 192.2 in (4882 mm), width 70.8 in (1798 mm), height 54.3 in (1379 mm), wheelbase 196.0 in (2692 mm).

Performance (est): Maximum speed 112 mph (180 km/h); Fuel consumption overall (est), 22 mpg.

Features: Optional engine is 3.8-litre V6. Good equipment includes air conditioning, with electronic climate control as an option. **Summary:** The full-width 'lamp-bar' at the front is original and brings a fresh look to the Sable, which was among the first of the American saloons to go to an aerodynamic shape.

MITSUBISHI (J)   Colt 1500-12V GLX

Identity: At Birmingham 1990 an important development in the ever-improving Mitsubishi range was the introduction of new 12-valve engines for the carburettor versions of the Colt and Lancer, giving more power with better response. The Colt is a three-door hatchback, available with this engine or the 1300, also with 12 valves.

Engine: Front-mounted transverse four-cylinder with alloy head and belt-driven single ohc working two inlet and one exhaust valves per cylinder, using roller rockers. Varying venturi carb. Bore 75.5 mm, stroke 82.0 mm; capacity 1468 cc. Power 87 PS (64 kW) at 6000 rpm; torque 87 lb ft (120 Nm) at 4000 rpm. Compression 9.4-to-1. Catalyst: not available.

Transmission: Front-wheel drive; five-speed manual gearbox. Automatic, optional extra. Top gear speed at 1000 rpm: 21.1 mph (34.0 km/h).

Suspension: Front, independent, MacPherson struts, anti-roll bar. Rear, semi-independent, torsion beam axle with three-link location; coil springs.

Steering: Rack and pinion. Power assistance: optional. **Brakes:** Solid discs front, drums rear. ABS: not available. **Tyres:** 175/70 R 13. **Fuel tank:** 11.0 Imp. gall (50 litres). **Unladen weight:** 2046 lb (930 kg).

Dimensions: Length 155.5 in (3950 mm), width 65.7 in (1670 mm), height 54.3 in (1380 mm), wheelbase 93.9 in (2385 mm).

Performance Works: Maximum speed 104 mph (167 km/h); 0 to 62 mph (100 km/h) 11.9 sec. Fuel consumption at constant 75 mph (120 km/h): 39.2 mpg.

Features: Electric windows are standard, but the Colt does not get central locking; tailgate is self-locking with floor release. Driver's seat-height adjustment was introduced for 1990. **Summary:** Capable, roomy and easy to drive, the Colt in this new 1.5-litre form gains a useful improvement in performance. Big-selling feature for Mitsubishis in the UK is the three-year unlimited mileage warranty.

MITSUBISHI (J)   Colt 1800 GTi-16V

Identity: At the same time as the 12-valve engines were introduced at Birmingham 1990, the Colt also became available in GTi 16-valve form. It offers vigorous performance and, incidentally, all the ingredients for a good tow-car, confirmed when it won its class in the Caravan Club Towcar of the Year awards.

Engine: Front-mounted transverse four-cylinder with alloy head and twin belt-driven ohc working four valves per cylinder, using roller. Electronic multi-point fuel injection. Bore 81.5 mm, stroke 88.0 mm; capacity 1836 cc. Power 136 PS (100 kW) at 6500 rpm; torque 119 lb ft (165 Nm) at 4500 rpm. Compression 10.5-to-1. Catalyst: not available.

Transmission: Front-wheel drive; five-speed manual gearbox. Automatic, not available. Top gear speed at 1000 rpm: 19.1 mph (30.7 km/h).

Suspension: Front, independent, MacPherson struts, anti-roll bar. Rear, semi-independent, torsion beam axle with three-link location; coil springs.

Steering: Rack and pinion. Power assistance: standard. **Brakes:** Vented discs front, solid discs rear. ABS: not available. **Tyres:** 195/60 HR 14. **Fuel tank:** 11.0 Imp. gall (50 litres). **Unladen weight:** 2293 lb (1040 kg).

Dimensions: Length 155.9 in (3960 mm), width 65.7 in (1670 mm), height 54.3 in (1380 mm), wheelbase 93.9 in (2385 mm).

Performance Works: Maximum speed 125 mph (201 km/h); 0 to 62 mph (100 km/h) 7.9 sec. Fuel consumption at constant 75 mph (120 km/h): 34.9 mpg.

Features: This engine also has the Mitsubishi system of counter-rotating balance shafts, making it exceptionally smooth. Alloy wheels identify the GTi. **Summary:** After driving this new Colt as a judge on the Towcar awards I was so impressed that I used one again for further journeys involving towing, and was delighted at the way it performed and handled.

MITSUBISHI (J)   Galant Coupé Dynamic Four

Identity: Following the successful launch of four-wheel drive and four-wheel steering on the Galant saloon in May 1989, the same specification was extended to the attractively styled Galant Coupé, Geneva 1990. Four-wheel drive is permanently engaged; rear steering effect is rather restricted, and occurs only above 31 mph.

Engine: Front-mounted transverse four-cylinder with alloy head and twin ohc working four valves per cylinder. Electronic multi-point fuel injection. Bore 85.0 mm, stroke 88.0 mm; capacity 1997 cc. Power 150 PS (110 kW) at 6750 rpm; torque 129 lb ft (178 Nm) at 5500 rpm. Compression 9.8-to-1. Catalyst: standard.

Transmission: Four-wheel drive; five-speed manual gearbox. Automatic, optional extra. Top gear speed at 1000 rpm: 19.5 mph (31.4 km/h).

Suspension: Front, independent, MacPherson struts, anti-roll bar. Rear, independent, wishbones with trailing arms and concentric coil springs; anti-roll bar.

Steering: Rack and pinion. Power assistance: standard. **Brakes:** Vented discs front, solid discs rear. ABS: standard. **Tyres:** 195/60 R 15 87V. **Fuel tank:** 13.7 Imp. gall (62 litres). **Unladen weight:** 2954 lb (1340 kg).

Dimensions: Length 180.0 in (4570 mm), width 66.7 in (1695 mm), height 55.5 in (1410 mm), wheelbase 102.4 in (2600 mm).

Performance *Autocar & Motor* test (saloon): Maximum speed 118 mph (190 km/h); 0 to 60 mph (97 km/h) 9.4 sec; 80 mph (130 km/h) 16.7 sec. Fuel consumption at constant 75 mph (120 km/h): 31.7 mpg; overall test, 21.4 mpg.

Features: Rear wheels turn always in the same direction as the front ones, returning to straight ahead below 31 mph. Full equipment.

Summary: A very capable and reassuring car to drive. But one drawback is that the air conditioning and electronic suspension control options are not available for the Dynamic Four.

MITSUBISHI (J)

Lancer 1800 GLXi 4WD Liftback

Identity: New in the Mitsubishi line-up at Motorfair 1989 was the Lancer in four-wheel drive form, with lively new 1.8-litre injection engine (later to be offered also in the Colt, but with front-drive only). The Liftback is also available with new 12-valve 1500 and 16-valve 1800 engines.

Engine: Front-mounted transverse four-cylinder with alloy head and belt-driven ohc; two-valves per cylinder. Electronic fuel injection. Bore 80.6 mm, stroke 86.0 mm; capacity 1755 cc. Power 95 PS (71 kW) at 5500 rpm; torque 104 lb ft (141 Nm) at 4000 rpm. Compression 9.5-to-1. Catalyst: standard.

Transmission: Four-wheel drive; five-speed manual gearbox. Automatic, not available. Top gear speed at 1000 rpm: 19.8 mph (31.9 km/h).

Suspension: Front, independent, MacPherson struts, anti-roll bar. Rear, live axle with five link location and coil springs; anti-roll bar.

Steering: Rack and pinion. Power assistance: standard. **Brakes:** Vented discs front, drums rear. ABS: not available. **Tyres:** 175/70 HR 13. **Fuel tank:** 11.0 Imp. gall (50 litres). **Unladen weight:** 2500 lb (1134 kg).

Dimensions: Length 166.7 in (4235 mm), width 65.7 in (1670 mm), height 56.1 in (1425 mm), wheelbase 96.7 in (2455 mm).

Performance *Autocar & Motor* test: Maximum speed 103 mph (166 km/h); 0 to 60 mph (97 km/h) 11.7 sec; 80 mph (130 km/h) 23.4 sec. Fuel consumption at 75 mph (120 km/h): 30.4 mpg; overall test, 24.6 mpg.

Features: Viscous couplings are used as the centre and rear differentials for the four-wheel drive, which is permanently engaged. Equipment is generous, and there are no options. **Summary:** Four-wheel drive contributes to the stability and handling of the Lancer in this version, but it combined with the catalyst to take away most of the expected power advantage over the 1.5. At Birmingham 1990 the twin-cam 16-valve engine became available, front-drive only.

MITSUBISHI   (J)   Shogun Turbo D

Identity: When the new V6 Shogun was introduced in mid-1989, the diesel version was given extra power and torque, but continued with leaf-spring front suspension. Later, the same coil-spring suspension as that of the V6 was adopted for the diesel, and it won the Caravan Club's 1991 Best Diesel Towcar award.

Engine: Front-mounted longitudinal four-cylinder with single ohc and twin counter-rotating balance shafts; turbocharger and intercooler. Bore 91.1 mm, stroke 95.0 mm; capacity 2477 cc. Power 95 PS (70 kW) at 4200 rpm; torque 173 lb ft (239 Nm) at 2000 rpm. Compression 21.0-to-1. Catalyst: not available.

Transmission: Four-wheel drive; five-speed manual gearbox. Automatic, optional extra. Low ratio transfer gearbox. Top gear speed at 1000 rpm: 20.8 mph (33.5 km/h).

Suspension: Front, independent, wishbones and torsion bars, anti-roll bar. Rear, live axle with three-link location with coil springs; twin anti-roll bars.

Steering: Recirculating ball. Power assistance: standard. **Brakes:** Vented discs front, drums rear. ABS: not available. **Tyres:** 205 R 16. **Fuel tank:** 20.2 Imp. gall (92 litres). **Unladen weight:** 4012 lb (1820 kg).

Dimensions: Length 181.1 in (4600 mm), width 66.1 in (1680 mm), height 74.0 in (1880 mm), wheelbase 106.1 in (2695 mm).

Performance *Autocar & Motor* test: Maximum speed 85 mph (137 km/h); 0 to 60 mph (97 km/h) 18.8 sec. Fuel consumption at constant 75 mph (120 km/h): 19.9 mpg; overall test, 20.2 mpg.

Features: Four-wheel drive is selectable, and self-cancelling freewheeling hubs save energy by stopping the front transmission when not in use.
Summary: With a very refined diesel engine, the Shogun is easy and relaxing to drive, despite its size. Excellent at towing, thanks to the good stability and generous torque of the turbo diesel engine.

MITSUBISHI (J)   Sigma

Identity: Moving upmarket into the luxury saloon class, Mitsubishi launched the Sigma at Paris 1990; on the British market from spring 1991. It introduces a number of new features, including Mitsubishi's Traction Control system and Trace control, adjusting traction and cornering forces in relation to available grip.

Engine: Front-mounted transverse V6-cylinder with alloy block and heads; twin ohc working 24 valves, electronic fuel injection, and varying induction control. Bore 91.1 mm, stroke 76.0 mm; capacity 2972 cc. Power 205 PS (151 kW) at 6000 rpm; torque 195 lb ft (270 Nm) at 3000 rpm. Compression 10.0-to-1. Catalyst: standard.

Transmission: Front-wheel drive; five-speed manual gearbox. Automatic, optional extra. Top gear speed at 1000 rpm: 24.0 mph (38.6 km/h).

Suspension: Front, independent, MacPherson struts, anti-roll bar. Computer control. Rear, independent, multi-link location, with coil springs and anti-roll bar. Computer control.

Steering: Rack and pinion. Power assistance: standard. **Brakes:** Vented discs front and rear. ABS: standard. **Tyres:** 205/65 R 15. **Fuel tank:** 15.8 Imp. gall (72 litres). **Unladen weight:** 3252 lb (1475 kg).

Dimensions: Length 187.0 in (4750 mm), width 69.9 in (1775 mm), height 56.5 in (1435 mm), wheelbase 107.1 in (2720 mm).

Performance Works: Maximum speed 143 mph (230 km/h); 0 to 62 mph (100 km/h) 8.1 sec. Fuel consumption at constant 75 mph (120 km/h): 31.7 mpg.

Features: Every conceivable item of luxury equipment is included plus many not so easily imagined, such as the four-wheel steering, advanced suspension control and anti-skid systems. **Summary:** Experienced on snowy roads in Switzerland, it gave traction and cornering grip that I would not have believed possible in such conditions with only two-wheel drive.

Identity: Launch of a new Morgan is a rare event indeed, as this company is steeped in tradition, and keeps on building the same unchanged sports cars year after year; but May 1988 brought a new version using the Rover M16 engine with four valves per cylinder. Choice of two or four seats.

Engine: Front-mounted longitudinal four-cylinder with belt-driven twin ohc operating four valves per cyl.; Lucas electronic injection and digital ignition. Bore 84.5 mm, stroke 89.0 mm; capacity 1994 cc. Power 140 PS (103 kW) at 6000 rpm; torque 131 lb ft (181 Nm) at 4500 rpm. Compression 10.0-to-1. Catalyst: not available.

Transmission: Rear-wheel drive; five-speed manual gearbox. Automatic, not available. Top gear speed at 1000 rpm: 25.5 mph (41.0 km/h).

Suspension: Front, independent, sliding pillars and coil springs. Rear, live axle on leaf springs with lever arm dampers.

Steering: Worm and roller. Power assistance: not available. **Brakes:** Solid discs front, drums rear. ABS: not available. **Tyres:** 195/60 R 15. **Fuel tank:** 12.5 Imp gall (56 litres). **Unladen weight:** 1984 lb (900 kg).

Dimensions: Length 153.1 in (3890 mm), width 59.0 in (1500 mm), height 50.0 in (1270 mm), wheelbase 96.0 in (2440 mm).

Performance *Autocar & Motor* test: Maximum speed 109 mph (175 km/h); 0 to 60 mph (97 km/h) 7.7 sec; 80 mph (130 km/h) 13.6 sec. Fuel consumption: no data.

Features: Very basic weather protection, but this is essentially a fun car, bought for prestige and show rather than for serious all-weather motoring. **Summary:** Rover's beefy 16-valve engine suits the character of the Morgan very well, and tried at Brands Hatch circuit it proved exciting to drive, reaching 100 mph on the top straight. But limitations of ride and handling remain.

NISSAN (J)   Maxima

Identity: Quietly introduced to the market with minimal publicity in mid-1989, the Maxima contends for the executive market and tries to compete with exotic European cars which it cannot beat on sheer pleasure of driving, although it is very strong on comfort and refinement.

Engine: Front-mounted transverse V6-cylinder with alloy head and single ohc per bank. Electronic fuel injection. Bore 87.0 mm, stroke 83.0 mm; capacity 2960 cc. Power 172 PS (126 kW) at 5600 rpm; torque 182 lb ft (252 Nm) at 2800 rpm. Compression 10.0-to-1. Catalyst: not available.

Transmission: Front-wheel drive; four-speed automatic, standard. Top gear speed at 1000 rpm: 29.2 mph (47.0 km/h).

Suspension: Front, independent, MacPherson struts, anti-roll bar. Rear, independent, struts with parallel transverse links; anti-roll bar.

Steering: Rack and pinion. Power assistance: standard. **Brakes:** Vented discs front, solid discs rear. ABS: standard. **Tyres:** 205/65 VR 15. **Fuel tank:** 15.4 Imp. gall (70 litres). **Unladen weight:** 3130 lb (1420 kg).

Dimensions: Length 188.2 in (4780 mm), width 69.3 in (1760 mm), height 55.3 in (4470 mm), wheelbase 104.3 in (2649 mm).

Performance *Autocar & Motor* test: Maximum speed 119 mph (192 km/h); 0 to 60 mph (97 km/h) 9.4 sec; 80 mph (130 km/h) 16.6 sec. Fuel consumption at constant 75 mph (120 km/h): 32.1 mpg; overall test, 16.8 mpg.

Features: Comfortably furnished and comprehensively equipped, with such items as electric seat adjustment, air conditioning and cruise control. **Summary:** A car of strong appeal to those who want an impressive specification with no extras to pay for; but I thought the ride disappointing and the car generally a little uninspiring.

NISSAN   (J)   Prairie 4 × 4

Identity: A much more stylish and aerodynamic version of the spacious multi-seat Prairie was launched Paris 1988. It is a more advanced vehicle, with choice of front-wheel or four-wheel drive, and there are two trim levels, LX and SLX. 2-litre engine with carb. or injection.

Engine: Front-mounted longitudinal four-cylinder with single overhead camshaft and electronic fuel injection. Bore 84.5 mm, stroke 88.0 mm; capacity 1973 cc. Power 91 PS (67 kW) at 5200 rpm; torque 107 lb ft (148 Nm) at 2800 rpm. Compression 8.5-to-1. Catalyst: not available.

Transmission: Four-wheel drive; five-speed manual gearbox. Automatic, four-speed optional.

Suspension: Front, independent, MacPherson struts. Rear, independent, MacPherson struts and parallel links; anti-roll bar.

Steering: Rack and pinion. Power assistance: standard. **Brakes:** Vented discs front, drums rear. ABS: not available. **Tyres:** 185/70 R 14. **Fuel tank:** 13.2 Imp. gall (60 litres). **Unladen weight:** 2668 lb (1210 kg).

Dimensions: Length 171.2 in (4350 mm), width 66.5 in (1690 mm), height 64.0 in (1625 mm), wheelbase 102.8 in (2610 mm).

Performance *Autocar & Motor* test (front drive, automatic): maximum speed 97 mph (156 km/h); 0 to 60 mph (97 km/h) 14.4 sec; 80 mph (130 km/h) 30.4 sec. Fuel consumption at constant 75 mph (120 km/h): 31.4 mpg; overall test, 20.6 mpg.

Features: Four-wheel drive version has viscous coupling for centre diff. Wide range of options, including electric sunroof. **Summary:** Original concept of the Prairie, to carry people in spacious comfort, applies as before, and there is the same versatility to fold seats forward for extra luggage space, or to rearrange them as a bed. Two versions offer seating for five or seven to choice. With the automatic, top speed was reached in third.

NISSAN   (GB, J)   Primera 1.6LS

Identity: This new range of saloon and hatchback models was launched Birmingham 1990, to succeed the Bluebird. Front-wheel drive and choice of 1.6- or 2.0-litre engines, both with 16 valves. Best value is at the lower end of the range. Choice of L, LS, GS, GSX and even ZX trim.

Engine: Front-mounted transverse four-cylinder with alloy head and twin ohc working four valves per cylinder. Twin-choke carb. Bore 76.0 mm, stroke 86.0 mm; capacity 1597 cc. Power 95 PS (70 kW) at 6000 rpm; torque 100 lb ft (138 Nm) at 4000 rpm. Compression 9.8-to-1. Catalyst: optional.

Transmission: Front-wheel drive; five-speed manual gearbox. Automatic, optional extra on 2-litre only. Top gear speed at 1000 rpm: 22.7 mph (36.6 km/h).

Suspension: Front, independent, MacPherson struts with multi-link location; anti-roll bar. Rear, independent, struts with parallel links; anti-roll bar.

Steering: Rack and pinion. Power assistance: standard. **Brakes:** Vented discs front, solid discs rear. ABS: not available. **Tyres:** 165 R 13. **Fuel tank:** 13.2 Imp. gall (60 litres). **Unladen weight:** 2375 lb (1077 kg).

Dimensions: Length 173.2 in (4400 mm), width 66.9 in (1700 mm), height 54.7 in (1390 mm), wheelbase 100.4 in (2550 mm).

Performance *Autocar & Motor* test: Maximum speed 111 mph (179 km/h); 0 to 60 mph (97 km/h) 12.4 sec; 80 mph (130 km/h) 22.1 sec. Fuel consumption at constant 75 mph (120 km/h): 42.2 mpg; overall test, 29.2 mpg.

Features: Neat finish and quite generous equipment, even at the LS level, includes such items as sunroof and tilt-adjustable steering column. **Summary:** Perhaps it's because the Primera does everything unobtrusively well that it seems somewhat lacking in character; even with the 16-valve engine, performance is unremarkable. The engine is extremely smooth, and all controls are precise, making it an easy car to drive.

NISSAN (J)   Sunny 100NX 1.6 Coupé

Identity: Replacement Sunny range introduced February 1991 offers 1.4 LS with three, four or five doors, 1.6 GS four- or five-door, and this attractive little coupé, the 100 NX. There are deep scoops for the headlamps; otherwise it's pleasantly styled.

Engine: Front-mounted transverse four-cylinder with alloy block and twin ohc working four valves per cylinder; single point fuel injection. Bore 76.0 mm, stroke 88.0 mm; capacity 1597 cc. Power 95 PS (70 kW) at 6000 rpm; torque 97 lb ft (134 Nm) at 4000 rpm. Compression 9.8-to-1. Catalyst: standard.

Transmission: Front-wheel drive; five-speed manual gearbox. Automatic, optional extra. Top gear speed at 1000 rpm: 21.1 mph (33.9 km/h).

Suspension: Front, independent, MacPherson struts. Rear, independent, parallel links.

Steering: Rack and pinion. Power assistance: standard. **Brakes:** Vented discs front, drums rear. ABS: not available. **Tyres:** 155 SR 13. **Fuel tank:** 11.0 Imp. gall (50 litres). **Unladen weight:** 2072 lb (940 kg).

Dimensions: Length 162.8 in (4135 mm), width 65.7 in (1670 mm), height 51.6 in (1310 mm), wheelbase 95.7 in (2430 mm).

Performance Works: Maximum speed 112 mph (180 km/h); 0 to 62 mph (100 km/h) 10.8 sec. Fuel consumption at constant 75 mph (120 km/h): 40.9 mpg.

Features: Sporty appearance inside, with wrap-round seats and good instrumentation. T-bar roof with removable panels as illustrated is an option. **Summary:** The unhappy dispute between the European HQ and the British importer put rather a damper on the launch. The new Sunny appeared clearly over-priced, taking away the attraction, with the Coupé priced over £15,000 with UK taxes.

Identity: Replacement for the Silvia Turbo 1.8ZX, the 200 SX was launched Birmingham 1988; on market early 1989 as a stylish 2 + 2 sports coupé, again with 1.8 turbo engine. Bumpers are colour keyed, and there are deeply recessed side and indicator lamps, with pop-up headlamps.

Engine: Front-mounted longitudinal four-cylinder with twin ohc operating four valves per cylinder. Electronic injection/ignition and turbocharger. Bore 83.0 mm, stroke 83.6 mm; capacity 1809 cc. Power 171 PS (126 kW) at 6400 rpm; torque 165 lb ft (228 Nm) at 4000 rpm. Compression 8.5-to-1. Catalyst: not available.

Transmission: Rear-wheel drive; five-speed manual gearbox. Automatic, four-speed optional. Top gear speed at 1000 rpm: 23.6 mph (37.9 km/h).

Suspension: Front, independent, MacPherson struts, anti-roll bar. Rear, independent, multi-link location; coil springs, anti-roll bar.

Steering: Rack and pinion. Power assistance: standard. **Brakes:** Vented discs front, solid discs rear, servo-assisted. ABS: standard. **Tyres:** 195/60 VR 15. **Fuel tank:** 13.2 Imp. gall (60 litres). **Unladen weight:** 2623 lb (1190 kg).

Dimensions: Length 178.5 in (4535 mm), width 66.5 in (1690 mm), height 50.8 in (1290 mm), wheelbase 97.4 in (2475 mm).

Performance *Autocar & Motor* test: Maximum speed 140 mph (225 km/h); 0 to 60 mph (97 km/h) 7.2 sec; 80 mph (130 km/h) 11.9 sec. Fuel consumption at constant 75 mph (120 km/h): 34.9; overall test, 19.3 mpg.

Features: Boomerang-shaped rear spoiler and generally smooth shape contribute to 0.30 CD factor. Full instrumentation and equipment.
Summary: A most exciting GT to drive, with vigorous performance and very pleasing handling and controls. It achieved a well-deserved place in the Guild's Top Ten for 1990.

NISSAN (J)   300 ZX

Identity: Supplementing the successful and widely acclaimed 200 SX, Nissan launched another exciting GT at Geneva 1989. Called the 300 ZX, it has very shapely styling for its 2 + 2 bodywork, and offers very high performance. As for the 200 SX, it has rear drive. In UK February 1990.

Engine: Front-mounted longitudinal V6-cylinder with alloy heads and twin ohc per bank, working four valves per cylinder. Electronic fuel injection. Twin turbochargers. Bore 87.0 mm, stroke 83.0 mm; capacity 2960 cc. Power 280 PS (205 kW) at 6400 rpm; torque 269 lb ft (372 Nm) at 3600 rpm. Compression 8.5-to-1. Catalyst: standard.

Transmission: Rear-wheel drive; five-speed manual gearbox. Automatic, optional extra. Top gear speed at 1000 rpm: 23.4 mph (37.7 km/h).

Suspension: Front, independent, multi-link wheel location with coil springs and anti-roll bar. Rear, independent, multi-link location, coil springs; anti-roll bar.

Steering: Rack and pinion with computer-controlled rear-wheel steering. Power assistance: standard. **Brakes:** Vented discs front, and rear. ABS: standard. **Tyres:** 225/50 (front), 245/45 (rear) ZR 16. **Fuel tank:** 15.8 Imp. gall (72 litres). **Unladen weight:** 3494 lb (1585 kg).

Dimensions: Length 178.0 in (2570 mm), width 70.9 in (1800 mm), height 49.4 in (1255 mm), wheelbase 101.2 in (2570 mm).

Performance *Autocar & Motor* test: Maximum speed 143 mph (230 km/h); 0 to 60 mph (97 km/h) 7.0 sec; 80 mph (130 km/h) 11.9 sec. Fuel consumption at 75 mph (120 km/h): 26.9 mpg; overall test, 19.2 mpg.

Features: Called Super HICAS, the four-wheel steering system is ingeniously arranged to contribute better high speed stability. Luxurious interior and very comprehensive specification. **Summary:** A very interesting car, introducing a number of novel features in addition to the computer-controlled all-wheel steering. Minor controls on pods within reach of hands on the wheel, double-cone synchromesh in the gearbox, and optional five-speed automatic.

OLDSMOBILE (USA)   Bravada

Identity: Described as 'another new Oldsmobile thrust into a fresh area of the marketplace', the Bravada was added to the range for 1991, featuring a V6 engine and permanent four-wheel drive. It is not very inspiring to look at, but promises roominess and ruggedness.

Engine: Front-mounted longitudinal V6-cylinder with central camshaft and pushrod overhead valves; hydraulic tappets. Electronic fuel injection. Bore 101.6 mm, stroke 88.4 mm; capacity 4300 cc. Power 162 PS (119 kW) at 4000 rpm; torque 230 lb ft (318 Nm) at 2800 rpm. Compression 9.3-to-1. Catalyst: standard.

Transmission: Four-wheel drive; four-speed automatic, standard. Electronically controlled torque converter lock-up. Top gear speed at 1000 rpm: 34.2 mph (55.0 km/h).

Suspension: Front, independent, wishbones and torsion bars; anti-roll bar. Rear, live axle on semi-elliptic leaf springs.

Steering: Recirculating ball. Power assistance: standard. **Brakes:** Solid discs front, drums rear. ABS: standard. **Tyres:** P235/75 R 15. **Fuel tank:** 16.7 Imp. gall (76 litres). **Unladen weight:** 3720 lb (1687 kg).

Dimensions: Length 178.9 in (4544 mm), width 65.2 in (1656 mm), height 65.6 in (1666 mm), wheelbase 107.0 in (2717 mm).

Performance (est): Maximum speed 105 mph (169 km/h); 0 to 60 mph (97 km/h) 12.0 sec. Fuel consumption overall (est): 20 mpg.

Features: Four-wheel drive is permanently engaged, using a centre viscous coupling. Bucket seats are fitted, with leather trim optional. **Summary:** This is a fairly late entry into a market already well supplied with a big choice of Japanese and British off-road vehicles. A more original design might have been expected from the vast Oldsmobile resources.

PEUGEOT (F)   *205 CTI Cabriolet*

Identity: At the end of summer 1986, Peugeot brought the charming little CTI convertible to the British market. Performance and sporting handling of the 1.6-litre GTI three-door, with open bodywork, and I am the delighted owner of one. Fixed roll bar; electric hood operation was introduced Geneva 1990. Not available as 1.9.

Engine: Front-mounted transverse four-cylinder with alloy head and block; wet cylinder liners. Belt-driven ohc. Bosch L-Jetronic fuel injection. Bore 83.0 mm, stroke 73.0 mm; capacity 1580 cc. Power 115 PS (86 kW) at 6250 rpm; torque 98 lb ft (135 Nm) at 4000 rpm. Compression 9.8-to-1. Catalyst: not available.

Transmission: Front-wheel drive; five-speed manual gearbox. No automatic transmission option. Top gear speed at 1000 rpm: 18.7 mph (30.1 km/h).

Suspension: Front, independent, MacPherson struts; anti-roll bar. Rear, independent, trailing arms and transverse torsion bars; telescopic dampers; anti-roll bar.

Steering: Rack and pinion. Power assistance: not available. **Brakes:** Vented discs front, drums rear. ABS: not available. **Tyres:** 185/60 HR 14. **Fuel tank:** 11.0 Imp. gall (50 litres). **Unladen weight:** 1953 lb (884 kg).

Dimensions: Length 145.9 in (3706 mm), width 61.9 in (1572 mm), height 53.3 in (1354 mm), wheelbase 95.3 in (2421 mm).

Performance *Autocar & Motor* test: Maximum speed 116 mph (187 km/h); 0 to 60 mph (97 km/h) 8.9 sec; 80 mph (130 km/h) 15.6 sec. Fuel consumption at constant 75 mph (120 km/h): 37.7 mpg; overall test, 30.7 mpg.

Features: Teppelux-lined PVC hood with flexible rear window. Rear side windows can be lowered. Rear seats fold to extend boot space.
Summary: Very pleasant to drive with hood down, yet also snug and draughtproof when closed, although there is then a lot of extra wind noise.

PEUGEOT   (F)   205 D Turbo

Identity: Having a Peugeot 205 GRD in the family, I have often wondered what it would be like if the turbocharged version of the 1.8-litre diesel could be squeezed in. Then, at Paris 1990, this very concept was added to the range, though without intercooler. On the British market early 1991.

Engine: Front-mounted transverse four-cylinder with alloy head and belt-driven ohc. Bosch or Lucas fuel injection, and KKK-K14 turbocharger. Bore 80.0 mm, stroke 88.0 mm; capacity 1769 cc. Power 78 PS (57.5 kW) at 4300 rpm; torque 114 lb ft (157 Nm) at 2100 rpm. Compression 22.0-to-1. Catalyst: not available.

Transmission: Front-wheel drive; five-speed manual gearbox. Automatic, not available. Top gear speed at 1000 rpm: 24.5 mph (39.4 km/h).

Suspension: Front, independent, MacPherson struts, anti-roll bar. Rear, independent, trailing arms and transverse torsion bars.

Steering: Rack and pinion. Power assistance: optional. **Brakes:** Solid discs front, drums rear. ABS: not available. **Tyres:** 165/65 R 14. **Fuel tank:** 11.0 Imp. gall (50 litres). **Unladen weight:** 2030 lb (920 kg).

Dimensions: Length 145.9 in (3706 mm), width 61.9 in (1572 mm), height 53.9 in (1369 mm), wheelbase 95.3 in (2421 mm).

Performance Works: Maximum speed 109 mph (175 km/h); 0 to 62 mph (100 km/h) 12.2 sec. Fuel consumption at constant 75 mph (120 km/h): 42.8 mpg.

Features: GTI-type skirt is fitted at the front, housing two long-range spot lamps. The name on the boot shows '205 D' in grey, and 'Turbo' in red. **Summary:** Improved instrumentation for this more sporty version of the popular 205 diesel includes a rev counter, and seats are upholstered in two-tone velour. The D Turbo should prove an ideal long-distance commuting car.

PEUGEOT (F)   205 GTI 1.9

Identity: During 1986 the power of the 1-6-litre GTI engine was increased to 115 PS, and then a new high performance version with 1.9-litre injection engine was launched Birmingham 1986, in production December—a superb little flyer! Supplementing the 205 GTI 1.6, it came on to the British market from beginning of 1987.

Engine: Front-mounted transverse four-cylinder with alloy head and block; wet cylinder liners. Belt-driven ohc. Bosch L-Jetronic fuel injection. Bore 83.0 mm, stroke 88.0 mm; capacity 1905 cc. Power 130 PS (96 kW) at 6000 rpm; torque 119 lb ft (165 Nm) at 4750 rpm. Compression 9.6-to-1. Catalyst: optional.

Transmission: Front-wheel drive; five-speed manual gearbox. No automatic transmission option. Top gear speed at 1000 rpm: 20.9 mph (33.6 km/h).

Suspension: Front, independent, MacPherson struts; anti-roll bar. Rear, independent, trailing arms and transverse torsion bars; anti-roll bar.

Steering: Rack and pinion. Power assistance: not available. **Brakes:** Vented discs front, solid rear. ABS: not available. **Tyres:** 185/55 VR 15. **Fuel tank:** 11.0 Imp. gall (50 litres). **Unladen weight:** 1929 lb (875 kg).

Dimensions: Length 145.9 in (3706 mm), width 61.9 in (1572 mm), height 53.3 in (1354 mm), wheelbase 95.3 in (2421 mm).

Performance *Autocar & Motor* test: Maximum speed 120 mph (193 km/h); 0 to 60 mph (97 km/h) 7.8 sec; 80 mph (130 km/h) 13.7 sec. Fuel consumption at constant 75 mph (120 km/h): 36.7 mpg. Overall test, 28.1 mpg.

Features: Luxury interior, including leather-trimmed wheel, and seats with velour facings and leather side cushions. Sunroof optional. **Summary:** Delightful car to drive with its very responsive and smooth engine bringing new boost of power to the already quick GTI. Contender for the title of 'most desirable hot hatchback'.

Identity: One of the criticisms of Peugeot's superbly responsive and fast 309 GTI was answered at Motorfair 1989 when the tailgate was continued down between the tail lamps, making loading up easier. The spoiler, previously at the base of the rear window, became a separate wing at the back.

Engine: Front-mounted transverse four-cylinder with alloy block and head. Single ohc and Bosch LE2 fuel injection. Bore 83.0 mm, stroke 88.0 mm; capacity 1905 cc. Power 130 PS (96 kW) at 6000 rpm; torque 119 lb ft (165 Nm) at 4750 rpm. Compression 9.6-to-1. Catalyst: optional.

Transmission: Front-wheel drive; five-speed manual gearbox. Automatic, not available. Top gear speed at 1000 rpm: 20.9 mph (33.6 km/h).

Suspension: Front, independent, MacPherson struts, anti-roll bar. Rear, independent, trailing arms and transverse torsion bars, anti-roll bar.

Steering: Rack and pinion. Power assistance: standard. **Brakes:** Vented discs front, solid discs rear. ABS: not available. **Tyres:** 185/55 HR 15. **Fuel tank:** 12.1 Imp. gall (55 litres). **Unladen weight:** 2050 lb (930 kg).

Dimensions: Length 159.4 in (4051 mm), width 64.0 in (1628 mm), height 54.3 in (1380 mm), wheelbase 97.2 in (2469 mm).

Performance *Autocar & Motor* test: Maximum speed 119 mph (191 km/h); 0 to 60 mph (97 km/h) 8.7 sec; 80 mph (130 km/h) 15.6 sec. Fuel consumption at constant 75 mph (120 km/h): 36.2 mpg; overall test, 28.2 mpg.

Features: Improved specification for 1990 brought in electric windows and central locking as standard, previously options. Sliding glass sunroof is also provided. **Summary:** Very attractive car offering a good combination of speed, handling and comfort. Tends to get a bit busy on a motorway journey, but great fun on twisting roads, with the inevitable penalty of rather firm ride.

PEUGEOT (GB, F) 405 GL × 4

Identity: Impressive four-wheel drive versions were added to the 405 range in March 1989, and the GL × 4 is essentially a 'working' car, rather than a prestige model, to give very competent road behaviour and the traction to keep going in all conditions.

Engine: Front-mounted transverse four-cylinder with alloy block and head. Single ohc carburettor. Bore 83.0 mm, stroke 88.0 mm; capacity 1905 cc. Power 110 PS (81 kW) at 6000 rpm; torque 119 lb ft (165 Nm) at 3000 rpm. Compression 9.3-to-1. Catalyst: not available.

Transmission: Four-wheel drive; five-speed manual gearbox. Automatic, not available. Lockable centre and rear diffs. Top gear speed at 1000 rpm: 22.0 mph (35.4 km/h).

Suspension: Front, independent, MacPherson struts, anti-roll bar. Rear, independent, trailing arms and electrically pressurised gas springs with hydrauulic self-levelling; anti-roll bar.

Steering: Rack and pinion. Power assistance: standard. **Brakes:** Vented discs front, solid discs rear. ABS: optional. **Tyres:** 185/65 R 14T. **Fuel tank:** 15.4 Imp. gall (70 litres). **Unladen weight:** 2557 lb (1160 kg).

Dimensions: Length 173.5 in (4408 mm), width 67.5 in (1714 mm), height 55.1 (1400 mm), wheelbase 105.0 in (2667 mm).

Performance *Autocar & Motor* test: Maximum speed 115 mph (185 km/h); 0 to 60 mph (97 km/h) 10.9 sec; 80 mph (130 km/h) 20.3 sec. Fuel consumption at constant 75 mph (120 km/h): 34.5 mpg; overall test, 24.4 mpg.

Features: Equipment is the same as for the front-drive GL and includes remote control central locking and electric glass sunroof. **Summary:** Four-wheel drive plus the oleo-pneumatic rear suspension with self-levelling achieves a tremendous improvement to the handling of the already good 405, and makes this a most attractive and competent car.

PEUGEOT (F, GB)   405 GTDT

Identity: In July 1988 I ran an extended economy test for Lucas on a Peugeot 405 GTDT equipped with their new Epic fuel pump, and travelled 1,118 miles on a tankful, at 73.4 mpg. Later, the same car lapped Millbrook test track at 113 mph—highly impressive for a 1.8-litre diesel.

Engine: Front-mounted transverse four-cylinder with cast iron block and alloy head; belt-driven single ohc. KKK or Garrett Turbocharger, with inter-cooler. Bore 80.0 mm, stroke 88.0 mm; capacity 1769 cc. Power 92 PS (67 kW) at 4300 rpm; torque 132 lb ft (183 Nm) at 2200 rpm. Compression 22.0-to-1. Fuel: Derv.

Transmission: Front-wheel drive; five-speed manual gearbox. Automatic, not available. Top gear speed at 1000 rpm: 25.3 mph (40.7 km/h).

Suspension: Front, independent, MacPherson struts, anti-roll bar. Rear, independent, trailing arms, transverse torsion bars; anti-roll bar.

Steering: Rack and pinion. Power assistance: standard. **Brakes:** Vented discs front, drums rear. ABS: optional. **Tyres:** 185/66 HR 14. **Fuel tank:** 15.4 Imp. gall (70 litres). **Unladen weight:** 2680 lb (1215 kg).

Dimensions: Length 173.5 in (4408 mm), width 66.6 in (1694 mm), height 55.4 in (1406 mm), wheelbase 105.1 in (2669 mm).

Performance *Autocar & Motor* test: Maximum speed 108 mph (174 km/h); 0 to 62 mph (100 km/h) 12.2 sec; 80 mph (130 km/h) 23.5 sec. Fuel consumption at constant 75 mph (120 km/h): 45.6 mpg; overall test, 31.3 mpg.

Features: This is the top diesel of the 405 range, and it is well-equipped to the same level as the GTX. **Summary:** On that extended test run, the 405 GTDT proved very comfortable during long hours at the wheel, and the turbocharged diesel engine copes manfully with this big saloon.

Identity: As well as the GL version, the 405 is also available with four-wheel drive in Mi16 form, and with this 16-valve 160 bhp engine, the performance and handling are outstandingly good. Badge in red at rear of boot identifies the 4 × 4 version, and it differs from the GL in having a viscous coupling and Torsen rear diff.

Engine: Front-mounted transverse four-cylinder with alloy block and head. Twin ohc working four valves per cylinder; Bosch Motronic fuel injection. Bore 83.0 mm, stroke 88.0 mm; capacity 1905 cc. Power 160 PS (116 kW) at 6500 rpm; torque 133 lb ft (183 Nm) at 5000 rpm. Compression 10.4-to-1. Catalyst: optional.

Transmission: Four-wheel drive; five-speed manual gearbox. Automatic, not available. Self-blocking viscous differential control. Top gear speed at 1000 rpm: 20.0 mph (32.2 km/h).

Suspension: Front, independent, MacPherson struts, anti-roll bar. Rear, independent, trailing arms and electrically pressurised gas springs with hydraulic self-levelling; anti-roll bar.

Steering: Rack and pinion. Power assistance: standard. **Brakes:** Vented discs front, solid discs rear. ABS: standard. **Tyres:** 195/55 R 15V. **Fuel tank:** 15.4 Imp. gall (70 litres). **Unladen weight:** 2734 lb (1240 kg).

Dimensions: Length 173.5 in (4408 mm), width 67.6 in (1716 mm), height 55.1 in (1400 mm), wheelbase 105.0 in (2667 mm).

Performance *Autocar & Motor* test: Maximum speed 127 mph (204 km/h); 0 to 60 mph (97 km/h) 9.5 sec; 80 mph (130 km/h) 16.5 sec. Fuel consumption at constant 75 mph (120 km/h): 33.2 mpg; overall test, 26.0 mpg.

Features: Equipment is the same as for the front-drive Mi16, and is very comprehensive; air conditioning and leather seats with heating are about the only options to be considered. **Summary:** An outstandingly safe car with magnificent handling, and still very fast although of course the extra weight and resistance take away some of the Mi16 sparkle.

Identity: France's new big car—in addition to the Citroen XM—to fight back against Jaguar, BMW, Mercedes, is the 605, launched Frankfurt 1989, and on British market from May 1990. In this form as the SRi, it is aimed firmly at the executive fleet market. It bears family resemblance to the 405, but is sufficiently different not to be confused with it.

Engine: Front-mounted transverse four-cylinder with alloy head and single ohc. Bosch LE2 fuel injection. Bore 86.0 mm, stroke 86.0 mm; capacity 1998 cc. Power 94 PS (68 kW) at 5600 rpm; torque 175 lb ft (242 Nm) at 4800 rpm. Compression 8.8-to-1. Catalyst: standard.

Transmission: Front-wheel drive; five-speed manual gearbox. Automatic, not available. Top gear speed at 1000 rpm: 20.3 mph (32.7 km/h).

Suspension: Front, independent, MacPherson struts, anti-roll bar. Rear, independent, wishbones and coil springs; anti-roll bar.

Steering: Rack and pinion. Power assistance: standard. **Brakes:** Vented discs front, solid discs rear. ABS: optional. **Tyres:** 195/65 R 15H. **Fuel tank:** 17.6 Imp. gall (80 litres). **Unladen weight:** 2920 lb (1325 kg).

Dimensions: Length 185.9 in (4723 mm), width 70.8 in (1799 mm), height 55.8 in (1417 mm), wheelbase 110.2 in (2800 mm).

Performance *Autocar & Motor* test: Maximum speed 121 mph (195 km/h); 0 to 60 mph (97 km/h) 11.8 sec; 80 mph (130 km/h) 20.2 sec. Fuel consumption at constant 75 mph (120 km/h): 32.1 mpg; overall test, 24.7 mpg.

Features: SRi is the sporting model of the 605 range and has intermediate level equipment with such features as outside temperature gauge, and seats with height adjustment. **Summary:** Smooth, rapid transport with generous five-seater space, and good handling. The optional four-speed automatic transmission is also outstandingly good.

PEUGEOT (F)   605 SV24

Identity: Luxury model of the new 605 range is the SV24, with 24-valve V6 engine, giving really vigorous performance. There is also an intermediate V6 with 12 valves, offered in the SR3.0 and SV3.0. The standard 3-litre goes well, but as the SV24 with the multi-valve heads it's very quick indeed.

Engine: Front-mounted transverse V6-cylinder with alloy heads and block; single ohc per bank, working four valves per cylinder. Fenix 4 fuel injection. Bore 93.0 mm, stroke 73.0 mm; capacity 2975 cc. Power 147 PS (106 kW) at 6000 rpm; torque 260 lb ft (360 Nm) at 4800 rpm. Compression 9.5-to-1. Catalyst: standard.

Transmission: Front-wheel drive; five-speed manual gearbox. Automatic, optional. Top gear speed at 1000 rpm: 22.9 mph (36.9 km/h).

Suspension: Front, independent, MacPherson struts with automatic damper control; anti-roll bar. Rear, independent, wishbones and coil springs with automatic damper control; anti-roll bar.

Steering: Rack and pinion. Power assistance: standard. **Brakes:** Vented discs front, solid discs rear. ABS: standard. **Tyres:** 205/55 R 16V. **Fuel tank:** 17.6 Imp. gall (80 litres). **Unladen weight:** 3220 lb (1460 kg).

Dimensions: Length 185.9 in (4723 mm), width 70.8 in (1799 mm), height 55.5 in (1411 mm), wheelbase 110.2 in (2800 mm).

Performance Works: Maximum speed 146 mph (235 km/h); 0 to 62 mph (100 km/h) 8.0 sec. Fuel consumption at constant 75 mph (120 km/h): 29.4 mpg.

Features: Luxurious trim and equipment in this top version of the 605, includes leather upholstery and electric sunroof. **Summary:** With the 24-valve engine, the 605 gives really vigorous response and is a strong contender for the senior executive market. On the launch in Egypt I was most impressed by the SV24's comfort and stability when cruising at 120 mph.

PONTIAC (USA)   Trans Sport SE

Identity: Until it appeared in the new Pontiac line-up, I had never thought of the word 'transport' as a 'sport' derivative; but it's appropriate for this stylish looking multi-seater from GM. It is very similar to the Oldsmobile Silhouette, but there are differences, and SE gets six individual seats. Larger, electrically adjustable mirrors added for 1991.

Engine: Front-mounted transverse V6-cylinder with alloy heads and central camshaft; pushrod ohv and hydraulic tappets. Rochester throttle body fuel injection. Bore 88.9 mm, stroke 84.0 mm; capacity 3128 cc. Power 120 PS (88 kW) at 4200 rpm; torque 175 lb ft (242 Nm) at 2200 rpm. Compression 8.9-to-1. Catalyst: standard.

Transmission: Front-wheel drive; three-speed automatic, standard. Top gear speed at 1000 rpm: 25.5 mph (41.0 km/h).

Suspension: Front, independent, MacPherson struts, anti-roll bar. Rear, dead beam axle on trailing arms with coil springs and anti-roll bar. Self-levelling standard on SE.

Steering: Rack and pinion. Power assistance: standard. **Brakes:** Vented discs front, drums rear. ABS: not available. **Tyres:** P195/70 R 15. **Fuel tank:** 16.7 Imp. gall (76 litres). **Unladen weight:** 3500 lb (1588 kg).

Dimensions: Length 194.5 in (4940 mm), width 74.2 in (1885 mm), height 65.5 in (1664 mm), wheelbase 109.9 in (2791 mm).

Performance (est): Maximum speed 105 mph (169 km/h). Fuel consumption overall (est), 25.0 mpg.

Features: Main difference between SE and standard Trans Sport is that the SE gets 'modular' seating; standard has a mid-mounted bench seat. **Summary:** In America this body style is referred to as a 'minivan'; but it's more of an Espace-style spacious executive or family high-top with low-drag shape. The body, as for the Silhouette, is in composite.

Identity: Traditionally, the 'RS' designation is reserved by Porsche for lighter and more powerful versions of a standard model; the 911 Carrera in RS form was launched Birmingham 1990. It has 10 PS extra power, while weight is reduced by 10 per cent. Production begins summer 1991.

Engine: Rear-mounted longitudinal flat six-cylinder with air cooling and dry sump lubrication. Bosch Motronics and twin ignition system. Bore 100.0 mm, stroke 76.4 mm; capacity 3600 cc. Power 260 PS (191 kW) at 6100 rpm; torque 227 lb ft (314 Nm) at 5000 rpm. Compression 11.3-to-1. Catalyst: standard.

Transmission: Rear-wheel drive; five-speed manual gearbox. Automatic, not available for RS. Top gear speed at 1000 rpm: 24.1 mph (38.9 km/h).

Suspension: Front, independent, struts with torsion bars; anti-roll bar. Rear, independent, semi-trailing arms and torsion bars; anti-roll bar.

Steering: Rack and pinion. Power assistance: standard. **Brakes:** Vented and cross-drilled discs front and rear. ABS: standard. **Tyres:** 205/50 (front); 255/40 (rear) ZR 17. **Fuel tank:** 16.7 Imp. gall (76 litres). **Unladen weight:** 2755 lb (1250 kg).

Dimensions: Length 168.9 in (4291 mm), width 65.0 in (1650 mm), height 51.6 in (1310 mm), wheelbase 89.5 in (2273 mm).

Performance Works: Maximum speed 162 mph (261 km/h); 0 to 62 mph (100 km/h) 5.4 sec. Fuel consumption at constant 75 mph (120 km/h): 29.7 mpg.

Features: Manually adjustable turbo-look mirrors are one of the few external distinguishing features of the RS. Front bonnet is in aluminium. Rear spoiler rises automatically at 50 mph. **Summary:** This is the Porsche for the driver who wants to get a move on! Chassis is tuned for the higher performance, with stiffer springs and dampers, and ride height is lowered by 40 mm.

Identity: So successful did the 928 GT prove after its introduction in early 1989 that it was decided to cease other versions of the 928 and concentrate on the GT. It was developed from the 928S Series 4 featured in the 1989 edition, but power went up again, now 330 bhp.

Engine: Front-mounted longitudinal V8-cylinder with all alloy construction. Chain and toothed belt drive to twin ohc each bank, working four valves per cylinder. Bosch LH Jetronic injection. Bore 100.0 mm, stroke 78.9 mm; capacity 4957 cc. Power 330 PS (243 kW) at 6200 rpm; torque 317 lb ft (430 Nm) at 4100 rpm. Compression 10.0-to-1. Catalyst: standard.

Transmission: Rear-wheel drive; five-speed manual gearbox. Automatic, optional extra. Top gear speed at 1000 rpm: 26.1 mph (42.0 km/h).

Suspension: Front, independent, wishbones and coil springs; anti-roll bar. Rear, independent, semi-trailing arms and upper transverse links; coil springs with self-levelling provision; anti-roll bar.

Steering: Rack and pinion. Power assistance: standard. **Brakes:** Vented discs front, and rear. ABS: standard. **Tyres:** 225/50 (front), 245/45 (rear) ZR 16. **Fuel tank:** 19.0 Imp. gall (86 litres). **Unladen weight:** 3484 lb (1580 kg).

Dimensions: Length 177.9 in (4520 mm), width 72.8 in (1836 mm), height 50.5 in (1282 mm), wheelbase 98.4 in (2500 mm).

Performance *Autocar & Motor* test: Maximum speed 165 mph (266 km/h); 0 to 60 mph (97 km/h) 5.6 sec; 80 mph (130 km/h) 8.9 sec. Fuel consumption at constant 75 mph (120 km/h): 23.5 mpg; overall test, 14.2 mpg.

Features: Gearbox is rear-mounted in transaxle. Tyre pressure monitoring system standard. Facia has been revised to allow possible future fitting of an air bag safety system. **Summary:** Still one of the fastest and safest cars on the road; but with the higher performance and catalyst, consumption has now become rather tediously heavy. Electronically controlled rear diff. lockup is standard.

PORSCHE (D)   944 S2 3.0

Identity: Originally, the Porsche 944 was a 2½-litre; but in this form with catalyst, it has 3-litre capacity and gives 211 bhp. It is available with cabriolet bodywork, and electric hood, as covered in the 1989 edition, or as this coupé with the characteristic rounded rear window.

Engine: Front-mounted longitudinal four-cylinder with all-alloy construction and belt-driven twin ohc working four valves per cylinder. Bosch Motronics. Bore 104.0 mm, stroke 88.0 mm; capacity 2990 cc. Power 211 PS (155 kW) at 5800 rpm; torque 207 lb ft (280 Nm) at 4100 rpm. Compression 10.9-to-1. Catalyst: standard.

Transmission: Rear-wheel drive; five-speed manual gearbox. Automatic, not available. Top gear speed at 1000 rpm: 23.9 mph (38.5 km/h).

Suspension: Front, independent, MacPherson struts; anti-roll bar. Rear, independent, semi-trailing arms and torsion bars; anti-roll bar.

Steering: Rack and pinion. Power assistance: standard. **Brakes:** Vented discs front and rear. ABS: standard. **Tyres:** 205/55 (front), 225/50 (rear) ZR 16. **Fuel tank:** 17.6 Imp. gall (80 litres). **Unladen weight:** 2955 lb (1340 kg).

Dimensions: Length 165.3 in (4200 mm), width 68.3 in (1735 mm), height 50.2 in (1275 mm), wheelbase 94.5 in (2400 mm).

Performance *Autocar & Motor* test: Maximum speed 146 mph (235 km/h); 0 to 60 mph (97 km/h) 6.0 sec; 80 mph (130 km/h) 9.7 sec. Fuel consumption at constant 75 mph (120 km/h): 31.0 mpg; overall test, 20.7 mpg.

Features: Gearbox is rear-mounted in a transaxle. Bodywork is the same as for the 944 Turbo; fog and driving lamps are mounted in the impact-absorbing nose section. **Summary:** More advanced and refined version of the 944, supplied as standard with anti-theft system, automatic heating control, and electric height adjustment for front seats. Exciting performance to match the phenomenal road grip.

PROTON (MAL)   1.5 SE Triple Valve

Identity: The first new model to be launched in 1991 was Proton's new range with triple-valve engines, released at one minute past midnight on 31 December. I think most people may have been thinking of something else, or singing, at that time, but the new Proton is worth singing about!

Engine: Front-mounted transverse four-cylinder with alloy head and belt-driven single ohc working three valves per cylinder. Single choke carb. Bore 75.5 mm, stroke 82 mm; capacity 1468 cc. Power 87 PS (64 kW) at 6000 rpm; torque 87 lb ft (120 Nm) at 4000 rpm. Compression 9.5-to-1. Catalyst: not available.

Transmission: Front-wheel drive; five-speed manual gearbox. Automatic, optional extra. Top gear speed at 1000 rpm: 20.0 mph (32.2 km/h).

Suspension: Front, independent, MacPherson struts, anti-roll bar. Rear, independent, trailing arms and coil springs; anti-roll bar.

Steering: Rack and pinion. Power assistance: standard. **Brakes:** Solid discs front, drums rear. ABS: not available. **Tyres:** 155 SR 13. **Fuel tank:** 10.0 Imp. gall (45.5 litres). **Unladen weight:** 2172 lb (985 kg).

Dimensions: Length 169.7 in (4311 mm), width 64.8 in (1645 mm), height 53.5 in (1360 mm), wheelbase 93.7 in (2380 mm).

Performance *Autocar & Motor* test: Maximum speed 98 mph (158 km/h); 0 to 60 mph (97 km/h) 12.4 sec. Fuel consumption at constant 75 mph (120 km/h): 32.8 mpg; overall test, 28.5 mpg.

Features: Many detail improvements were introduced at the same time as the 12-valve engines, including new centre console and better seats.
Summary: Assessed before the launch, in 1990, the new 12-valve Protons appeared substantially improved, and effectively even better value for money, especially with power steering on the 1.5. The 1.3 is also available, but does not get power steering.

RENAULT (F)   19 Chamade TXE

Identity: Following the 1988 launch of the Renault 19 hatchback, the Chamade saloon followed in December 1989, in a range of six models. The 1397 cc engine is not available, choice being the 1390 'Energy' unit, 1721 cc with carb. or injection, and the 1870 diesel. TXE is top of the range, except for the new 16-valve version.

Engine: Front-mounted transverse four cylinder with alloy head and twin-choke carb, electrically heated for cold start warm-up. Bore 81.0 mm, stroke 83.5 mm; capacity 1721 cc. Power 92 PS (67 kW) at 5750 rpm; torque 97 lb ft (134 Nm) at 3000 rpm. Compression 9.5-to-1. Catalyst: not available.

Transmission: Front-wheel drive; five-speed manual gearbox. Automatic, not available. Top gear speed at 1000 rpm; 19.9 mph (32.1 km/h).

Suspension: Front, independent, MacPherson struts, anti-roll bar. Rear, independent, trailing arms and transverse torsion bars; anti-roll bar.

Steering: Rack and pinion. Power assistance: optional. **Brakes:** Solid discs front, drums rear. ABS: optional. **Tyres:** 175/70 R 13T. **Fuel tank:** 12.1 Imp. gall (55 litres). **Unladen weight:** 2127 lb (965 kg).

Dimensions: Length 167.7 in (4260 mm), width 66.5 in (1689 mm), height 55.9 in (1420 mm), wheelbase 100.4 in (2550 mm).

Performance *Autocar & Motor* test: Maximum speed 110 mph (177 km/h); 0 to 60 mph (97 km/h) 11.4 sec; 80 mph (130 km/h) 22.0 sec. Fuel consumption at constant 75 mph (120 km/h): 42.8 mpg; overall test, 30.9 mpg.

Features: Anti-lock brake option was introduced in 1990. TXE is well-equipped, with remote locking and electric glass sunroof. **Summary:** On test in France towards the end of 1989, the Chamade proved comfortable, responsive and quite fast, but there was a disappointingly high degree of wheel thump on poor roads, and excessive understeer.

RENAULT   (F)   19 Chamade 1.7 16v

Identity: Renault first unveiled the 19 with more powerful 16-valve engine at Geneva 1990, but it did not come on to the British market until February 1991. At Paris 1990, five-door and Chamade (saloon) versions with the 16-valve engine were added to the previous three-door 16v.

Engine: Front-mounted transverse four-cylinder with alloy head and twin ohc operating four valves per cylinder. Electronic multi-point fuel injection. Bore 82.0 mm, stroke 83.5 mm; capacity 1764 cc. Power 140 PS (103 kW) at 6500 rpm; torque 116 lb ft (161 Nm) at 4250 rpm. Compression 10.0-to-1. Catalyst: not available.

Transmission: Front-wheel drive; five-speed manual gearbox. Automatic, not available. Top gear speed at 1000 rpm: 20.3 mph (31.4 km/h).

Suspension: Front, independent, MacPherson struts; anti-roll bar. Rear, independent, trailing arms with four transverse torsion bars; anti-roll bar.

Steering: Rack and pinion. Power assistance: standard. **Brakes:** Vented discs front, solid discs rear. ABS: optional. **Tyres:** 195/50 R 15 V. **Fuel tank:** 12.1 Imp. gall (55 litres). **Unladen weight:** 2315 lb (1050 kg).

Dimensions: Length 167.7 in (4260 mm), width 66.5 in (1689 mm), height 55.9 in (1420 mm), wheelbase 100.4 in (2550 mm).

Performance Works: Maximum speed 134 mph (216 km/h); 0 to 62 mph (100 km/h) 8.2 sec. Fuel consumption at constant 75 mph (120 km/h): 38.2 mpg.

Features: Double headlamps, a front bumper with soft spoiler beneath and separate wing spoiler on the boot are features of the 16v. **Summary:** With its top speed of over 130 mph and impressive acceleration continuing right through the range, to cover a standing km in under 30 sec, this new 16-valve version of the 19 is a very fast car indeed.

RENAULT   (F)   **Clio 1.4 RT**

Identity: New at Birmingham 1990, Clio comes between 5 and 19 in the Renault range, and heralds a move to names instead of numbers. Three equipment levels – RL, RN and RT – and choice of 1.1, 1.2, 1.4, 1.7 and 1.9 diesel engines, though the 1.1 will not come to Britain. 1.8 injection version to be added later. UK launch was in spring 1991.

Engine: Front-mounted transverse four-cylinder with cast-iron block, renewable wet cylinder liners, and alloy head. Single ohc, eight valves, Weber twin-choke carb. Bore 75.8 mm, stroke 77.0 mm; capacity 1390 cc. Power 78 PS (57.5 kW) at 5750 rpm; torque 77 lb ft (107 Nm) at 3500 rpm. Compression 9.5-to-1. Catalyst: optional.

Transmission: Front-wheel drive; five-speed manual gearbox. Automatic, optional extra. Top gear speed at 1000 rpm: 21.7 mph (34.9 km/h).

Suspension: Front, independent, MacPherson struts, anti-roll bar. Rear, independent, trailing arms and two transverse torsion bars; anti-roll bar.

Steering: Rack and pinion. Power assistance: optional. **Brakes:** Solid discs front, drums rear. ABS: optional on 1.7 only. **Tyres:** 165/65 R 13T. **Fuel tank:** 9.5 Imp. gall (43 litres). **Unladen weight:** 1870 lb (850 kg).

Dimensions: Length 146.0 in (3709 mm), width 64.0 in (1625 mm), height 54.9 in (1395 mm), wheelbase 97.3 in (2472 mm).

Performance Works: Maximum speed 109 mph (175 km/h); 0 to 62 mph (100 km/h) 11.2 sec. Fuel consumption at constant 75 mph (120 km/h): 42.8 mpg.

Features: The special appeal of the Clio is its generous equipment level, especially in RT (Renault Top) form, with such items as remote central locking, but not electric windows or sunroof – these are options. **Summary:** In the busy time just before the September Show I went out to France to drive the Clio, and enjoyed its smoothness and high standard of comfort. An important addition to the small–medium car sector.

RENAULT (F)   Espace Quadra TXE

Identity: Intriguing addition to the new kind of vehicle, termed 'people carriers' as first offered by some Japanese makes. Renault's contribution has an aerodynamic body, is very pleasant to drive, and can carry seven or a 1300 lb payload. TXE is top version. Styling changes Spring 1988, and four-wheel drive versions in UK from February 1989.

Engine: Front-mounted longitudinal four-cylinder with aluminium block and head. Electronic ignition. Weber 32 DARA carb. Bore 88.0 mm, stroke 82.0 mm; capacity 1995 cc. Power 120 PS (87 kW) at 5500 rpm; torque 119 lb ft (164 Nm) at 3000 rpm. Compression 9.2-to-1. Catalyst: not available.

Transmission: Four-wheel drive; five-speed manual gearbox. Top gear speed at 1000 rpm: 22.8 mph (36.7 km/h).

Suspension: Front, independent, wishbones, coil springs, anti-roll bar. Rear, torsion beam axle on trailing arms, with Panhard rod; varying rate coil springs.

Steering: Rack and pinion. Power assistance: standard. **Brakes:** Solid discs front, drums rear. ABS: not available. **Tyres:** 185/65 R 14. **Fuel tank:** 14.0 Imp. gall (65 litres). **Unladen weight:** 2602 lb (1177 kg).

Dimensions: Length 167.3 in (4250 mm), width 70.0 in (1277 mm), height 65.4 in (1660 mm), wheelbase 101.6 in (2580 mm).

Performance *Autocar and Motor* test (4 × 4): Maximum speed 105 mph (169 km/h); 0 to 60 mph (97 km/h) 11.2 sec; 80 mph (130 km/h) 22.0 sec. Fuel consumption at constant 75 mph (120 km/h): 28.7 mpg; overall test, 24.3 mpg.

Features: Unusual construction, using Polyester sheet reinforced with glass fibre on zinc-protected metal sub-frame. Ingenious provision for seats to be rearranged or removed as required. Low drag, Cd 0.32. **Summary:** Very versatile vehicle with high degree of refinement and comfort, offering ability to carry a large number of people and a mass of luggage, or to take on a load-carrying role.

RENAULT   (F)   GTA V6 Turbo Le Mans

Identity: One of my most enjoyable trips in 1986 was a drive in the GTA V6 Turbo to Dieppe to see the Alpine factory where this remarkable car is made, with lightweight bodyshell in laminated polyester on a steel backbone chassis. Special Le Mans version illustrated has exhaust catalyst as standard.

Engine: Mid-mounted longitudinal 90-deg V6 cylinder with alloy block and heads. Chain-driven ohc each bank. Renix electronic fuel injection and Garrett T3 turbocharger with air-air intercooler. Bore 91.0 mm, stroke 63.0 mm; capacity 2458 cc. Power 188 PS (138 kW) at 5750 rpm; torque 214 lb ft (285 Nm) at 2500 rpm. Comp. 8.0-to-1. Catalyst: standard.

Transmission: Rear-wheel drive; five-speed manual gearbox. No automatic transmission option. Speed at 1000 rpm: 26.5 mph (42.6 km/h).

Suspension: Front, independent, wishbones, with coil spring and damper units bearing on to upper wishbone; anti-roll bar. Rear, independent, wishbones with coil spring and damper units bearing on to upper wishbone; anti-roll bar.

Steering: Rack and pinion. Power assistance: not available. **Brakes:** Vented discs front and rear. ABS: optional. **Tyres:** 195/50 R 15 (front); 255/45 R 15. Emergency thin spare. **Fuel tank:** 15.8 Imp. gall (72 litres). **Unladen weight:** 2668 lb (1210 kg).

Dimensions: Length 170.5 in (4331 mm), width 69.1 in (1755 mm), height 47.1 in (1196 mm), wheelbase 92.1 in (2340 mm).

Performance *Autocar & Motor* test: Maximum speed 146 mph (235 km/h); 0 to 60 mph (97 km/h) 6.8 sec; 80 mph (130 km/h) 12.9 sec. Fuel consumption at 75 mph (120 km/h); 31.4 mpg; overall test, 20.3 mpg.

Features: Unusual interior design, and most elaborate layout including 6-speaker hi-fi and comprehensive computer. Restricted luggage space. Two occasional rear seats. **Summary:** Worthy successor to the former Alpine (name not used for the GTA in Britain). Wanders on straight at speed, but marvellous cornering. Non-turbo version also available.

RENAULT (F)   21 1.7 GTS Hatchback

Identity: For Frankfurt 1989, Renault added a hatchback version to the 21 range, previously available only as saloon or estate car; and it came to the British market at Motorfair. Choice of 1.7- or 2-litre engine, plus 1.9-litre diesel. The 1.7 is a particularly attractive car.

Engine: Front-mounted transverse four-cylinder with alloy head and belt-driven ohc; eight valves. Twin-choke carb. Bore 81.0 mm, stroke 83.5 mm; capacity 1721 cc. Power 92 PS (66 kW) at 5750 rpm; torque 99 lb ft (135 Nm) at 3000 rpm. Compression 9.5-to-1. Catalyst: not available.

Transmission: Front-wheel drive; five-speed manual gearbox. Automatic, not available. Top gear speed at 1000 rpm: 23.2 mph (37.3 km/h).

Suspension: Front, independent, MacPherson struts, anti-roll bar. Rear, independent, trailing arms and transverse torsion bars; anti-roll bar.

Steering: Rack and pinion. Power assistance: optional. **Brakes:** Vented discs front, drums rear. ABS: not available. **Tyres:** 175/70 TR 13. **Fuel tank:** 14.5 Imp. gall (66 litres). **Unladen weight:** 2388 lb (1084 kg).

Dimensions: Length 175.6 in (4460 mm), width 67.9 in (1724 mm), height 55.1 in (1399 mm), wheelbase 104.7 in (2659 mm).

Performance *Autocar & Motor* test: Maximum speed 111 mph (179 km/h); 0 to 60 mph (97 km/h) 11.6 sec; 80 mph (130 km/h) 22.1 sec. Fuel consumption at constant 75 mph (120 km/h): 41.5 mpg; overall test, 28.1 mpg.

Features: Hatchback has the same rear seat folding arrangement as in the estate car, with easy conversion for extra load space. Electric sunroof is included in relatively generous equipment. **Summary:** Very comfortable car with low noise level, extremely good ride and very level and easily manageable handling. Small spoiler is attached to the tailgate. The 1.7 engine is installed transversely and gives best handling; 2.0 versions have longitudinal engine layout.

RENAULT (F)   21 2L Turbo Quadra

Identity: Although the 21 2L Turbo impressed as a superbly fast and well-equipped car, it was a bit of a handful in the wet; this problem was answered with the introduction of the four-wheel drive Quadra version in June 1990, a very safe and impressive GT saloon.

Engine: Front-mounted longitudinal four-cylinder with all-alloy construction and wet cylinder liners. Toothed belt ohc, eight valves and Garrett T3 turbocharger. Bore 88.0 mm, stroke 82.0 mm; capacity 1995 cc. Power 175 PS (129 kW) at 5200 rpm; torque 195 lb ft (270 Nm) at 3000 rpm. Compression 8.0-to-1. Catalyst: not available.

Transmission: Four-wheel drive; five-speed manual gearbox. Automatic, not available. Top gear speed at 1000 rpm: 23.9 mph (38.5 km/h).

Suspension: Front, independent, MacPherson struts with anti-dive geometry, anti-roll bar. Rear, independent, trailing arms and Panhard rod; coil springs and anti-roll bar.

Steering: Rack and pinion. Power assistance: standard. **Brakes:** Vented discs front, solid discs rear. ABS: standard. **Tyres:** 195/55 R 15Z. **Fuel tank:** 13.6 Imp. gall (62 litres). **Unladen weight:** 2965 lb (1345 kg).

Dimensions: Length 178.2 in (4528 mm), width 69.3 in (1726 mm), height 55.1 in (1400 mm), wheelbase 102.3 in (2600 mm).

Performance *Autocar & Motor* test: Maximum speed 138 mph (222 km/h); 0 to 60 mph (97 km/h) 7.8 sec; 80 mph (130 km/h) 12.9 sec. Fuel consumption at constant 75 mph (120 km/h): 32.1 mpg; overall test, 22.1 mpg.

Features: Viscous coupling for the centre differential is housed in the rear of the gearbox, giving 65 per cent of torque to the front wheels. Rear diff. can be locked. Lavish equipment, including leather trim. **Summary:** A very pleasant car to live with, combining high-speed ability with excellent handling and brakes. It is also a very comfortable and relaxing car on a long journey.

RENAULT (F)   25 2.9 V6 Baccara

Identity: First launched Geneva 1984, the 25 range came in for some improvements in May 1990, including the addition of a luxury Baccara version of the V6 automatic, replacing the former 25 Turbo. The 25 V6 was the first Renault to be offered in the UK with a catalyst.

Engine: Front-mounted longitudinal V6-cylinder with all-alloy construction and single ohc per bank. Multi-point fuel injection. Bore 91.0 mm, stroke 73.0 mm; capacity 2849 cc. Power 153 PS (113 kW) at 5400 rpm; torque 163 lb ft (225 Nm) at 2500 rpm. Compression 9.5-to-1. Catalyst: standard.

Transmission: Front-wheel drive; four-speed automatic standard. Top gear speed at 1000 rpm: 26.8 mph (43.1 km/h).

Suspension: Front, independent, wishbones and coil springs; anti-roll bar. Rear, independent, semi-trailing arms and coil springs; anti-roll bar.

Steering: Rack and pinion. Power assistance: standard. **Brakes:** Vented discs front, solid discs rear. ABS: standard. **Tyres:** 195/60 R 15V. **Fuel tank:** 15.8 Imp. gall (72 litres). **Unladen weight:** 2866 lb (1300 kg).

Dimensions: Length 185.5 in (4713 mm), width 71.1 in (1806 mm), height 55.7 in (1415 mm), wheelbase 107.2 in (2723 mm).

Performance *Autocar & Motor* test: Maximum speed 128 mph (206 km/h); 0 to 60 mph (97 km/h) 9.5 sec; 80 mph (130 km/h) 16.6 sec. Fuel consumption at constant 75 mph (120 km/h): 31.4 mpg; overall test, 21.2 mpg.

Features: Baccara gets grey leather interior and wood trim on doors and facia, special Baccara alloy wheels and air conditioning. **Summary:** A frequently under-rated car, the 25 V6 offers luxurious travel and high performance. Elaborate interior includes every kind of warning system, plus a fully built-in audio system with graphic equaliser.

Identity: Launched at the end of December 1990, Tempest results from an attempt to produce the best and fastest two-seater sports car so far. It is the work of former Panther founder Robert Jankel and his company Robert Jankel Design. It is developed from the Chevrolet Corvette L98.

Engine: Front-mounted longitudinal V8-cylinder with alloy heads and block. Carroll supercharger, and water injection. Tuned-port fuel injection. Bore 105.5 mm, stroke 95.3 mm; capacity 6665 cc. Power 535 PS (394 kW) at 5250 rpm; torque 608 lb ft (841 Nm) at 4000 rpm. Compression 10.0-to-1. Catalyst: standard.

Transmission: Rear-wheel drive; six-speed manual gearbox. Automatic, optional extra. Top gear speed at 1000 rpm: 29.6 mph (47.6 km/h).

Suspension: Front, independent, forged aluminium upper and lower control arms and transverse monoleaf spring; anti-roll bar. Rear, independent, five-link location and monoleaf filament-wound carbon fibre composite spring. Gas-filled dampers with three-position electronic ride control.

Steering: Rack and pinion. Power assistance: standard. **Brakes:** Vented discs front and rear. ABS: standard. **Tyres:** P275-40 17 (front); P315-35 17 (rear). **Fuel tank:** 20.0 Imp. gall (91 litres). **Unladen weight:** 3270 lb (1483 kg).

Dimensions: Length 176.5 in (4483 mm), width 71.0 in (1803 mm), height 46.7 in (1186 mm), wheelbase 96.2 in (2444 mm).

Performance Works: Maximum speed 200 mph (322 km/h); 0 to 60 mph (97 km/h) 3.3 sec; 120 mph (193 km/h) 12.0 sec. Fuel: no data.

Features: Very comprehensive specification, including climate control air conditioning, top level Bose audio system, and Connolloy hide upholstery or other materials to choice. **Summary:** Hailed as a 'new statement in sports car performance', this is certainly a most exciting specification, well thought-out and brilliantly designed. UK price at launch was £98,000.

ROLLS-ROYCE (GB)   Silver Spirit II

Identity: With the important changes announced for Motorfair 1989, including the introduction of Automatic Ride Control, all Rolls-Royce models took the 'II' designation, which was not applied to Bentley cars. Many subtle changes to the world's most distinguished car were made at the same time.

Engine: Front-mounted longitudinal V8-cylinder with alloy block and heads, and pushrod ohv; hydraulic tappets. Bosch K-Motronic fuel injection. Bore 104.1 mm, stroke 99.1 mm; capacity 6750 cc. Power and torque: no data released. Compression 8.0-to-1. Catalyst: optional.

Transmission: Rear-wheel drive; three-speed GM automatic, with R-R column-mounted control. Speed at 1000 rpm: 30.0 mph (48.3 km/h).

Suspension: Front, independent, wishbones and coil springs with compliant controlled upper levers and electronic damper control; anti-roll bar. Rear, independent, semi-trailing arms; coil springs and self-levelling struts with electronically controlled dampers; anti-roll bar.

Steering: Rack and pinion. Power assistance: standard. **Brakes:** Vented discs front, solid discs rear. ABS: standard. **Tyres:** 235/70 R 15. **Fuel tank:** 23.5 Imp. gall (107 litres). **Unladen weight:** 5180 lb (2350 kg).

Dimensions: Length 207.4 in (5268 mm), width 74.0 in (1879 mm), height 58.5 in (1485 mm), wheelbase 120.5 in (3061 mm).

Performance *Autocar & Motor* test: Maximum speed 126 mph (203 km/h); 0 to 60 mph (97 km/h) 10.4 sec; 80 mph (130 km/h) 17.9 sec. Fuel consumption at 75 mph (120 km/h): 17.6 mpg; overall test, 13.8 mpg.

Features: Redesigned facia with new warning module, improved air conditioning, and still better audio system were among the many 1989 improvements to an already superb car. **Summary:** Big efforts are being made to keep the Rolls-Royce abreast of latest developments, such as remote control anti-theft alarm, now standard. Perhaps we might look forward to out-of-sight parking for the windscreen wipers.

Identity: When the Rover 200-Series was first introduced, there was no version with the Honda 1.6-litre twin ohc engine. This first appeared in the Rover range in the 416GTi, the saloon model, but at Birmingham 1990 the three-door Rover 200 was launched including a 216GTi with this engine.

Engine: Front-mounted transverse four-cylinder with all-alloy construction and belt-driven twin ohc working four valves per cylinder. Honda PGM F-1 fuel injection. Bore 75.0 mm, stroke 90.0 mm; capacity 1590 cc. Power 130 PS (96 kW) at 6800 rpm; torque 105 lb ft (145 Nm) at 5700 rpm. Compression: 9.5-to-1. Catalyst: not available.

Transmission: Front-wheel drive; five-speed manual gearbox. Automatic, optional extra. Top gear speed at 1000 rpm: 18.5 mph (29.8 km/h).

Suspension: Front, independent, MacPherson struts, anti-roll bar. Rear, independent, wishbones with compensating trailing arm, coil springs; anti-roll bar.

Steering: Rack and pinion. Power assistance: standard. **Brakes:** Vented discs front, solid discs rear. ABS: optional. **Tyres:** 185/60 HR 14. **Fuel tank:** 12.1 Imp. gall (55 litres). **Unladen weight:** 2489 lb (1130 kg).

Dimensions: Length 166.0 in (4220 mm), width 66.1 in (1680 mm), height 55.0 in (1400 mm), wheelbase 100.4 in (2550 mm).

Performance *Autocar & Motor* test (416GTi): Maximum speed 120 mph (193 km/h); 0 to 60 mph (97 km/h) 10.0 sec; 80 mph (130 km/h) 17.7 sec. Fuel consumption at constant 75 mph (120 km/h): 33.2 mpg; overall test, 25.1 mpg.

Features: Three-door body gives a sporty look to the 216GTi and in this form it is well-equipped, including central locking and electric sunroof. **Summary:** Power steering as standard on this model is a big improvement. With the Honda 16-valve engine, power output is commendably high for a 1.6, making it a vigorous and sporty car to drive.

ROVER (GB)

414SLi

Identity: In the 400 saloon range, there is no GSi version with 1.4-litre engine, as there is in the 200 hatchback line-up. This SLi model is the better and dearer of the two 1.4-litre saloons (the other being the 414Si), though differences are confined to fittings and trim.

Engine: Front-mounted transverse four-cylinder with all-alloy construction and belt-driven single ohc working four valves per cylinder. Single point fuel injection. Bore 75.0 mm, stroke 79.0 mm; capacity 1396 cc. Power 95 PS (70 kW) at 6250 rpm; torque 91 lb ft (126 Nm) at 4000 rpm. Compression 9.5-to-1. Catalyst: optional.

Transmission: Front-wheel drive; five-speed manual gearbox. Automatic, not available. Top gear speed at 1000 rpm: 19.8 mph (31.9 km/h).

Suspension: Front, independent, MacPherson struts; anti-roll bar. Rear, independent, wishbones with compensating trailing arm, coil springs; anti-roll bar.

Steering: Rack and pinion. Power assistance: not available. **Brakes:** Solid discs front, drums rear. ABS: optional. **Tyres:** 175/65 X 14TR. **Fuel tank:** 12.1 Imp. gall (55 litres). **Unladen weight:** 2300 lb (1043 kg).

Dimensions: Length 166.0 in (4220 mm), width 66.1 in (1680 mm), height 55.0 in (1400 mm), wheelbase 100.4 in (2550 mm).

Performance *Autocar & Motor* test: Maximum speed 101 mph (163 km/h); 0 to 60 mph (97 km/h) 11.5 sec; 80 mph (130 km/h) 21.3 sec. Fuel consumption at constant 75 mph (120 km/h): 42.4 mpg; overall test, 32.7 mpg.

Features: At this level in the 400 range, the Rover gets a winding sunroof which can be optionally upgraded to electric; interior trim is pleasing. **Summary:** With its good performance (for a 1.4) and high-quality finish, this version of the mid-range Rover is proving a good choice for company-car buyers who want to keep in Band 1 (under 1400 cc). An attractive car, but beginning to look expensive.

Identity: In a reduction of the 800 line-up for Birmingham 1990, the eight-valve Fastback and versions of the saloon and Fastback with single point injection were dropped. The range now starts with the 820i with multi-point fuel injection and availability of both body styles.

Engine: Front-mounted transverse four-cylinder with alloy head and twin ohc working four valves per cylinder; Lucas multi-point fuel injection. Bore 84.5 mm, stroke 89.0 mm; capacity 1994 cc. Power 140 PS (103 kW) at 6000 rpm; torque 131 lb ft (178 Nm) at 4500 rpm. Compression 10.0-to-1. Catalyst: optional.

Transmission: Front-wheel drive; five-speed manual gearbox. Automatic, optional extra. Top gear speed at 1000 rpm: 21.7 mph (34.9 km/h).

Suspension: Front, independent, wishbones and coil springs with coaxial dampers; anti-roll bar. Rear, independent, transverse and trailing links; coil springs and anti-roll bar.

Steering: Rack and pinion. Power assistance: standard. **Brakes:** Vented discs front, solid discs rear. ABS: optional. **Tyres:** 195/70 HR 14. **Fuel tank:** 15.0 Imp. gall (68 litres). **Unladen weight:** 3010 lb (1365 kg).

Dimensions: Length 184.8 in (4694 mm), width 68.1 in (1730 mm), height 55.0 in (1398 mm), wheelbase 108.6 in (2759 mm).

Performance *Autocar & Motor* test: Maximum speed 125 mph (201 km/h); 0 to 60 mph (97 km/h) 9.1 sec; 80 mph (130 km/h) 15.8 sec. Fuel consumption at constant 75 mph (120 km/h): 34.3 mpg; overall test, 29.8 mpg.

Features: All of the 800 series now get an anti-theft alarm, delay in headlamp and courtesy light switching off, and programmed wash/wipe. **Summary:** Impressively quiet car, with good handling and extremely level ride. Well-planned control layout and pleasant interior trim.

Identity: Although there's a diesel version of the Rover O-Series engine in the range, for the diesel version of the 800-series the Italian VM unit was chosen again, as previously fitted in the 2400SD as well as the Range Rover diesel. Available as Fastback only, it was launched Birmingham 1990, and has the same specification as the revised 820i.

Engine: Front-mounted transverse four-cylinder with cast-iron block and head, and pushrod ohv. Garrett T2 turbocharger. Bore 90.5 mm, stroke 97.0 mm; capacity 2495 cc. Power 120 PS (88 kW) at 4200 rpm; torque 198 lb ft (274 Nm) at 2100 rpm. Compression 21.0-to-1. Catalyst: not available.

Transmission: Front-wheel drive; five-speed manual gearbox. Automatic, optional extra. Top gear speed at 1000 rpm: 28.6 mph (46.0 km/h).

Suspension: Front, independent, wishbones and coil springs with coaxial dampers; anti-roll bar. Rear, independent, transverse and trailing links; coil springs and anti-roll bar.

Steering: Rack and pinion. Power assistance: standard. **Brakes:** Vented discs front, solid discs rear. ABS: optional. **Tyres:** 195/70 HR 14. **Fuel tank:** 15.0 Imp. gall (68 litres). **Unladen weight:** 3240 lb (1470 kg).

Dimensions: Length 184.8 in (4694 mm), width 68.1 in (1730 mm), height 55.0 in (1398 mm), wheelbase 108.6 in (2759 mm).

Performance *Autocar & Motor* test: Maximum speed 116 mph (187 km/h); 0 to 60 mph (97 km/h) 11.7 sec; 80 mph (130 km/h) 21.6 sec. Fuel consumption at constant 75 mph (120 km/h): 45.2 mpg; overall test, 36.2 mpg.

Features: Central locking, manual-wind glass sunroof, electric front windows and a good audio unit are all standard. The finish is also very good. **Summary:** Enormous torque is developed at low revs with this big turbo diesel, helping to make the 825D easy to drive and deceptively fast. It is, nevertheless, economical: *Diesel Car* magazine obtained 36.7 mpg on test, close to the *Autocar & Motor* figure.

ROVER (GB)   Metro 1.1C

Identity: 1990 was a busy year for Rover, and one of the most significant launches came in May. The Metro appeared then in much-improved form, with restyled body and an eight-valve version of the K-Series all-alloy engine. Best value seemed at the bottom of the range, in this 1.1C.

Engine: Front-mounted transverse four-cylinder with all-alloy construction and belt-driven single ohc; eight valves, and KIF carb. Bore 75.0 mm, stroke 63.0 mm; capacity 1120 cc. Power 60 PS (44 kW) at 3500 rpm; torque 66 lb ft (91 Nm) at 3500 rpm. Compression 9.75-to-1. Catalyst: optional.

Transmission: Front-wheel drive; four-speed manual gearbox (five-speed optional). Automatic, not available. Top gear speed at 1000 rpm: 16.1 mph (25.9 km/h); fifth: 19.9 mph (32.0 km/h).

Suspension: Front, independent, wishbones and Hydragas spring-damper units linked front to rear. Rear, independent, trailing arms and Hydragas linked spring-damper units.

Steering: Rack and pinion. Power assistance: not available. **Brakes:** Solid discs front, drums rear. ABS: not available. **Tyres:** 155/65 R 13. **Fuel tank:** 7.7 Imp. gall (35.5 litres). **Unladen weight:** 1795 lb (815 kg).

Dimensions: Length 138.6 in (3521 mm), width 69.8 in (1775 mm), height 54.2 in (1377 mm), wheelbase 89.3 in (2269 mm).

Performance *Autocar & Motor* test: Maximum speed 97 mph (156 km/h); 0 to 60 mph (97 km/h) 13.7 sec; 80 mph (130 km/h) 27.2 sec. Fuel consumption at constant 75 mph (120 km/h): 45.8 mpg; overall test, 31.9 mpg.

Features: Equipment is fairly simple at this base level, with even rear wash/wipe listed as an option and no audio as standard; choice of three-or five-door body. **Summary:** Performance is very respectable, showing the efficiency of the K-Series engine, and maximum speed is in fourth. The five-speed gearbox comes with lower ratio, so fifth is not much higher than fourth on the four-speed model.

ROVER (GB)   MG Maestro 2.0i

Identity: Long ago it was presumed that the Maestro would be discontinued to make way for the increasing number of new Rovers, but it goes on. The MG version is well-liked, and is available with turbocharged engine or in this non-turbo 2-litre form.

Engine: Front-mounted transverse four-cylinder with alloy head, belt-driven ohc, and eight valves; Lucas electronic fuel injection. Bore 84.5 mm, stroke 89.0 mm; capacity 1994 cc. Power 115 PS (85 kW) at 5500 rpm; torque 134 lb ft (185 Nm) at 2800 rpm. Compression 9.1-to-1. Catalyst: optional.

Transmission: Front-wheel drive; five-speed manual gearbox. Automatic, not available. Top gear speed at 1000 rpm: 21.9 mph (35.2 km/h).

Suspension: Front, independent, MacPherson struts, anti-roll bar. Rear, semi-independent, trailing arms and torsion beam; coil springs and anti-roll bar.

Steering: Rack and pinion. Power assistance: optional. **Brakes:** Vented discs front, drums rear. ABS: not available. **Tyres:** 185/55 HR 15. **Fuel tank:** 11.0 Imp. gall (50 litres). **Unladen weight:** 2295 lb (1040 kg).

Dimensions: Length 159.5 in (4050 mm), width 66.4 in (1687 mm), height 56.4 in (1433 mm), wheelbase 98.7 in (2507 mm).

Performance *Autocar & Motor* test: Maximum speed 114 mph (183 km/h); 0 to 60 mph (97 km/h) 8.4 sec; 80 mph (130 km/h) 14.9 sec. Fuel consumption at constant 75 mph (120 km/h): 34.8 mpg; overall test, 33.4 mpg.

Features: Bumpers are in body colour, and alloy wheels are standard. Traditional MG red piping on doors, and a sporty look to the interior. **Summary:** This version of the Maestro appeals to those who appreciate the MG image and like the blend of sporty pretensions, swift performance and restrained styling.

ROVER (GB)   Sterling

Identity: Top version of the new Rover range which was launched July 1986, the Sterling has every item of equipment one could wish for in a fine car. Expensive, but not if account is taken of performance and luxurious specification. Honda V6 engine increased to 2.7 litre, Feb. 1988.

Engine: Front-mounted transverse V6-cylinder with alloy head and single ohc per bank working four valves per cyl. Honda PGM-FI multi-point fuel injection. Bore 87.0 mm, stroke 75.0 mm; capacity 2675 cc. Power 177 PS (130 kW) at 6000 rpm; torque 168 lb ft (228 Nm) at 4500 rpm. Compression 9.0-to-1. Catalyst: optional.

Transmission: Front-wheel drive; five-speed manual gearbox. Four-speed selectable automatic transmission alternative at no extra cost. Top gear speed at 1000 rpm: 22.9 mph (36.8 km/h). Automatic: 21.3 mph (34.2).

Suspension: Front, independent, wishbones and coil springs, with coaxial dampers; anti-roll bar. Rear, independent, transverse and trailing links; coil springs; anti-roll bar. Self-levelling standard.

Steering: Rack and pinion. Power assistance: standard, speed proportional. **Brakes:** Vented discs front, solid rear. ABS: standard. **Tyres:** 195/65 VR 15. **Fuel tank:** 15.0 Imp. gall (68 litres). **Weight:** 3086 lb (1400 kg).

Dimensions: Length 184.8 in (4694 mm), width 76.6 in (1946 mm), height 55 .0 in (1398 mm), wheelbase 108.6 in (2759 mm).

Performance *Autocar & Motor* test: Maximum speed 130 mph (209 km/h); 0 to 60 mph (97 km/h) 9.3 sec; 80 mph (130 km/h) 16.2 sec. Fuel consumption at constant 75 mph (120 km/h): 28.3 mpg; overall test, 21.3 mpg.

Features: At touch of a button, seats and door mirrors adjust to any of four programmed settings; this exemplifies the lavish equipment on the Sterling. **Summary:** Very smooth, quiet and comfortable car, with good performance and relatively good economy. Figures are for automatic with catalyst.

ROVER (GB)   Vitesse

Identity: Better air flow over the sloping tail of the new Fastback body shape for the 800 Series was improved still more on the top model, Vitesse, by addition of a spoiler at the rear. This gives slightly lower drag, and hence the highest top speed of the range.

Engine: Front-mounted transverse V6-cylinder with alloy head and single ohc per bank working four valves per cyl. Honda PGM-FI multi-point fuel injection. Bore 87.0 mm, stroke 75.0 mm; capacity 2675 cc. Power 177 PS (130 kW) at 6000 rpm; torque 168 lb ft (228 Nm) at 4500 rpm. Compression 9.4-to-1. Catalyst: optional.

Transmission: Front-wheel drive; five-speed manual gearbox. Automatic, four-speed Honda, optional. Top gear speed at 1000 rpm: 22.6 mph (36.4 km/h).

Suspension: Front, independent, wishbones and coil springs with coaxial dampers, anti-roll bar. Rear, independent, transverse and trailing links; coil springs, anti-roll bar.

Steering: Rack and pinion. Power assistance: standard, speed proportional. **Brakes:** Vented discs front, solid discs rear. ABS: standard. **Tyres:** 205/60 VR 15. **Fuel tank:** 15.0 Imp. gall (68 litres). **Unladen weight:** 3142 lb (1425 kg).

Dimensions: Length 184.8 in (4694 mm), width 68.1 in (1730 mm), height 55.0 in (1398 mm), wheelbase 108.6 in (2759 mm).

Performance *Autocar & Motor* test: Maximum speed 137 mph (220 km/h); 0 to 60 mph (97 km/h) 8.0 sec; 80 mph (130 km/h) 13.5 sec. Fuel consumption at constant 75 mph (120 km/h): 31.6 mpg; overall test, 22.1 mpg.

Features: Well equipped and since Birmingham 1990, the Vitesse gets the same luxury equipment as the Sterling. Leather upholstery and such items as electric sunroof all standard. **Summary:** Very satisfying car, available either with five-speed manual as detailed here, or with the very good Honda S4 automatic.

Identity: By continuing the 'old' body style in production, Saab manage to offer a wide range. They increased the attraction of the 900 in September 1990 by making the 16-valve turbocharged engine available, in what is described as 'Light Pressure Turbo' form, giving 145 PS.

Engine: Front-mounted longitudinal four-cylinder with alloy head and twin chain-driven ohc working four valves per cylinder, and water-cooled turbocharger delivering mild boost of only 0.5 bar. Bore 90.0 mm, stroke 78.0 mm; capacity 1985 cc. Power 145 PS (107 kW) at 5500 rpm; torque 145 lb ft (200 Nm) at 3000 rpm. Compression 9.0-to-1. Catalyst: standard.

Transmission: Front-wheel drive; five-speed manual gearbox. Automatic, optional extra. Top gear speed at 1000 rpm: 22.0 mph (35.4 km/h).

Suspension: Front, independent, wishbones and coil springs; anti-roll bar. Rear, dead beam axle on four trailing links with Panhard rod and coil springs.

Steering: Rack and pinion. Power assistance: standard. **Brakes:** Vented discs front, solid discs rear. ABS: optional. **Tyres:** 185/65 R 15 87H. **Fuel tank:** 15.0 Imp. gall (68 litres). **Unladen weight:** 2646 lb (1200 kg).

Dimensions: Length 184.3 in (4680 mm), width 66.5 in (1690 mm), height 55.1 in (1400 mm), wheelbase 99.1 in (2517 mm).

Performance Works: Maximum speed 127 mph (205 km/h); 0 to 62 mph (100 km/h) 9.6 sec. Fuel consumption at constant 75 mph (120 km/h): 26.2 mpg.

Features: Rear spoiler is standard, and equipment includes electric action for windows, mirrors and sunroof; alloy wheels. **Summary:** Although the 900 body seems very dated when one is behind the wheel, with rather low screen top, it remains popular on account of good pricing. In this form it offers good performance with high response at relatively low engine speeds.

SAAB (S)   9000 2.3 Turbo

Identity: An interesting launch, bringing a long, fast Continental drive in autumn 1990, gave an excellent introduction to the new turbocharged version of the 2.3. This model offers impressive performance for its engine size, yet behaves with great safety and in very relaxed fashion. The best Saab yet.

Engine: Front-mounted transverse four-cylinder with alloy head and twin ohc working four valves per cylinder. Direct ignition with an individual coil on each sparking plug, and Garrett T25 turbocharger. Bore 90.0 mm, stroke 90.0 mm; capacity 2290 cc. Power 200 PS (147 kW) at 5000 rpm; torque 243 lb ft (336 Nm) at 2000 rpm. Compression 8.5-to-1. Catalyst: standard.

Transmission: Front-wheel drive; five-speed manual gearbox. Automatic, optional extra. Top gear speed at 1000 rpm: 24.0 mph (38.6 km/h).

Suspension: Front, independent, MacPherson struts, anti-roll bar. Rear, dead beam axle on four longitudinal links, with Panhard rod; coil springs and anti-roll bar.

Steering: Rack and pinion. Power assistance: standard. **Brakes:** Vented discs front and rear. ABS: standard. **Tyres:** 205/55 VR 15. **Fuel tank:** 13.7 Imp. gall (62 litres). **Unladen weight:** 3050 lb (1383 kg).

Dimensions: Length 188.1 in (4777 mm), width 69.4 in (1763 mm), height 55.9 in (1420 mm), wheelbase 105.2 in (2672 mm).

Performance *Autocar & Motor* test: Maximum speed 140 mph (225 km/h); 0 to 60 mph (97 km/h) 7.5 sec; 80 mph (130 km/h) 11.5 sec. Fuel consumption at constant 75 mph (120 km/h): 30.3 mpg; overall test, 19.7 mpg.

Features: Still quite a lot of extras to be paid for, including air conditioning and electric seat adjustment, otherwise it's a well-equipped car with an attractive specification. **Summary:** Usually a turbocharged engine suffers a noticeable delay before any response to the throttle is felt, but with the new engine this is reduced to a minimum.

Identity: Named after Eric Carlsson, former rally driver and now an industrious ambassador for Saab, the Carlsson special edition range was widened for 1991. There are 2.3 Turbo Carlssons in both 9000 (hatchback) and CD (saloon) format, as well as the 900 Turbo. For the 9000 and CD, power is increased to 220 bhp.

Engine: Front-mounted transverse four-cylinder with alloy head and twin ohc working four valves per cylinder. Turbocharger and APC (Automatic Performance Control). Bore 90.0 mm, stroke 90.0 mm; capacity 2290 cc. Power 220 PS (162 kW) at 5600 rpm; torque 210 lb ft (290 Nm) at 3000 rpm. Compression 10.0-to-1. Catalyst: standard.

Transmission: Front-wheel drive; five-speed manual gearbox. Automatic, no-cost option. Top gear speed at 1000 rpm: 24.4 mph (39.3 km/h).

Suspension: Front, independent, MacPherson struts; anti-roll bar. Rear, dead beam axle on four longitudinal links with Panhard rod; coil springs, anti-roll bar.

Steering: Rack and pinion. Power assistance: standard. **Brakes:** Vented discs front, solid discs rear. ABS: standard. **Tyres:** 205/50 ZR 16. **Fuel tank:** 13.6 Imp. gall (62 litres). **Unladen weight:** 2921 lb (1325 kg).

Dimensions: Length 183.7 in (4667 mm), width 69.4 in (1764 mm), height 55.9 in (1420 mm), wheelbase 105.2 in (2672 mm).

Performance (est): Maximum speed 142 mph (229 km/h); 0 to 60 mph (97 km/h) 7.2 sec; 80 mph (130 km/h) 10.9 sec. Fuel consumption at constant 75 mph (120 km/h): 31.4 mpg; overall test, 19.0 mpg.

Features: Special 'aero' wheels are standard with the Carlsson, and suspension is specially tuned for optimum handling; suede leather seats.
Summary: As Saab seem reluctant to quote any performance figures, those given above are estimates, based on the expected improvement of the extra 20 bhp over the standard car tested by *Autocar & Motor*. Traction control system is standard, but for manual Carlssons only.

Identity: Always good performers in relation to their engine size, Seat cars were joined by the new injection model in July 1989, offering 100 bhp output in the small Ibiza three-door body. Special alloy wheels and SXi badge on front are identity features. Restyled body introduced Geneva 1991.

Engine: Front-mounted transverse four-cylinder with alloy head and belt-driven ohc operating eight valves. Bosch LE2 multi-point fuel injection. Bore 83.0 mm, stroke 67.5 mm; capacity 1461 cc. Power 100 PS (72 kW) at 5900 rpm; torque 94 lb ft (128 Nm) at 4700 rpm. Compression 11.0-to-1. Catalyst: not available.

Transmission: Front-wheel drive; five-speed manual gearbox. Automatic, not available. Top gear speed at 1000 rpm: 19.9 mph (32.0 km/h).

Suspension: Front, independent, MacPherson struts, anti-roll bar. Rear, independent, lower wishbones and transverse leaf spring.

Steering: Rack and pinion. Power assistance: not available. **Brakes:** Vented discs front, drums rear. ABS: not available. **Tyres:** 185/60 SR 14. **Fuel tank:** 11.0 Imp. gall (50 litres). **Unladen weight:** 2039 lb (925 kg).

Dimensions: Length 143.2 in (3638 mm), width 63.3 in (1610 mm), height 54.8 in (1394 mm), wheelbase 96.3 m (2443 mm).

Performance *Autocar & Motor* test: Maximum speed 107 mph (172 km/h); 0 to 60 mph (97 km/h) 10.3 sec; 80 mph (130 km/h) 19.4 sec. Fuel consumption at constant 75 mph (120 km/h): 40.9 mpg; overall test, 34.9 mpg.

Features: Quite a lot of extra equipment is included with the SXi package, including electric front windows and central locking, but no sunroof. **Summary:** Lively performance for a 1.5-litre, accompanied by a harsh snarl of exhaust when accelerating hard. But the red-on-black instruments are not easy to read, and steering very heavy.

Identity: After years of inflicting a tail-heavy rear-engined design on buyers of the low-cost Czech car, Skoda unveiled their new front-drive model at Geneva 1989, on UK market from June. Vastly improved, it deservedly found its way into the Top Ten selected for the final year of the UDT Guild of Motoring Writers' Top Car award.

Engine: Front-mounted transverse four-cylinder with all-alloy construction and pushrod ohv. Pierburg twin-choke carb. Bore 76.8 mm, stroke 72.0 mm; capacity 1289 cc. Power 62 PS (46 kW) at 5000 rpm; torque 73 lb ft (100 Nm) at 3000 rpm. Compression 9.7-to-1. Catalyst: not available.

Transmission: Front-wheel drive; five-speed manual gearbox. Automatic, not available. Top gear speed at 1000 rpm: 23.0 mph (37.0 km/h).

Suspension: Front, independent, MacPherson struts. Rear, semi-independent, trailing arms and torsion beam; coil springs.

Steering: Rack and pinion. Power assistance: not available. **Brakes:** Solid discs front, drums rear. ABS: not available. **Tyres:** 165/70 SR 13. **Fuel tank:** 10.3 Imp. gall (47 litres). **Unladen weight:** 2070 lb (939 kg).

Dimensions: Length 150.0 in (3815 mm), width 63.7 in (1620 mm), height 55.7 in (1415 mm), wheelbase 96.4 in (2450 mm).

Performance *Autocar & Motor* test: Maximum speed 92 mph (148 km/h); 0 to 60 mph (97 km/h) 14.3 sec; 80 mph (130 km/h) 33.2 sec. Fuel consumption at constant 75 mph (120 km/h): 40.4 mpg; overall test, 32.3 mpg.

Features: Rather simple interior trim and basic finish, but clever design offering a lot of load space, plus many ingenious features. **Summary:** With its fairly high gearing for a 1.3, the Favorit reaches top speed in fourth gear, with fifth for cruising. Acceptable standards of ride comfort and handling, though rather pronounced understeer and body roll on corners. Unquestionably good value.

SKODA (CS)   **Favorit Roadster**

Identity: An estate car was launched by Skoda at Birmingham 1990, and there was also the prototype of this unusually styled convertible, the Roadster. A joint production of Skoda and Metalex, a specialist firm north of Prague, the Roadster was expected to go into production in 1991.

Engine: Front-mounted transverse four-cylinder with alloy block and head; pushrod ohv. Jikov twin-choke carb. Bore 75.5 mm, stroke 72.0 mm; capacity 1289 cc. Power 62 PS (46 kW) at 5000 rpm; torque 74 lb ft (102 Nm) at 3000 rpm. Compression 9.7-to-1. Catalyst: standard.

Transmission: Front-wheel drive; five-speed manual gearbox. Automatic, not available. Top gear speed at 1000 rpm: 23.0 mph (37.0 km/h).

Suspension: Front, independent, MacPherson struts. Rear, semi-independent, trailing arms and torsion beam axle; coil springs.

Steering: Rack and pinion. Power assistance: not available. **Brakes:** Solid discs front, drums rear. ABS: not available. **Tyres:** 165/70 R 13. **Fuel tank:** 10.3 Imp. gall (47 litres). **Unladen weight:** 1950 lb (885 kg).

Dimensions: Length 150.3 in (3815 mm), width 63.8 in (1620 mm), height 55.8 in (1415 mm), wheelbase 96.5 in (2450 mm).

Performance *Autocar & Motor* test (saloon): Maximum speed 92 mph (148 km/h); 0 to 60 mph (97 km/h) 14.3 sec; 80 mph (130 km/h) 33.2 sec. Fuel consumption at constant 75 mph (120 km/h): 39.8 mpg; overall test, 32.4 mpg.

Features: The Roadster will have a catalyst as standard; equipment includes electric windows, central locking and sports wheel. **Summary:** Individual roll-over protection bars are mounted behind the front seats. Side sills continue the air-flow line from the front spoiler beneath the bumper. The car looked quite promising at Birmingham but, as always with Skoda, the price will be the key.

SUBARU   (J)   Justy GLII 4WD

Identity: Small car for those who have to tackle tricky going and don't want to get stuck, the Justy has front-wheel drive in normal running but adds rear drive when a button on top of the gear lever is pressed. Interesting addition for Motorfair 1989 was the availability of continuously variable automatic transmission with electronic control.

Engine: Front-mounted transverse three-cylinder with alloy head and belt-driven ohc working three valves per cylinder. Twin-choke carb. Bore 78.0 mm, stroke 83.0 mm; capacity 1189 cc. Power 67 PS (49 kW) at 5600 rpm; torque 71 lb ft (98 Nm) at 3600 rpm. Compression 9.1-to-1. Catalyst: not available.

Transmission: Four-wheel drive; five-speed manual gearbox. Automatic, optional extra. Automatic is of ECVT type, using continuously variable belts and pulleys under electronic control. Top gear speed at 1000 rpm: 17.6 mph (28.3 km/h).

Suspension: Front, independent, MacPherson struts, anti-roll bar. Rear, independent, wishbones and coil springs; anti-roll bar.

Steering: Rack and pinion. Power assistance: not available. **Brakes:** Vented discs front, drums rear. ABS: not available. **Tyres:** 165/65 R 13. **Fuel tank:** 7.7 Imp. gall (35 litres). **Unladen weight:** 1874 lb (850 kg).

Dimensions: Length 145.5 in (3695 mm), width 60.4 in (1534 mm), height 55.9 in (1420 mm), wheelbase 90.0 in (2285 mm).

Performance *Autocar & Motor* test: Maximum speed 90.0 mph (145 km/h); 0 to 60 mph (97 km/h) 14.4 sec; 80 mph (130 km/h) 31.0 sec. Fuel consumption at constant 75 mph (120 km/h): 35.3 mpg; overall test, 31.0 mpg.

Features: Choice of three- or five-door body; equipment is reasonable for this class of car, and interior materials appear durable. **Summary:** The combination of four-wheel drive (easily engaged at the touch of a switch), with optional automatic transmission is unique to Subaru; economy is claimed to be as good, or better, with the automatic version.

SUBARU (J)   Legacy 2.2 GX 4WD

Identity: New at Frankfurt 1989, the Legacy moves Subaru farther up the market into the executive class, with an elegantly styled and very promising design, available as saloon or estate car. Spacious car, still with horizontally opposed engine, and permanent four-wheel drive.

Engine: Front-mounted longitudinal four-cylinder with horizontally opposed layout (boxer engine) and alloy block and heads; single ohc each bank working four valves per cylinder. Multi-point fuel injection. Bore 96.9 mm, stroke 75.0 mm; capacity 2212 cc. Power 134 PS (98 kW) at 6000 rpm; torque 139 lb ft (193 Nm) at 4800 rpm. Compression 9.5-to-1. Catalyst: not available.

Transmission: Four-wheel drive; five-speed manual gearbox. Automatic, optional extra. Top gear speed at 1000 rpm: 20.8 mph (33.4 km/h).

Suspension: Front, independent, MacPherson struts, anti-roll bar. Rear, independent, trailing arms and dual transverse links; coil springs and anti-roll bar.

Steering: Rack and pinion. Power assistance: standard. **Brakes:** Vented discs front, solid discs rear. ABS: standard. **Tyres:** 185/70 R 14. **Fuel tank:** 13.2 Imp. gall (60 litres). **Unladen weight:** 2822 lb (1280 kg).

Dimensions: Length 177.6 in (4510 mm), width 66.5 in (1690 mm), height 55.1 in (1400 mm), wheelbase 101.6 in (2580 mm).

Performance *Autocar & Motor* test: Maximum speed 116 mph (187 km/h); 0 to 60 mph (97 km/h) 10.8 sec; 80 mph (130 km/h) 20.3 sec. Fuel consumption at constant 75 mph (120 km/h): 30.1 mpg; overall test, 25.0 mpg.

Features: Estate cars with automatic transmission have air suspension and self-levelling provision under computer control, with choice of high or normal settings. **Summary:** Interesting design, with low front and good weight distribution as a result of the boxer engine, and luxurious equipment and interior furnishing. Automatic versions get variable front/rear distribution of torque to suit conditions and demands.

SUZUKI (J)   Vitara JLX

Identity: New at Birmingham 1988, Vitara is an additional four-wheel drive compact cross-country car, supplementing the existing SJ410 and its Spanish-built equivalent, Santana. It has a larger and more powerful 1.6-litre engine, with selectable four-wheel drive. Automatic transmission option introduced April 1990.

Engine: Front-mounted longitudinal four-cylinder with single ohc, alloy head, and twin-choke carb. Bore 75.0 mm, stroke 90.0 mm; capacity 1590 cc. Power 75 PS (55 kW) at 5250 rpm; torque 89 lb ft (123 Nm) at 3100 rpm. Compression 8.9-to-1. Catalyst: not available.

Transmission: Four-wheel drive; five-speed manual gearbox. Automatic, optional extra. Top gear speed at 1000 rpm: 17.8 mph (28.6 km/h).

Suspension: Front, independent, MacPherson struts, anti-roll bar. Rear, independent, trailing links with centre wishbone; coil springs and telescopic dampers.

Steering: Ball and nut. Power assistance: optional. **Brakes:** Solid discs front, drums rear. ABS: not available. **Tyres:** 195 SR 15. **Fuel tank:** 9.5 Imp. gall (43 litres). **Unladen weight:** 2227 lb (1010 kg).

Dimensions: Length 142.5 in (3620 mm), width 64.2 in (1630 mm), height 75.6 in (1665 mm), wheelbase 86.6 in (2200 mm).

Performance *Autocar & Motor* test: Maximum speed 87 mph (140 km/h); 0 to 60 mph (97 km/h) 14.5 sec; 80 mph (130 km/h) 34.7 sec. Fuel consumption at constant 75 mph (120 km/h): 24.8 mpg; overall test, 24.2 mpg.

Features: Two-speed transfer gearbox and four-wheel drive control. Good equipment including electric mirrors; power pack adds power steering, central locking, electric windows and alloy wheels. **Summary:** Quite a lively ride on rough going, but the Vitara certainly has impressive traction, and it's an attractive vehicle for farmers and others needing a compact, low-cost go-anywhere vehicle.

TOYOTA   (J)   Celica 2.0 GT-Four

Identity: Fifth generation to carry the Celica name was launched November 1989, with sleek styling, and again with pop-up headlamps and choice of front- or four-wheel drive. Mechanically much as before but with a better and stronger body, making use of galvanealed steel.

Engine: Front-mounted transverse four-cylinder with alloy head and twin ohc working four valves per cylinder. Electronic injection and turbocharger with air-air inter-cooler. Bore 86.0 mm, stroke 86.0 mm; capacity 1998 cc. Power 204 PS (150 kW) at 6000 rpm; torque 199 lb ft (275 Nm) at 3200 rpm. Compression 8.8-to-1. Catalyst: standard.

Transmission: Four-wheel drive; five-speed manual gearbox. Automatic, not available. Top gear speed at 1000 rpm: 28.5 mph (45.9 km/h).

Suspension: Front, independent, MacPherson struts, anti-roll bar. Rear, independent, MacPherson struts, anti-roll bar.

Steering: Rack and pinion. Power assistance: standard. **Brakes:** Vented discs front, solid discs rear. ABS: standard. **Tyres:** 215/50 VR 15. **Fuel tank:** 13.2 Imp. gall (60 litres). **Unladen weight:** 4166 lb (1890 kg).

Dimensions: Length 174.4 in (4430 mm), width 68.7 in (1745 mm), height 51.2 in (1300 mm), wheelbase 99.4 in (2525 mm).

Performance *Autocar & Motor* test (4 × 2): Maximum speed 132 mph (212 km/h); 0 to 60 mph (97 km/h) 8.1 sec; 80 mph (130 km/h) 13.9 sec. Fuel consumption at constant 75 mph (120 km/h): 37.1 mpg; overall test, 22.5 mpg.

Features: Exciting appearance, and very well-equipped car including air conditioning and an advanced audio system. **Summary:** My last and perhaps most exciting overseas test drive of 1989 was in the Celica GT-Four in France; I also enjoyed the standard front-drive model (test figures above), which is available with automatic, but the enthusiast will appreciate the superb handling and performance of the turbocharged GT-Four.

TOYOTA (J)   Corolla GT-i

Identity: In the new Corolla range at Frankfurt 1987 was, as usual, a performance model, now called the GT-i. It has similar 16-valve engine to the Executive, but with fuel injection. This is the 4A-GE engine, giving very lively performance. Many other changes to make the GT-i more sporting.

Engine: Front-mounted transverse four-cylinder with alloy head and twin ohc operating four valves per cyl. Bosch D-Jetronic fuel injection. Bore 81.0 mm, stroke 77.0 mm; capacity 1587 cc. Power 123 PS (90 kW) at 6600 rpm; torque 107 lb ft (148 Nm) at 5000 rpm. Compression 10.0-to-1. Catalyst: not available.

Transmission: Front-wheel drive; five-speed manual gearbox. Automatic, not available. Top gear speed at 1000 rpm: 19.9 mph (32.0 km/h).

Suspension: Front, independent, MacPherson struts, anti-roll bar. Rear, independent, MacPherson struts, anti-roll bar.

Steering: Rack and pinion. Power assistance: standard. **Brakes:** Vented discs front, solid discs rear. ABS: not available. **Tyres:** 185/60 HR 14. **Fuel tank:** 11.0 Imp. gall (50 litres). **Unladen weight:** 2083 lb (945 kg).

Dimensions: Length 165.9 in (4215 mm), width 65.1 in (1655 mm), height 53.7 in (1365 mm), wheelbase 95.6 in (2430 mm).

Performance *Autocar & Motor* test: Maximum speed 121 mph (195 km/h); 0 to 60 mph (97 km/h) 9.2 sec; 80 mph (130 km/h) 15.6 sec. Fuel consumption at constant 75 mph (120 km/h): 36.2 mpg; overall test, 35.1 mpg.

Features: GT-i gets much extra equipment such as electric adjustment for door mirrors. Extra spoilers and side sills reveal identity. **Summary:** Impressively lively car to drive, with exceptionally good handling and general road behaviour. Excellent controls. Rather noisy, but not out of keeping with its sporting character. A good 'fun' car.

TOYOTA (J)   Corolla 4WD Estate

Identity: Replacing the former Tercel 4WD, the new Corolla in 4 × 4 form offers a remarkable combination of off-road ability with dual purpose utility and spaciousness. Four-wheel drive is permanently engaged, and although the gearbox does not have the emergency low ratio provided with the Tercel, it copes very well in tough going.

Engine: Front-mounted transverse four-cylinder with alloy head and twin ohc operating four valves per cylinder. Electronic fuel injection. Bore 81.0 mm, stroke 77.8 mm; capacity 1587 cc. Power 94 PS (69 kW) at 6000 rpm; torque 100 lb ft (136 Nm) at 3600 rpm. Compression 9.5-to-1. Catalyst: not available.

Transmission: Four-wheel drive; five-speed manual gearbox. Automatic, not available. Top gear speed at 1000 rpm: 19.8 mph (31.9 km/h).

Suspension: Front, independent, MacPherson struts, anti-roll bar. Rear, live axle on trailing arms with Panhard rod; coil springs and telescopic dampers.

Steering: Rack and pinion. Power assistance: standard. **Brakes:** Vented discs front, drums rear. ABS: not available. **Tyres:** 185/70 SR 13. **Fuel tank:** 11.0 Imp. gall (50 litres). **Unladen weight:** 2575 lb (1165 kg).

Dimensions: Length 167.3 in (4250 mm), width 65.2 in (1655 mm), height 57.1 in (1450 mm), wheelbase 95.7 in (2430 mm).

Performance *Autocar & Motor* test: Maximum speed 94 mph (151 km/h); 0 to 60 mph (97 km/h) 12.1 sec; 80 mph (130 km/h) 23.8 sec. Fuel consumption at constant 75 mph (120 km/h): 32.8 mpg; overall test, 21.3 mpg.

Features: Roof level locker at rear provides useful out-of-sight stowage space, and equipment is good, including sunroof and electric windows. **Summary:** Very good family vehicle with the ability to keep going when conditions get tough, thanks to the extra ground clearance and permanent four-wheel drive. Also pleasant enough to drive in ordinary road conditions, except for rather a lot of roll on corners.

TOYOTA (J)   LEXUS LS400

Identity: Toyota offers the Lexus as a separate brand, but it seems to belong more amongst the Ts than the Ls, despite being a very individual and luxurious car. Good though Toyotas are, Lexus marked a major adventure into a very different field – as a new rival for Jaguar and Mercedes – when it was launched here in May.

Engine: Front-mounted longitudinal V8-cylinder with alloy block and heads, and twin ohc each bank working four valves per cylinder; electronic fuel injection. Bore 87.5 mm, stroke 82.5 mm; capacity 3969 cc. Power 241 PS (177 kW) at 5400 rpm; torque 258 lb ft (357 Nm) at 4400 rpm. Compression 10.0-to-1. Catalyst: standard.

Transmission: Rear-wheel drive; four-speed automatic, standard. Top gear speed at 1000 rpm: 27.1 mph (43.6 km/h).

Suspension: Front, independent, wishbones and coil springs, anti-roll bar. Rear, independent wishbones and coil springs, anti-roll bar.

Steering: Rack and pinion. Power assistance: standard. **Brakes:** Vented discs front and rear. ABS: standard. **Tyres:** 205/65 ZR 15. **Fuel tank:** 18.7 Imp. gall (85 litres). **Unladen weight:** 3890 lb (1765 kg).

Dimensions: Length 196.6 in (4995 mm), width 71.6 in (1820 mm), height 56.1 in (1425 mm), wheelbase 110.8 in (2815 mm).

Performance *Autocar & Motor* test: Maximum speed 147 mph (237 km/h); 0 to 60 mph (97 km/h) 8.3 sec; 80 mph (130 km/h) 13.2 sec. Fuel consumption at constant 75 mph (120 km/h): 27.4 mpg; overall test, 19.7 mpg.

Features: In any list of standard features, the Lexus scores 'full house', having everything from the neat remote central locking, with sender built into the key, to air conditioning. **Summary:** Quietness and refinement are what I chiefly remember from driving the Lexus. It also stood out as a very fast car, always trying to go soaring into three-figure speeds, and a very safe one as well. I thoroughly enjoyed testing it.

171

TOYOTA (J)   **MR2 GT T-Bar**

Identity: Sleek, purposeful and eye-catching styling came to the mid-engined Toyota sports GT in April 1990, when the new version with much more rounded body shape was introduced. Engine size was increased to 2-litre, and there is a choice of two power output levels, standard or GT. The T-Bar body is available only with GT engine.

Engine: Mid-mounted transverse four-cylinder with twin ohc working four valves per cylinder and varying induction, by altering lift and opening time of valves. Electronic fuel injection. Bore 86.0 mm, stroke 86.0 mm; capacity 1998 cc. Power 160 PS (118 kW) at 6600 rpm; torque 140 lb ft (194 Nm) at 4800 rpm. Compression 10.0-to-1. Catalyst: standard.

Transmission: Rear-wheel drive; five-speed manual gearbox. Automatic, optional extra on standard model only; not available on GT. Top gear speed at 1000 rpm: 21.2 mph (34.1 km/h).

Suspension: Front, independent, MacPherson struts, anti-roll bar. Rear, MacPherson struts, anti-roll bar.

Steering: Rack and pinion. Power assistance: not available. **Brakes:** Vented discs front and rear. ABS: not available. **Tyres:** 195/60 R 14 85V (front); 205/60R 14 88V (rear). **Fuel tank:** 12.1 Imp. gall (55 litres). **Unladen weight:** 2810 lb (1275 kg).

Dimensions: Length 164.6 in (4180 mm), width 66.9 in (1700 mm), height 48.8 in (1240 mm), wheelbase 94.5 in (2400 mm).

Performance *Autocar & Motor* test (fixed head): Maximum speed 137 mph (220 km/h); 0 to 60 mph (97 km/h) 6.7 sec; 80 mph (130 km/h) 9.9 sec. Fuel consumption at constant 75 mph (120 km/h): 37.7 mpg; overall test, 27.2 mpg.

Features: Complex seven-way adjustment of driving seat is provided, and top-level audio is fitted. T-Bar gets removable glass roof panels and has leather upholstery as standard. **Summary:** Accommodation is a bit restricted, but the MR2 is adequate for two, and offers a small luggage space at each end. Exceptional roadholding and an exciting car to drive.

Identity: Cleverly designed replacement for the Spacecruiser, launched in UK Birmingham 1990, Previa has its engine mid-mounted beneath the floor, with ancillaries such as the alternator shaft-driven at the front. Spacious and comfortable eight-seater, yet relaxing to drive.

Engine: Mid-mounted longitudinal four-cylinder with twin overhead camshafts and 16 valves; fuel injection. Bore 95.0 mm, stroke 86.0 mm; capacity 2438 cc. Power 134 PS (99 kW) at 5000 rpm; torque 152 lb ft (210 Nm) at 4000 rpm. Compression 9.3-to-1. Catalyst: not available.

Transmission: Rear-wheel drive; five-speed manual gearbox. Automatic, optional extra. Top gear speed at 1000 rpm: 22.1 mph (35.6 km/h).

Suspension: Front, independent, MacPherson struts; anti-roll bar. Rear, independent, wishbones and coil springs.

Steering: Rack and pinion. Power assistance: standard. **Brakes:** Vented discs front and rear. ABS: not available. **Tyres:** 215/65 R15 96H. **Fuel tank:** 16.5 Imp. gall (75 litres). **Unladen weight:** 3968 lb (1800 kg).

Dimensions: Length 187.0 in (4750 mm), width 70.9 in (1800 mm), height 71.3 in (1810 mm), wheelbase 112.6 in (2860 mm).

Performance *Autocar & Motor* test: Maximum speed 109 mph (175 km/h); 0 to 60 mph (97 km/h) 12.9 sec; 80 mph (130 km/h) 22.9 sec. Fuel consumption at constant 75 mph (120 km/h): 24.1 mpg; overall test, 21.6 mpg.

Features: Sliding side door and large tailgate; pop-up front sunroof and electric sliding roof over centre of vehicle. Generous equipment.
Summary: Futuristic fascia design and sleek appearance give a very modern look to this advanced multi-seater. Centre row of seats has reach adjustment and rear seats fold against the sides for extra load space. Most impressive design.

TOYOTA   (J)   Supra 3.0i Turbo

Identity: Following the launch of the completely new Supra in 1986, a very fast turbocharged model was added in early 1989. In this form, Supra can challenge the world's fastest cars, and it presents an exciting appearance with its flat deck front, rear wing, and removable roof panels.

Engine: Front-mounted longitudinal six-cylinder with all-alloy construction and belt-driven twin ohc working four valves per cylinder. Multipoint fuel injection. Turbocharger and inter-cooler. Bore 83.0 mm, stroke 91.0 mm; capacity 2954 cc. Power 232 PS (173 kW) at 5600 rpm; torque 254 lb ft (345 Nm) at 3200 rpm. Compression 8.4-to-1. Catalyst: standard.

Transmission: Rear-wheel drive; five-speed manual gearbox. Automatic, optional extra. Top gear speed at 1000 rpm: 25.7 mph (41.4 km/h).

Suspension: Front, independent, wishbones and coil springs; anti-roll bar. Rear, independent, wishbones and coil springs; anti-roll bar.

Steering: Rack and pinion. Power assistance: standard. **Brakes:** Vented discs front, and rear. ABS: standard. **Tyres:** 225/50 VR 16. **Fuel tank:** 15.4 Imp. gall (70 litres). **Unladen weight:** 3470 lb (1575 kg).

Dimensions: Length 181.9 in (4620 mm), width 68.7 in (1745 mm), height 51.6 in (1310 mm), wheelbase 102.4 in (2600 mm).

Performance *Autocar & Motor* test: Maximum speed 144 mph (232 km/h); 0 to 60 mph (97 km/h) 6.9 sec; 80 mph (130 km/h) 11.4 sec. Fuel consumption at constant 75 mph (120 km/h): 27.4 mpg; overall test, 18.8 mpg.

Features: Excellent standard equipment including air conditioning, leaving automatic transmission as about the only extra listed. **Summary:** Extremely fast and competent 2+2 to rival some of the world's top super-cars, although its interior finish and standards of furnishing are not up to the same level.

TVR (GB)   Griffith

Identity: Eye-catching new shape on the TVR stand at Birmingham in 1990 was the completely new Griffith. TVR say it was developed to meet market demand for a very high-performance V8 model, and it evolved in conjunction with the TVR racing programme.

Engine: Front-mounted longitudinal V8-cylinder with alloy block and heads, and pushrod ohv. Electronic fuel injection. Bore 94.0 mm, stroke 71.1 mm; capacity 3947 cc. Power 240 PS (177 kW) at 6250 rpm; torque 270 lb ft (373 Nm) at 2600 rpm. Compression 10.5-to-1. Catalyst: optional.

Transmission: Rear-wheel drive; five-speed manual gearbox. Automatic, not available. Top gear speed at 1000 rpm: 26.8 mph (43.2 km/h).

Suspension: Front, independent, wishbones and coil springs; anti-roll bar. Rear, independent, semi-trailing arms with coil springs and anti-roll bar.

Steering: Rack and pinion. Power assistance: not available. **Brakes:** Vented discs front, solid discs rear. ABS: not available. **Tyres:** 215/60 XR 15. **Fuel tank:** 11.8 Imp. gall (53.6 litres). **Unladen weight:** 2095 lb (950 kg).

Dimensions: Length 152.8 in (3882 mm), width 67.0 in (1701 mm), height 46.1 in (1172 mm), wheelbase 90.6 in (2300 mm).

Performance Works: Maximum speed 148 mph (238 km/h); 0 to 60 mph (97 km/h) 4.9 sec; 80 mph (130 km/h) 8.6 sec. Fuel consumption: no data.

Features: Semi-frameless electric windows and folding rear-quarter hood with removable targa roof panel. Trim in ambla, leather optional.
Summary: After its Birmingham appearance, the show car was stripped down preparatory to setting up for production, but the Griffith is expected to be as fast as its exciting looks and preliminary figures suggest.

Identity: Originally launched as the S in 1986, this TVR appeared in 3C form at Birmingham 1990. It brings back into production the body style of past TVRs, to appeal to a public which now appreciates the styling of the 60s. Main difference from the S2C is the engine, with standard fitting of a catalyst.

Engine: Front-mounted longitudinal V6-cylinder with cast-iron block and heads; pushrod ohv. Bosch L-Jetronic fuel injection. Bore 93.0 mm, stroke 72.0 mm; capacity 2933 cc. Power 170 PS (125 kW) at 6000 rpm; torque 172 lb ft (238 Nm) at 3000 rpm. Compression 9.0-to-1. Catalyst: standard.

Transmission: Rear-wheel drive; five-speed manual gearbox. Automatic, not available. Top gear speed at 1000 rpm: 23.4 mph (37.7 km/h).

Suspension: Front, independent, wishbones and coil springs; anti-roll bar. Rear, independent, semi-trailing arms and coil springs; anti-roll bar.

Steering: Rack and pinion. Power assistance: not available. **Brakes:** Vented discs front, drums rear. ABS: not available. **Tyres:** 205/60 VR 15. **Fuel tank:** 12.0 Imp. gall (55 litres). **Unladen weight:** 2070 lb (940 kg).

Dimensions: Length 155.8 in (3958 mm), width 65.6 in (1665 mm), height 48.1 in (1223 mm), wheelbase 90.0 in (2286 mm).

Performance *Autocar & Motor* test: Maximum speed 128 mph (206 km/h); 0 to 60 mph (97 km/h) 7.6 sec; 80 mph (130 km/h) 13.5 sec. Fuel consumption at constant 75 mph (120 km/h): 30.1 mpg; overall test, 27.3 mpg.

Features: Although the S2C also had a catalyst, the S3C uses the larger Ford engine and has a three-way catalyst with low pressure drop exhaust system, to avoid any power loss. **Summary:** Sporting two-seater with neat hood action and glass-fibre body on tubular steel chassis. The S filled in the gap at the bottom of the range when the prices for the later-bodied 400 moved upwards.

VAUXHALL (B, D, GB) Astra GTE 2.0i Cabriolet

Identity: First seen at Frankfurt, 1985, the new Opel Kadett convertible was followed by the British equivalent—Vauxhall Astra convertible—at Birmingham a year later; on market spring 1987. Choice of 1600 cc low-end torque engine, or 2-litre 115 bhp unit similar to the engine of the Cavalier CD. Conversion is by Bertone of Italy. New model due 1991.

Engine: Front-mounted transverse four-cylinder with alloy head and single ohc operating hydraulic tappets. Bosch LE Jetronic fuel injection. Bore 86.0 mm, stroke 86.0 mm; capacity 1998 cc. Power 115 PS (85 kW) at 5600 rpm; torque 129 lb ft (178 Nm) at 3000 rpm. Comp. 9.2-to-1. Catalyst: not available.

Transmission: Front-wheel drive; five-speed manual gearbox. No automatic option. Top gear speed at 1000 rpm: 20.8 mph (33.5 km/h).

Suspension: Front, independent, MacPherson struts with gas-filled dampers; anti-roll bar. Rear, independent, trailing arms and torsion beam (compound crank); minibloc coil springs and gas dampers; anti-roll bar.

Steering: Rack and pinion. Power assistance: standard. **Brakes:** Vented discs front, drums rear. ABS: standard. **Tyres:** 185/60 HR 14. **Fuel tank:** 11.4 Imp. gall (52 litres). **Unladen weight:** 2326 lb (1055 kg).

Dimensions: Length 157.4 in (3997 mm), width 65.3 in (1658 mm), height 53.5 in (1359 mm), wheelbase 99.2 in (2520 mm).

Performance *Autocar & Motor* test (Hatchback): Maximum speed 123 mph (198 km/h); 0 to 60 mph (97 km/h) 8.4 sec; 80 mph (130 km/h) 14.0 sec. Fuel consumption at constant 75 mph (120 km/h): 38.7 mpg; overall test, 33.4 mpg.

Features: Hood in grey or beige, and includes glass rear window with heating element. Frameless front doors with fixed quarter windows. **Summary:** Extensive reinforcement has been added in sill panels, pillars, doors and rear floor pan to retain rigidity of the structure. Padded roll bar. Rear seat is divided and folds, with release in boot for security.

VAUXHALL (GB, D)   Calibra 2.0i 16V

Identity: Launched Frankfurt 1989, and revealed again at Motorfair, Calibra went into production 1990 as an excitingly sleek new coupé shape in the Vauxhall range, as well as Opel Calibra in Germany. Standard model has 2-litre 8-valve engine; 16-valve and four-wheel drive versions also available.

Engine: Front-mounted transverse four-cylinder with alloy head and twin ohc working four valves per cylinder. Bosch Motronic M 1.5 injection. Bore 86.0 mm, stroke 86.0 mm; capacity 1998 cc. Power 150 PS (110 kW) at 6000 rpm; torque 145 lb ft (196 Nm) at 4800 rpm. Compression 10.5-to-1. Catalyst: standard.

Transmission: Front- or four-wheel drive; five-speed manual gearbox. Automatic, not available. Top gear speed at 1000 rpm: 22.1 mph (35.6 km/h).

Suspension: Front, independent, MacPherson struts, anti-roll bar. Rear, independent, semi-trailing arms and coil springs; anti-roll bar.

Steering: Rack and pinion. Power assistance: standard. **Brakes:** Vented discs front, solid discs rear. ABS: standard. **Tyres:** 205/55 VR 15. **Fuel tank:** 14.3 Imp. gall (65 litres). **Unladen weight:** 2964 lb (1344 kg).

Dimensions: Length 176.8 in (4490 mm), width 66.9 in (1700 mm), height 55.1 in (1400 mm), wheelbase 102.4 in (2600 mm).

Performance *Autocar & Motor* test: Maximum speed 137 mph (220 km/h); 0 to 60 mph (97 km/h) 8.1 sec; 80 mph (130 km/h) 13.5 sec. Fuel consumption at constant 75 mph (120 km/h): 39.2 mpg; overall test, 25.5 mpg.

Features: Slightly longer than Cavalier, Calibra has a rounded, energy-absorbing front with integrated bumpers. Rear seats fold for extra luggage space. Generous standard equipment on top model. **Summary:** Calibra offers an exceptionally low drag factor of 0.26, and is a most exciting but reassuringly safe car to drive. A bit noisy, but very responsive.

Identity: Improved model in the Vauxhall range, launched Birmingham 1990, is the Carlton. It has a new engine, enlarged to 2.6-litre capacity, and features the same 'dual ram' induction system as first introduced by GM on the Senator 3.0i-24v. All Carltons now have ABS.

Engine: Front-mounted longitudinal six-cylinder with cylinders in-line and alloy head; single ohc working eight valves. Dual-stage induction, changing at 4,000 rpm. Bosch M1.5 injection and ignition system. Bore 88.8 mm, stroke 69.8 mm; capacity 2594 cc. Power 150 PS (110 kW) at 5600 rpm; torque 162 lb ft (224 Nm) at 3800 rpm. Compression 9.2-to-1. Catalyst: twin, standard.

Transmission: Rear-wheel drive; five-speed manual gearbox. Automatic, optional extra. Top gear speed at 1000 rpm: 23.2 mph (37.3 km/h); auto 27.8 mph (44.7 km/h).

Suspension: Front, independent, MacPherson struts with triangular control arms; anti-roll bar. Rear, independent, semi-trailing arms with transverse diagonal link each side; mini-block progressive rate coil springs and anti-roll bar.

Steering: Recirculating ball. Power assistance: standard. **Brakes:** Vented discs front, solid discs rear. ABS: standard. **Tyres:** 195/65 VR 14. **Fuel tank:** 16.5 Imp. gall (75 litres). **Unladen weight:** 3163 lb (1435 kg).

Dimensions: Length 184.5 in (4686 mm), width 69.8 in (1773 mm), height 57.8 in (1468 mm), wheelbase 107.5 in (2731 mm).

Performance Works: Maximum speed 134 mph (216 km/h); 0 to 62 mph (100 km/h) 9.8 sec. Fuel consumption at constant 75 mph (120 km/h): 30.1 mpg.

Features: Many improvements were made to the whole Carlton range at the same time as the 2.6 was introduced, and the CDX gets electrically heated seats and the ingenious Vauxhall computer. **Summary:** The company car tax limit for Band 4 (£19,250) makes the 2-litre limit irrelevant and this smooth new 2.6-litre takes advantage of the fact.

VAUXHALL   (B, D, GB)   Cavalier 2.0i 4 × 4

Identity: New adventure for GM in this range was introduction of a four-wheel drive version, on the market November 1988. It was initially packaged as a 'working' car for business use, with L specification, but later up-rated to GL trim.

Engine: Front-mounted transverse four-cylinder with alloy head and single belt-driven ohc. Bosch Motronic injection/ignition. Bore 86.0 mm, stroke 86.0 mm; capacity 1998 cc. Power 130 PS (95 kW) at 5600 rpm; torque 129 lb ft (175 Nm) at 4600 rpm. Compression 10.0-to-1. Catalyst: not available.

Transmission: Four-wheel drive; five-speed manual gearbox. Automatic, not available. Top gear speed at 1000 rpm: 20.3 mph (32.7 km/h).

Suspension: Front, independent, MacPherson struts, anti-roll bar. Rear, independent, semi-trailing arms with multi-axis support brackets; double-conical miniblock coil springs and twin-tube telescopic dampers; anti-roll bar.

Steering: Rack and pinion. Power assistance: standard. **Brakes:** Vented discs front, solid discs rear. ABS: optional. **Tyres:** 175/70 TR 14. **Fuel tank:** 13.4 Imp. gall (61 litres). **Unladen weight:** 2668 lb (1210 kg).

Dimensions: Length 174.4 in (4429 mm), width 66.9 in (1699 mm), height 55.1 in (1400 mm), wheelbase 102.4 in (2601 mm).

Performance *Autocar & Motor* test: Maximum speed 123 mph (198 km/h); 0 to 60 mph (97 km/h) 8.6 sec; 80 mph (130 km/h) 15.0 sec. Fuel consumption at constant 75 mph (120 km/h): 38.7 mpg, overall test, 28.3 mpg.

Features: Equipment is largely the same as for the front-drive models with GL specification; 2-litre gets power steering as standard. **Summary:** The 4 × 4 model is available only with saloon body and not as hatchback. Major improvement is the use of independent suspension at the rear, and when I first drove the new range I considered this model to be best of all.

VAUXHALL (D) Cavalier GSi 2.0i 16v 4 × 4

Identity: Although I was able to include details of the Cavalier 16V in the 1989 edition, based on the mechanically similar Opel Vectra, it did not arrive on the British market until September that year. Impressive combination of very high performance with safety, and good equipment.

Engine: Front-mounted transverse four-cylinder with alloy head and twin belt-driven ohc operating four valves per cyl. Bosch Motronic injection/ignition system. Bore 86.0 mm, stroke 86.0 mm; capacity 1998 cc. Power 150 PS (110 kW) at 6000 rpm; torque 145 lb ft (196 Nm) at 4800 rpm. Compression 10.5-to-1. Catalyst: standard.

Transmission: Four-wheel drive; five-speed manual gearbox. Automatic, not available. Top gear speed at 1000 rpm: 22.1 mph (35.6 km/h).

Suspension: Front, independent, MacPherson struts, anti-roll bar. Rear, independent, semi-trailing arms with transverse link each side; miniblock coil springs; anti-roll bar.

Steering: Rack and pinion. Power assistance: standard. **Brakes:** Vented discs front, solid discs rear. ABS: standard. **Tyres:** 205/55 VR 15. **Fuel tank:** 14.3 Imp. gall (65 litres). **Unladen weight:** 2890 lb (1311 kg).

Dimensions: Length 174.4 in (4430 mm), width 66.9 in (1700 mm), height 55.1 in (1400 mm), wheelbase 102.4 in (2600 mm).

Performance *Autocar & Motor* test: Maximum speed 128 mph (206 km/h); 0 to 60 mph (97 km/h) 8.5 sec; 80 mph (130 km/h) 14.8 sec. Fuel consumption at constant 75 mph (120 km/h): 34.9 mpg; overall test, 24.0 mpg.

Features: This was the first Vauxhall to have catalyst as standard, and it is also generously equipped, with such features as deadlocks, and electric sunroof. **Summary:** Vauxhall also offer the very powerful 16-valve engine with front-drive only, but four-wheel drive is well worth the extra for the added stability, making this a very fast yet extremely safe car to drive.

Identity: A few months after the Nova turbo diesel was launched at Motorfair 1988, the industrious new Vauxhall press manager asked me to see if I could get 100 mph and 100 mpg out of it. With RAC supervision I had a go, and managed it easily: 103 miles in the hour, and 105 miles on a gallon (obviously not at the same time!).

Engine: Front-mounted transverse four-cylinder with alloy head and single ohc; eight valves, and water-cooled turbocharger. Bore 76.0 mm, stroke 82.0 mm; capacity 1488 cc. Power 67 PS (49 kW) at 4600 rpm; torque 97 lb ft (135 Nm) at 2600 rpm. Compression 22.5-to-1. Catalyst: not available.

Transmission: Front-wheel drive; five-speed manual gearbox. Automatic, not available. Top gear speed at 1000 rpm: 24.2 mph (38.9 km/h).

Suspension: Front, independent, MacPherson struts. Rear, independent, compound crank with miniblock coil springs; anti-roll bar.

Steering: Rack and pinion. Power assistance: not available. **Brakes:** Solid discs front, drum rear. ABS: not available. **Tyres:** 165/70 R 13. **Fuel tank:** 9.2 Imp. gall (42 litres). **Unladen weight:** 1874 lb (850 kg).

Dimensions: Length 142.6 in (3622 mm), width 60.4 in (1534 mm), height 53.7 in (1363 mm), wheelbase 92.2 in (2342 mm).

Performance *Autocar & Motor* test: Maximum speed 101 mph (163 km/h); 0 to 60 mph (97 km/h) 12.2 sec; 80 mph (130 km/h) 24.2 sec. Fuel consumption at constant 75 mph (120 km/h): 50.4 mpg; overall test, 43.8 mpg.

Features: Nova 1.5TD comes only with Merit trim level and three-door hatchback body, but equipment is not too basic. One-piece rear seats fold for extra load space. **Summary:** With rather more mileage behind it, my car for the economy test went better than the road test figures suggest; it consistently lapped at over 104 mph, to give an average of 103.8 miles in the hour average speed from a standing start. A good commuting car.

VAUXHALL   (D)   Senator CD 3.0i 24v

Identity: Launched Germany in August, and on UK market from mid-November 1989, the revised Senator has the same Dual Ram engine as the Carlton GSi 3000, with many improvements. Small 24v badge and rectangular exhaust pipes identify the new Senator.

Engine: Front-mounted longitudinal six-cylinder with alloy head and twin ohc working 24 valves. Bosch Motronic ignition/injection, with separate induction pipes in groups of three, linked above 4,000 rpm. Bore 95.0 mm, stroke 69.6 mm; capacity 2969 cc. Power 204 PS (150 kW) at 6000 rpm; torque 199 lb ft (275 Nm) at 3600 rpm. Compression 10.0-to-1. Catalyst: standard.

Transmission: Rear-wheel drive; four-speed automatic, standard; five-speed manual is no-cost option. Top gear speed at 1000 rpm: 27.6 mph (44.4 km/h); manual: 24.4 mph (39.3 km/h).

Suspension: Front, independent, MacPherson struts with triangular controls arms and pendulum stabiliser. Rear, independent, semi-trailing arms with transverse diagonal link each side; mini-block progressive rate coil springs; anti-roll bar.

Steering: Recirculating ball. Power assistance: standard. **Brakes:** Vented discs front, solid discs rear. ABS standard. **Tyres:** 205/65 ZR 15. **Fuel tank:** 16.5 Imp. gall (75 litres). **Unladen weight:** 3404 lb (1544 kg).

Dimensions: Length 190.7 in (4844 mm), width 69.4 in (1763 mm), height 57.0 in (1448 mm), wheelbase 107.5 in (2731 mm).

Performance *Autocar & Motor* test: Maximum speed 139 mph (224 km/h); 0 to 60 mph (97 km/h) 9.1 sec; 80 mph (130 km/h) 14.3 sec. Fuel consumption at 75 mph (120 km/h): 31.4 mpg; overall test, 21.4 mpg.

Features: Available with leather trim, or at lower price with velour; choice of analogue or digital instruments. Lavish equipment including air conditioning, electric sunroof, and selectable suspension firmness.
Summary: Extremely fast yet very docile, quiet and comfortable car. The 'Dual Ram' feature reflects the switchover effect at 4,000 rpm.

VOLKSWAGEN (D)   Caravelle GL

Identity: After years of using rear-drive for the van and personnel carrier, Volkswagen launched the new front-drive model at Paris 1990. Choice of four-cylinder 2-litre engine, or five-cylinder 2½-litre; there is also a five-cylinder 2.3-litre diesel. Details follow for the 2½-litre GL.

Engine: Front-mounted transverse five-cylinder with single ohc and two valves per cylinder. Electronic fuel injection. Bore 81.0 mm, stroke 95.5 mm; capacity 2450 cc. Power 110 PS (81 kW) at 4500 rpm; torque 137 lb ft (190 Nm) at 2200 rpm. Compression 8.5-to-1. Catalyst: standard.

Transmission: Front-wheel drive; five-speed manual gearbox. Automatic, optional extra (from late 1991). Top gear speed at 1000 rpm: 21.4 mph (34.4 km/h).

Suspension: Front, independent, wishbones with longitudinal torsion bars. Rear, independent, semi-trailing arms and coil springs.

Steering: Rack and pinion. Power assistance: standard. **Brakes:** Solid discs front, drums rear. ABS: optional. **Tyres:** 195/70 R 15. **Fuel tank:** 17.6 Imp. gall (80 litres). **Unladen weight:** 3836 lb (1740 kg).

Dimensions: Length 183.3 in (4655 mm), width 72.6 in (1845 mm), height 72.4 in (1840 mm), wheelbase 115.0 in (2920 mm).

Performance Works: Maximum speed 100 mph (161 km/h). Acceleration: no data. Fuel consumption at constant 75 mph (120 km/h): 21.1 mpg.

Features: Wide choice of body styles and two wheelbase lengths to seat from six to as many as 12. One sliding side door standard, two optional. **Summary:** Although good in some respects, the former rear-drive Caravelle always lacked directional stability. It is to be hoped that the new one will handle much better, but at time of writing there had been no opportunity to drive it. UK launch: May 1991.

VOLKSWAGEN   (D)   Corrado 1.8 16V

Identity: Last year we featured the supercharged G60 version of the Corrado, but as it is clear there will never be a right-hand drive version of this, the 16-valve rhd model is perhaps more appropriate; it's not all that much slower.

Engine: Front-mounted transverse four-cylinder with alloy head and belt-driven twin ohc working four valves per cylinder. Multi-point fuel injection. Bore 81.0 mm, stroke 86.0 mm; capacity 1781 cc. Power 136 PS (100 kW) at 6300 rpm; torque 119 lb ft (165 Nm) at 4800 rpm. Compression 10.0-to-1. Catalyst: not available.

Transmission: Front-wheel drive; five-speed manual gearbox. Automatic, not available. Top gear speed at 1000 rpm: 19.8 mph (31.9 km/h).

Suspension: Front, independent, MacPherson struts, anti-roll bar. Rear, semi-independent, torsion beam with trailing arms and track correcting mountings; coil springs, anti-roll bar.

Steering: Rack and pinion. Power assistance: standard. **Brakes:** Vented discs front, solid discs rear. ABS: not available. **Tyres:** 185/55 VR 15. **Fuel tank:** 12.0 Imp. gall (55 litres). **Unladen weight:** 2544 lb (1155 kg).

Dimensions: Length 159.3 in (4048 mm), width 65.9 in (1674 mm), height 51.9 in (1318 mm), wheelbase 97.2 in (2470 mm).

Performance *Autocar & Motor* test: Maximum speed 131 mph (210 km/h); 0 to 60 mph (97 km/h) 8.7 sec; 80 mph (130 km/h) 14.5 sec. Fuel consumption at constant 75 mph (120 km/h): 40.9 mpg; overall test, 29.5 mpg.

Features: Rear spoiler moves upward at speed and down again on slowing down, motored electrically. **Summary:** In Germany, the spoiler does not go up until 75 mph, but for this country that would never do! So for Britain it goes up at only 45 mph, which proved most irritating. Otherwise it's an exciting car with good performance and delightful handling.

VOLKSWAGEN (D)   Golf CL Umwelt Diesel

Identity: One of the first small cars to be fitted with a diesel engine was the previous Golf model. A further stride of progress towards improving the image of the diesel came with the early 1990 launch of the Umwelt (meaning 'environmental') diesel, with catalyst.

Engine: Front-mounted transverse four-cylinder with single ohc and distributor injection pump; turbocharger. Bore 76.5 mm, stroke 86.4 mm; capacity 1588 cc. Power 60 PS (44 kW) at 4500 rpm; torque 80 lb ft (110 Nm) at 2400 rpm. Compression 23.0-to-1. Catalyst: standard.

Transmission: Front-wheel drive; five-speed manual gearbox. Automatic, not available. Top gear speed at 1000 rpm: 22.2 mph (35.7 km/h).

Suspension: Front, independent, MacPherson struts; anti-roll bar. Rear, semi-independent, torsion beam axle on semi-trailing arms; coil springs.

Steering: Rack and pinion. Power assistance: not available. **Brakes:** Solid discs front, drums rear. ABS: not available. **Tyres:** 155 R 13S. **Fuel tank:** 12.1 Imp. gall (55 litres). **Unladen weight:** 2170 lb (985 kg).

Dimensions: Length 156.9 in (3985 mm), width 65.6 in (1665 mm), height 55.7 in (1415 mm), wheelbase 97.4 in (2475 mm).

Performance Works: Maximum speed 94 mph (151 km/h); 0 to 62 mph (100 km/h) 16.9 sec. Fuel consumption at constant 75 mph (120 km/h): 42.8 mpg.

Features: Equipment for the Umwelt diesel is at CL level, and fairly basic, even lacking such items as a boot interior light. **Summary:** Turbocharging, a catalyst and a diesel engine all make a fairly rare combination, resulting in lively performance in a car whose exhaust is exceptionally free from pollution; a good choice for those with a genuine interest in the environment.

VOLKSWAGEN   (D)   Passat 2.0 GL Estate

Identity: For the big and roomy Passat, a 1.8-litre engine was always asking a bit much; it was good that Birmingham 1990 brought a replacement, with capacity increased to 1984 cc. The new engine is larger in both bore and stroke, and gives more power and extra torque at lower revs. 2.8-litre V6 was added at Geneva, 1991.

Engine: Front-mounted transverse four-cylinder with alloy head and single ohc. Digifant fuel injection. Bore 82.5 mm, stroke 92.8 mm; capacity 1984 cc. Power 116 PS (85 kW) at 5400 rpm; torque 120 lb ft (166 Nm) at 3200 rpm. Compression 10.0-to-1. Catalyst: standard.

Transmission: Front-wheel drive; five-speed manual gearbox. Automatic, optional extra. Top gear speed at 1000 rpm: 21.9 mph (35.2 km/h).

Suspension: Front, independent, MacPherson struts; anti-roll bar. Rear, independent, semi-trailing arms with struts; anti-roll bar.

Steering: Rack and pinion. Power assistance: standard. **Brakes:** Vented discs front, solid discs rear. ABS: not available. **Tyres:** 185/65 R 14. **Fuel tank:** 15.4 Imp. gall (70 litres). **Unladen weight:** 2546 lb (1155 kg).

Dimensions: Length 180.0 in (4573 mm), width 67.0 in (1704 mm), height 56.4 in (1432 mm), wheelbase 103.4 in (2627 mm).

Performance Works: Maximum speed 119 mph (191 km/h) ; 0 to 62 mph (100 km/h) 11.5 sec. Fuel consumption at constant 75 mph (120 km/h): 35.6 mpg.

Features: Optional automatic transmission features a 'mode selection' switch. Self-levelling option is also available, replacing steel springs with pneumatic units. **Summary:** In this new form the Passat GT should be able to cope much better than before, though the acceleration time to 62 mph is still not very sparkling. For brisker performance, the 16-valve is available.

Identity: Yet another new car launched at busy Birmingham 1990 was the restyled and re-engineered Polo, hailed as the first small car range to go all-catalyst. Choice of Fox, with 1.05 engine, CL with 1.05 or 1.3, and this GT model with a more powerful 1.3 engine.

Engine: Front-mounted transverse four-cylinder with alloy head, single ohc, eight valves, and Digifant fuel injection. Bore 75.0 mm, stroke 72.0 mm; capacity 1272 cc. Power 75 PS (55 kW) at 5900 rpm; torque 72 lb ft (99 Nm) at 3600 rpm. Compression 10.0-to-1. Catalyst: standard.

Transmission: Front-wheel drive; five-speed manual gearbox. Automatic, not available. Top gear speed at 1000 rpm: 17.9 mph (28.8 km/h).

Suspension: Front, independent, MacPherson struts with self-correcting geometry; anti-roll bar. Rear, dead beam axle on trailing arms from torsion beam; anti-roll bar.

Steering: Rack and pinion. Power assistance: not available. **Brakes:** Solid discs front, drums rear. ABS: not available. **Tyres:** 165/70 R 13S. **Fuel tank:** 9.2 Imp. gall (42 litres). **Unladen weight:** 1731 lb (785 kg).

Dimensions: Length 146.7 in (3725 mm), width 61.8 in (1570 mm), height 53.1 in (1350 mm), wheelbase 91.9 in (2335 mm).

Performance *Autocar & Motor* test: Maximum speed 104 mph (167 km/h); 0 to 60 mph (97 km/h) 11.7 sec; 80 mph (130 km/h) 21.9 sec. Fuel consumption at constant 75 mph (120 km/h): 39.2 mpg; overall test, 34.9 mpg.

Features: GT comes only as coupé or hatchback; the CL is available also as saloon. Sports steering wheel and sports seats standard.
Summary: With its firm suspension, the GT gave a pretty bumpy ride over some mediocre secondary roads (especially for a rear occupant), but still proved very responsive and fun to drive.

VOLVO (S) 460GLi

Identity: When the saloon model of the 440 hatchback was launched at Brussels 1990, it was pitched higher up the market – well-equipped, but rather expensive. When it came to the British market in March 1990, this version, with injection engine, seemed to offer best value of the range.

Engine: Front-mounted transverse four-cylinder with alloy head and single ohc; eight valves. Electronic fuel injection. Bore 81.0 mm, stroke 83.5 mm; capacity 1721 cc. Power 102 PS (75 kW) at 5600 rpm; torque 105 lb ft (145 Nm) at 3900 rpm. Compression 10.0-to-1. Catalyst: standard.

Transmission: Front-wheel drive; five-speed manual gearbox. Automatic, optional extra. Top gear speed at 1000 rpm: 21.5 mph (34.6 km/h).

Suspension: Front, independent, MacPherson struts, anti-roll bar. Rear, dead beam axle on longitudinal Watts linkage with Panhard rod; coil springs.

Steering: Rack and pinion. Power assistance: optional. **Brakes:** Vented discs front, solid discs rear. ABS: optional. **Tyres:** 175/70 HR 14. **Fuel tank:** 10.6 Imp. gall (48 litres). **Unladen weight:** 2153 lb (977 kg).

Dimensions: Length 173.4 in (4405 mm), width 66.5 in (1690 mm), height 54.3 in (1380 mm), wheelbase 98.5 in (2503 mm).

Performance *Autocar & Motor* test: Maximum speed 109 mph (175 km/h); 0 to 60 mph (97 km/h) 11.1 sec; 80 mph (130 km/h) 21.5 sec. Fuel consumption at constant 75 mph (120 km/h): 38.0 mpg; overall test, 26.4 mpg.

Features: All British imports of the 460 get electric sunroof as standard; but it is surprising that power steering is an option for this rather expensive car. **Summary:** Pleasant and refined to drive, the 460GLi appeals to the more traditional motorist looking for quality in a compact car. The Turbo version is available for those wanting more sparkling performance.

VOLVO (NL)   480 Turbo

Identity: There always seems to be an inordinate delay before new Volvos reach UK market, but 480 in turbocharged form arrived February 1989. Performance not all that much greater, but a little more in keeping with the sporty appeal of the 480 coupé.

Engine: Front-mounted transverse four-cylinder with alloy head and wet cylinder liners; electronic fuel injection. Water-cooled turbocharger with inter-cooler. Bore 81.0 mm, stroke 83.5 mm; capacity 1721 cc. Power 120 PS (88 kW) at 5400 rpm; torque 127 lb ft (175 Nm) at 4600 rpm. Compression 8.1-to-1. Catalyst: optional.

Transmission: Front-wheel drive; five-speed manual gearbox. Automatic, not available. Top gear speed at 1000 rpm: 21.3 mph (34.3 km/h).

Suspension: Front, independent, MacPherson struts, with eccentric coil springs; anti-roll bar. Rear, dead beam axle on longitudinal links with Panhard rod, coil springs; anti-roll bar.

Steering: Rack and pinion. Power assistance: standard. **Brakes:** Vented discs front, solid discs rear. ABS: standard. **Tyres:** 185/60 HR 14. **Fuel tank:** 10.1 Imp. gall (46 litres). **Unladen weight:** 2165 lb (982 kg).

Dimensions: Length 167.7 in (4260 mm), width 67.3 in (1710 mm), height 52.0 in (1320 mm), wheelbase 98.5 in (2502 mm).

Performance *Autocar & Motor* test: Maximum speed 124 mph (200 km/h); 0 to 62 mph (100 km/h) 9.6 sec; 80 mph (130 km/h) 15.0 sec. Fuel consumption at constant 75 mph (120 km/h): 34.9 mpg; overall test, 22.5 mpg.

Features: Turbo version gains oil-pressure gauge and colour-matched bumpers. Anti-lock brakes are an option for both models in some markets.
Summary: This very attractive GT offers wider appeal in turbo form, though it's still very much an elegant coupé rather than a GT or sports car. However, performance in this turbo form is good for a 1.7.

Identity: Although the reasons were not too convincingly explained, Volvo abandoned the V6 engine – although it continues in the 760 – and at Birmingham 1990 launchd the 960 with straight six engine, declaring a 'cylinders in line' policy from henceforth. Less angular tail end distinguishes the 960 from the 760.

Engine: Front-mounted longitudinal six-cylinder with all-alloy construction and twin ohc working four valves per cylinder. Bosch Motronic fuel injection. Bore 83.0 mm, stroke 90.0 mm; capacity 2922 cc. Power 204 PS (150 kW) at 6000 rpm; torque 193 lb ft (267 Nm) at 4300 rpm. Compression 10.7-to-1. Catalyst: standard.

Transmission: Rear-wheel drive; four-speed automatic, standard. Top gear speed at 1000 rpm: 25.8 mph (41.5 km/h).

Suspension: Front, independent, MacPherson struts; anti-roll bar. Rear, independent, multi-link location with coil springs and anti-roll bar. Self-levelling standard. Estate car has live rear axle.

Steering: Rack and pinion. Power assistance: standard. **Brakes:** Vented discs front, solid discs rear. ABS: standard. **Tyres:** 195/65 VR 15. **Fuel tank:** 17.6 Imp. gall (80 litres). **Unladen weight:** 3460 lb (1570 kg).

Dimensions: Length 191.7 in (4870 mm), width 68.8 in (1750 mm), height 55.5 in (1410 mm), wheelbase 109.0 in (2770 mm).

Performance *Autocar & Motor* test: Maximum speed 128 mph (206 km/h); 0 to 60 mph (97 km/h) 9.3 sec; 80 mph (130 km/h) 15.1 sec. Fuel consumption at constant 75 mph (120 km/h): 27.7 mpg; overall test, 18.4 mpg.

Features: Lavish equipment includes luxury interior trim and such items as air conditioning, electric sunroof, limited slip differential. Clever safety feature is the standard fitting of a child safety seat in the rear armrest. **Summary:** Extremely comfortable car with delightfully smooth and quiet engine; excellent transmission with good selector and triple mode control switch.

YUGO (YU)   Sana

Identity: Yugoslavia's car firm, Yugo, launched a new and much-improved model called the Florida at Frankfurt 1989. With that name reserved in Britain, it became the Sana when launched on the UK market November 1989. Roomy five-door body bearing a resemblance to Fiat's Tipo, on which it is based.

Engine: Front-mounted transverse four-cylinder with alloy head and single ohc. Twin-choke Weber carb. Bore 80.5 mm, stroke 67.4 mm; capacity 1372 cc. Power 71 PS (52 kW) at 6000 rpm; torque 78 lb ft (108 Nm) at 3000 rpm. Compression 9.2-to-1. Catalyst: not available.

Transmission: Front-wheel drive; five-speed manual gearbox. Automatic, not available. Top gear speed at 1000 rpm: 20.6 mph (33.2 km/h).

Suspension: Front, independent, MacPherson struts, anti-roll bar. Rear, independent, trailing arms and auxiliary cross member; coil springs and anti-roll bar.

Steering: Rack and pinion. Power assistance: not available. **Brakes:** Solid discs front, drums rear. ABS: not available. **Tyres:** 165/70 R 13. **Fuel tank:** 10.5 Imp. gall (47.7 litres). **Unladen weight:** 2006 lb (910 kg).

Dimensions: Length 154.8 in (3932 mm), width 65.3 in (1658 mm), height 55.5 in (1410 mm), wheelbase 98.4 in (2500 mm).

Performance *Autocar & Motor* test: Maximum speed (in fourth) 97 mph (153 km/h); 0 to 60 mph (97 km/h) 13.2 sec; 80 mph (130 km/h) 27.5 sec. Fuel consumption at constant 75 mph (120 km/h): 35.3 mpg; overall test, 28.1 mpg.

Features: Basically as Tipo, but with simpler levels of trim and materials. Good rear space, with the opening continued down to a level with the bottom of the tail lamp assemblies. **Summary:** Initially, Sana was fitted with the Fiat Tipo engine; but later production models have a Yugo-assembled similar unit. Sound design, with better rear-end appearance than the Fiat Tipo.